MARRIAGE, FAMILY, AND SOCIETY

A Reader

Studies in Sociology

✿✿✿✿✿

MARRIAGE, FAMILY, AND SOCIETY

A Reader

E D I T E D   B Y

Hyman Rodman

MERRILL-PALMER INSTITUTE

❀❀❀❀❀

Random House · New York

FIFTH PRINTING, AUGUST 1967

© *Copyright, 1965, by Random House, Inc.*

All rights reserved under International and Pan-American Copyright Conventions. Published in New York by Random House, Inc., and simultaneously in Toronto, Canada, by Random House of Canada Limited.

Library of Congress Catalog Card Number: 65-17448

MANUFACTURED IN THE UNITED STATES OF AMERICA

❧ PREFACE ❧

This book has been especially designed for the undergraduate course in family sociology. It is non-technical, and yet the sociological substance has been retained. It can therefore be used by the creative instructor in a variety of courses in which a sociological approach to the study of the family is thought to be desirable. For example, it might be used in an introductory sociology course in order to provide a more extended treatment of the family area. It might also be used in any professional course that focuses upon the family, in order to add a sociological dimension to the study of the family.

An attempt has been made to include only those selections that are clear, concise, and of long-term importance. An attempt has also been made to include a wide range of selections that cover many of the developmental areas in the family life cycle—the book deals with dating and mate selection, and moves on to cover husband-wife relations; parent-child relations; adolescents, siblings, and peers; and extended kinship relations. In addition, there are special sections on social class and family relations, and on the changing American family.

It is obviously impossible to incorporate all the selections one might wish to include in a reader. This is keenly felt in this case because of the attempt to put together a relatively short reader that could be adapted to a variety of teaching goals. There are two different ways in which I have tried to meet the problem:

1. Many of the selections have been especially adapted according to the primary purpose for which this text was designed. In many cases the original article was meant for a professional audience of social scientists, and it was therefore somewhat less than perfect for the introductory student of the family. In adapting

the selections for the student it has been possible to retain their basic substance, and yet to eliminate the more technical material. This has permitted me to present the material more briefly and more concisely.

2. Some of the selections have been especially prepared for this reader, and introductions have been written for each of the sections of the reader. This has made it possible to summarize a good deal of research in a short span of pages; to single out several major areas of importance in a way that complements the selections that have been included; and to make reference to many of the major studies that pertain to topics under consideration so that the student can readily follow up areas of interest.

To summarize, the present reader is unique in the extent to which adaptations have been used in order to provide articles of importance to a student audience: the articles are clear, concise, and non-technical. It is also unique in the extent to which introductory material has been provided in order to give additional background to some of the topics covered in the reader. Finally, the book is inexpensive, and can therefore readily be used along with a textbook, or in place of a textbook and along with a variety of other books or readings.

I am indebted to the authors of the selections included here for permission to use their material. Beyond that, I am indebted to many of them for their willingness to review my adaptations of their material, and for their kind words expressing satisfaction with the adaptations. I am also directly and indirectly indebted to many people who have helped me to edit and write the book—colleagues and friends, students and teachers. This includes many people I have known at McGill University, Harvard University, Boston University, and Merrill-Palmer Institute, as well as many people who have spent some time at Merrill-Palmer during the past several years. I regret that I cannot take the space to thank all of them individually and to indicate the nature of their help. Rather than omitting mention of them completely, however, I shall compromise by listing the following names alphabetically: Edna P. Amidon, Robert F. Bales, Muriel W. Brown, John G. Chantiny, Joan Ensink, Bernard Farber, Paul C. Glick, Oswald Hall, Grace Henderson, Alberta D. Hill, George C. Homans, John W. Hudson, Ruby Jo Reeves Kennedy, Pauline P. W. Knapp, Eleanore B.

Luckey, William W. McKee, Bernard N. Meltzer, John Mogey, Charles H. Page, Talcott Parsons, Paul J. Reiss, Florentina J. Roman, Aileen D. Ross, Constantina Safilios-Rothschild, Irving E. Sigel, Pitirim A. Sorokin, I. V. Sperry, Leland H. Stott, Marvin B. Sussman, Clark E. Vincent, and William A. Westley.

❧ CONTENTS ❧

✑ INTRODUCTION ❧

It is reported that the Thonga laughed when they first saw Europeans kissing: "Look at them—they eat each other's saliva and dirt." Ford and Beach* cite seven other societies besides the Thonga among whom kissing is unknown. To these groups of people the practice of kissing is strange, comical, and perhaps even somewhat disgusting.

To the Thonga, Europeans are an alien people, and kissing is an alien custom. And most people tend to react to alien people and to alien customs in an ethnocentric way. That is to say, one's own "ethnos" or society is thought to be superior, and other societies with different ways of doing things are thought to be inferior. In many societies, for example, the group name (such as the Zuni or the Skagit) is best translated as "the people"— as though to say that all others are not truly people.

Ethnocentric attitudes develop because the customs one learns are thought to represent the "natural" ways of doing things. Alien ways are thought to be "unnatural." But with the advent of a social scientific approach to behavior it has become clear that the customs one people regards as "natural" may be regarded as "unnatural" by other peoples. It is therefore better to talk about what is "cultural" rather than what is "natural." Such customs as kissing or dating or monogamy are cultural rather than natural. They are learned in certain societies, such as American society—but they may not be learned or practiced in other societies.

This book is almost entirely devoted to a discussion of marriage and the family in American society. It should therefore be borne

* Ford, Clellan S. and Frank A. Beach, *Patterns of Sexual Behavior,* New York: Harper, 1951, p. 49.

in mind throughout that the marriage and family patterns discussed here are guided by American cultural norms, and that the norms and patterns may be quite different in other societies. In the dominant Western societies, however, many of the marriage and family patterns are quite similar to the American patterns. As a consequence, the book will be of relevance to many European societies and to countries like England and Canada. Moreover, the material on the American family can be seen as a case study of one society, and contrasted with the patterns to be found elsewhere, in a way that may contribute to greater understanding of the societies being compared. For these reasons, cross-cultural similarities and differences are occasionally discussed in the book, and there are a number of references to cross-cultural materials that can be followed up by the student.

Some people say that to teach cultural relativity (that different things are right and wrong in different societies) is to promote anarchy. For example, if we teach that premarital sexual relationships are permitted in many societies, then we may be promoting such relationships in those societies where they are officially taboo. But there is an important distinction between teaching facts about a variety of societies and preaching about these facts. One of the instructor's major responsibilities is, after all, to teach facts to his students. And one of these facts may very well be that, in American society, premarital sexual relations, although not infrequent, are nevertheless contrary to the dominant moral standards. The student will get his facts on the street corner if he does not learn them at home or in the schoolroom. In the final analysis the student has to make up his own mind about a variety of things, and he must enjoy or suffer the consequences of his decisions. It would therefore seem best to give the student as many facts as possible in order that his decision can be made in a rational way. To make a rational decision, however, is not to ignore morality—because moral considerations, as well as other considerations, need to be taken into account.

The area of "marriage, family, and society" touches everyone personally in many respects. It is therefore an area about which feelings run high. The churches represent various points of view, *Playboy* magazine represents another, and there is a multitude of other views both more and less extreme. Philosophy and morality have their places in the study of marriage, family, and society. So do many other disciplines and approaches. In this book, however, we are concentrating upon the approach of the behavioral sciences—anthropology, psychology, and particularly sociology. We are not highlighting the question of morality, although it does come up from time to time. Our primary intention is to present sociological facts and the sociological approach to the study of marriage, family, and society. The substance and content of this sociological approach can undoubtedly be used and interpreted in many different ways.

In general, facts do not speak for themselves. They may be interpreted in different ways. Management and unions, for example, may come up with different interpretations of the same set of facts. This is also very much the case for groups with competing philosophies about the area of marriage, family, and society. As a result, several competing interpretations are elaborated upon in the book. In addition, other interpretations and elaborations of factual material are made where it seems necessary to do so.

One

DATING
RELATIONS
AND SEX
ROLES

✄ INTRODUCTION ❧

Girls: Marriage Versus Career

Each individual, as a member of various groups, is subject to the expectations of these groups. In a relatively simple society these groups may reinforce each other in the demands they make of an individual, and the individual therefore experiences little ambiguity or conflict. In a relatively complex society, such as American society, many ideas abound, and an individual may be subjected to conflicting demands from various individuals and groups. Shall a girl heed the relative who encourages her to study hard and to pursue a career? Or shall she heed the relative who encourages her to seek popularity, dates, and marriage while ignoring her books and studies? The selection by Komarovsky (2)* points to the existence of these conflicting demands upon college girls, and indicates the nature of the girls' reactions to these conflicting expectations. One reaction on the girls' part is to "play dumb" on dates—40 per cent of the girls questioned by Komarovsky indicated that they sometimes did "play dumb." In this way they fulfill the traditional expectation that the female should know less than the male and should need his help.

Conflicting expectations upon an individual may be more or less disconcerting. For example, if the conflicting expectations are held by two groups or individuals that the individual holds in high esteem, or if they refer to a matter that is important to the individual, or if the individual has internalized the conflicting expectations and expects them of himself, then the individual would be considerably more troubled. Wallin (1950) has found that many college women do face conflicting expectations and do

---

* This is the manner in which references to selections included in this book are made. See the table of contents for the numbers of the selections.

occasionally feign inferiority to men they are dating, and in this sense his data agree with Komarovsky's findings. But he also notes that the women are not much troubled by these conflicting expectations. One possible explanation is that Komarovsky's sample of Barnard College seniors may have had more career-oriented girls, and that they were therefore more troubled by a problem that is still usually resolved at the expense of a full-fledged career. Another possible explanation is that there have been changes through time such that the problem is no longer so charged with emotion, and permits various kinds of compromise solutions for the girl. Komarovsky (2; 1953, pp. 76–87) has suggested that the margin of superiority expected of men has narrowed and that more women are being placed under pressure to excel. Riesman's (3) references to the greater seriousness on dates and the lesser importance of a "line" also point in the direction of change through time.

One possible consequence of the changes that are occurring can be seen in Kammeyer's (1964) findings on the "inconsistent attitudes" of college girls. In elaborating upon Komarovsky's study, he distinguishes between attitudes about feminine role behavior, and attitudes about female personality traits. On the former, the traditional feminine attitude holds, for example, that "in marriage, the husband should make the major decisions"; on the latter, it holds that "women are more emotional then men." Kammeyer points out that one college girl out of every three in his sample holds traditional attitudes in one area and modern attitudes in the other, and that these "inconsistent" girls tend to be the ones who have had the least interaction with others. With more interaction and communication, the girls are likelier to recognize the inconsistency, and to adopt a consistently traditional or modern attitude. But whether the girls themselves hold inconsistent attitudes, the inconsistencies and the conflicting expectations in their social environment often remain.

How does the girl resolve the problem of marriage versus a career? The usual compromise solution is for the girl to maintain a primary orientation to marriage, while at the same time looking toward employment in a job traditionally held by females, such as teacher, typist, clerical worker, secretary, nurse, or social worker. In this way the girl can pursue a career if she must, she works at a "feminine" occupation, and she can adjust her working schedule to what she and her husband consider to be the needs of the family. Empey (1958), Stratton (1957), Weil (1962), Bell (1962), and Turner (1964) present data that strongly substantiate that the major orientation of American girls is toward marriage, along with a secondary orientation toward typically feminine jobs.* Nye and Hoffman (1963), moreover, point out that although the proportion of women who work has gone up, yet the proportion of women in professional and technical occupations has not increased in the past twenty-five years. Similarly, Bernard (1964) indicates that the proportion of women teaching on college faculties, and the proportion receiving higher degrees, have not increased in the past twenty-five years:

> For the proportion of master's degrees awarded to women, of Ph.D.'s awarded to women, and of academic faculties who were women, the trends tend to parallel one another. They were up from 1910 to about 1930 and down thereafter, with a possible upward trend in recent years. All were undoubtedly related to one another and to the headlong flight into maternity which characterized women in the 1940's and 1950's (p. 61).

One consequence of the girl's primary orientation to marriage is to be seen in her activities at school. She becomes a "sociometrist," in Riesman's terms, or a "human relations" expert, in Parsons' terms. This heightened interest in people, and in dating as a preliminary to marriage, are matched by a lowered interest in academic performance and in a career. As a result, as Coleman (1961) points out, potentially top scholars do not work too hard, and Kagan (1964) refers to a number of studies that show a decline in girls' academic performance from the early grades to the later school years. Intellectual competence and academic competition are often viewed as a facet of masculine aggression, and this inhibits many girls from pursuing academic excellence. This can also be seen as additional confirmation of Komarovsky's point. As Kagan (1964) puts it: "The girl's motivation toward mastery is decreasing with age as a result of anxiety over feeling intellectually more competent than the boy, and conflict over excessive competitiveness."

---

* For a comparative view see Myrdal and Klein (1956) and articles by Paul Chombart de Lauwe and others in *International Social Science Journal,* Vol. XIV, No. 1, 1962; for a brief historical review of the American scene, see Degler (1964).

By lowering her motivation, and by defaulting on the choice of a career that might confine her to a narrower range of potential husbands, a girl conforms to the traditional expectations of American society. As Riesman (1964) has said, girls "are prepared unconsciously if not consciously to surrender chances for personal distinction in order to be fairly sure of pleasing a larger range of men" from among whom they may draw a husband (see Douvan, 1960). Although most of the advice still tends to be traditional, and relates feminine fulfillment to a home and family, there are also prophets of change and proponents of "immodest proposals" that would play down the woman's special role as a homemaker and establish a far greater degree of sexual equality than presently exists in the United States (Rossi, 1964; see also below, pp. 255 ff.). Mannes, for example, suggests that marriage and procreation are neither duties nor responsibilities for a woman, and she wants the creative woman to maintain her independence without "trying to conform to society's image of a woman. . . . Girls who show marked talent and a strong desire for creative expression in any field should not be made to feel that they are unfeminine if they delay marriage for the sake of work or choose to experience a variety of involvements before they settle down." (Mannes, 1963, p. 129.)

The overall outlook is perhaps for further movement away from the problem of "marriage versus career" toward the solution of "marriage and career," at least for college-educated women. It should be noted that in discussing a career we have in mind an occupation for which a person has been especially trained and to which he is committed. In this sense, most working men are not pursuing a career, and similarly the question of a full-time career does not arise for most women. However, the question of a job after marriage is very likely to arise for almost all American women, and the possibility of a career is likely to exist for many women who have completed college, and for the girls who are in college or heading for college.

Both M. W. Riley *et al.* (1963) and Turner (1964) present data on high school girls indicating that approximately half of them are planning to combine a career with the role of homemaker. The conclusions of these investigators are remarkably similar, despite the fact that one study was carried out in New Jersey and the other in California. They point out that those girls who do plan to work look upon such work as being "inherently desirable" and as providing "intrinsic rewards." Material rewards, while not without significance, are presently less influential as a reason for working than in the past. This is especially true of women who have had, or who plan to have, a higher level of education. As a result, combining marriage and a career is now seen as compatible and desirable by many women, and their number is likely to increase as the number of women who go on to higher education increases.

Boys: Sexual Experience and Aggression

Riesman (*3, 14*) points out that students are often under pressure from adults or peers to have "experiences," and this leads to a lessening of freedom for those students who are not ready for, or interested in, these experiences. One such "experience," dating, is progressively being expected of youngsters at earlier ages, and a tremendous amount of emphasis is placed upon "successful dating." Stratton (1957) and Cameron and Kenkel (1960) point to age 14 as the median age of dating for American boys and girls. Lowrie (1952) reports the same median age for high school students, but a slightly higher median age, 15, for his sample of college students. This means that a considerable proportion of youngsters date, have "sweethearts," and have kissing experiences before 14 (Broderick and Fowler, 1961), and in general it means that there is a good deal of cross-sex interaction and experimentation in the pre-adolescent years quite aside from the formal dating relationship. As Burchinal (1964, pp. 625–626) points out in his summary of research by W. Breed, H. T. Christensen, J. R. Crist, and M. J. Williams, early dating is marked by feelings of inadequacy and anxiety, and in one study it was reported that most ninth-grade students said "they dated primarily because the group expected it, not because they wanted to."

As far as sexual behavior, particularly sexual intercourse, is concerned, boys are expected to have such experiences to a greater extent than girls. In this sense the double sexual standard has not faded away. The vast differences in the personal codes of males and females, as reported by Ehrmann (*1*), vividly testify to this double standard. Riesman (3) also points out the pressures upon boys to prove their masculinity through sexual relations with girls, and Tebor (1961) shows that male virgins are ridiculed by their peers and are reluctant to talk about their virginity with others.

Boys are also expected to be more aggressive than girls, and they are. Children and adults expect and receive "more dependence, passivity, and nurturance from females, more aggression from males" (Kagan, 1964). Males still continue to date girls of lower social status for purposes of sexual exploitation (Ehrmann, 1955; Breed, 1956; Ehrmann, 1), but at the same time, as Riesman (3) notes, they no longer rule out girls of the same social class as possible sexual partners. A considerable amount of sexual aggression by males on dates has been reported by college females—in the studies by Kanin (1957) and Kirkpatrick and Kanin (1957) more than half the girls reported at least one incident of erotic aggression, and approximately one in five reported forceful attempts at intercourse. It should be noted, however, that in many circles the boy is expected to go as far as he can, while the girl is expected to apply the restraint. Under such circumstances the boy's efforts to push the girl's defenses back one notch further may be perceived as legitimate dating behavior by some girls or as illegitimate aggression by others. This is not to deny, of course, that there may be a great deal of variation in the persuasiveness or force that a boy may use to try to break down a girl's resistance (see Kirkendall, 1961).

The Nature of Dating

The dating relationship is a typically American custom, and serves many different purposes. Above all, however, it is the relationship within which prospective mates meet and mingle, and it is through dating that a mate is usually selected. The American family leaves the individual relatively free to select a mate,* and the dating relationship has developed as a fairly efficient way in which to test out and to select a prospective mate. But, as Lowrie (1951) and Winch (1962) have noted, dating may also be an enjoyable end in itself, a means of gaining or maintaining prestige

---

* But far from completely free. See below, pp. 48 ff.

by dating popular partners, and an educational process in which each partner learns and develops as a result of interaction with the other.

In a widely known article by Waller (1937), the view was put forward that dating, especially among college students, is an exploitative relationship. Waller stressed that college students were not yet prepared to marry, and that they were merely seeking thrills in the dating relationship. He pointed out that the older morality, in which young people were inducted into marriage "by a series of progressive commitments," was breaking down, and that dating did not necessarily involve a commitment to one's partner. As a result, Waller felt that the woman might date a man "for the sake of presents and expensive amusements," while a man might date a woman for sexual purposes—hence, a mutually exploitative relationship. On the college campus, Waller pointed to yet another exploitative element in the relationship, which he signified by his much-used phrase, the "rating and dating complex." This refers to dating for prestige purposes, in which impersonal factors are important, such as access to a car and membership in a prestige fraternity for the male. Dating is competitive, and each student, in this "rating and dating complex," attempts to date highly desirable partners and to be seen with these partners. Waller acknowledges that in time the dating relationship may lose its competitive and exploitative nature and lead to personal involvement and possibly marriage, but it is the exploitative aspect of dating that he has emphasized. Margaret Mead (1955) has also emphasized this competitive and exploitative aspect of dating, and has suggested that the sexual controls expected of the dating partners, if well learned, may subsequently inhibit full sexual release in marriage.

In contrast to Waller and Mead, Lowrie (1951) has suggested that "exploitative relationships are a minor phase of the dating process." He points out that dating is an educational process in which the partners gain poise, learn to adjust to each other, and "obtain the training and experience needed for sensible selection of mates." Blood (1956) also presents evidence that counters the exploitative "rating and dating complex" elaborated by Waller. He points to several characteristics (for example, cheerfulness, good sportsmanship, naturalness, consideration) that are almost universally desired in a dating partner by the students in his sample, and "these are the sort of personality characteristics which make for relaxed and satisfying human interaction." (Cf. Donnelly, 1963.)

Do we go along with Waller and Mead and emphasize that dating is a competitive and exploitative experience? Or do we go along with Lowrie and Blood and emphasize that it is a mutually satisfying and educational experience? In actual fact, as most readers will readily recognize, the controversy is not as sharp as may first appear. All of the authors recognize that there are other aspects to the dating relationship than the one they emphasize. Both Lowrie (1951) and Blood (1956) point to a variety of different functions served by dating, and even Waller (1937) joins them by mentioning the possible variations that may exist from one group to another.

The problem of competitive-exploitative versus satisfying-educational dating is therefore one of emphasis and variation. To what extent do different groups or individuals vary in the extent to which they stress one or another aspect of the dating relationship? Blood (1956) shows that fraternity and sorority members on the college campus place somewhat more emphasis upon the competitive-exploitative aspect, while independent students place somewhat less emphasis upon it—although all students emphasize the satisfying-educational aspect, and this is true for both casual and serious dating. Riesman (3) suggests that one reason for the difference in emphasis between, say, Waller and Blood, is that there has been a change through time in the direction of more serious interests on the part of college students. There may, in addition, also be a change through time as the relationship between the dating partners develops. As Heiss (1962) puts it, "there is a general tendency toward decreased posing with increased intimacy." Insofar as this is the case the posing and feigning that takes place may be especially characteristic only of casual dating partners.

In addition to the social expectations that push youngsters toward early and chaste dating relationships, we must also note the biological drives of the youngsters that may propel them to seek some form of sexual release. The basic American sexual problem is that adolescents usually become physically mature and sexually driven long before marriage, while sexual intercourse is morally condemned (at least officially) outside of marriage. As a result, scholars have suggested a variety of solutions for adolescents, ranging from morally-based restraint and chastity to rationally-based release and sexual intercourse. Early marriage has been suggested as a possible solution by some (Leuba, 1948; Bee, 1959); trial marriage (Russell, 1929) and companionate marriage (Lindsey and Evans, 1927) have been suggested as solutions by others; petting to a climax has been referred to as a possible solution by yet others (LeMasters, 1957; Harper, 1961).

What do Americans actually do in the area of premarital sexual behavior? Ellis (1951) has demonstrated that this is an area about which there is a tremendous amount of ambiguity—it is hence difficult to say what *the* expectation is. Church leaders, club directors, textbook writers, and other official representatives of adult society usually urge restraint upon youngsters, and for the religiously devout youngster this is often the solution followed. It has been shown by Kinsey *et al.* (1953, pp. 278, 342; cf. Kavolis, 1962) that the chief restraint upon the petting and coital experiences of females is their religious devoutness. By age 20, for example, 17 per cent of the devout Protestant females in Kinsey's sample have petted to orgasm; and 14 per cent of the devout Protestant females have had premarital coitus. These figures are 20 and 25 per cent for inactive Protestants. For devout Catholics the figures are 15 and 12 per cent; for inactive Catholics, 31 and 41 per cent. For moderately religious Jews the figures are 27 and 11 per cent; for inactive Jews, 33 and 27 per cent. In all these instances, the devout females have a lower incidence of petting-to-orgasm or coital experiences than the moderately religious or inactive females. For petting experiences (that do not lead to orgasm) generally, the differences among females of varying degrees of devoutness is less marked, and the percentages of females who participate is much higher. For example, in Kinsey's sample 85 per cent or more of the females in all the above categories (Protestant, Catholic, Jewish; devout, moderate, inactive) had had petting experiences of some kind, from simple kissing to genital apposition, by age 20.

The sexual codes and behavior of middle-class Americans have been changing, and Ehrmann (*1*), Reiss (1960, 1964), and

Kirkendall (1961) all indicate what some of the present-day pre-marital trends are. There has, above all, been a gradually in-creasing acceptance of more intimate forms of premarital sexual behavior—toward what Reiss (1960) has called a standard of "permissiveness with affection." An important factor to consider is the extent to which it is possible to disassociate permissiveness regarding premarital intercourse from illegitimate births. As Pope and Knudsen (1965) point out, under those conditions where such a disassociation is possible—for example, through safe con-traceptive techniques or through a commitment to marry in case of premarital pregnancy—there is a greater likelihood of permis-sive standards.

Looking at the tremendous heterogeneity of American society, however, there still remains a great deal in the way of conflicting standards. One result is ambiguity on the part of many youngsters as to what is appropriate or moral. Another result, as Ehrmann clearly shows, is that many youngsters develop personal codes which indicate how far they are prepared to go on a date. Al-though these codes are personal, they are not usually idiosyncratic. There are rough social guides and expectations that have developed among youngsters, and their personal codes stem from these social expectations. In Ehrmann's selection, for example, we see that these codes are geared to the nature of one's date, so that one may be prepared to go farther or less far depending upon how close the dating relationship is. It is of interest to note that there are many different kinds of dates—group dating, double dating, dutch dating, casual dating, serious dating, steady dating, dating after being pinned, dating after being engaged, and so on (Herman, 1955; Hill, 1955; Heiss, 1960; Schnepp, 1960). These varieties of dating that have been elaborated by generations of youngsters point up the importance and complexity of what is meant by a dating relationship. Each of them is also associated, in a very general way, with certain typical expectations and pat-terns of behavior, including the degree of sexual intimacy that is appropriate to that relationship (Ehrmann, *1;* Poffenberger, 1961; Christensen and Carpenter, 1962).

Finally, it should be noted that we have been dealing with general trends and relationships, and that these do not account for all attitudes, expectations, or patterns of behavior. Some youngsters may be highly exploitative in their dating relationships; others may be highly sincere. Some girls, highly devout, may have premarital intercourse; other girls, religiously inactive, may not engage in any form of petting. In order to seek an explanation for some of these idiosyncratic patterns of behavior one would require considerable information about each individual. Take the highly devout religious girl who engages in premarital sexual intercourse: Does she belong to a religious group in which chastity is not so highly valued? Is she part of a high school group or gang that expects its members to have sexual intercourse? Does she have an especially strong physiological sex drive? Has she run into an especially persuasive dating partner? Did she lose control one night because she had been drinking? Is she deliberately using sex in order to try to catch a husband? Is she unconsciously reacting to a strict religious upbringing by acting out sexually? Many more such possibilities could be suggested—and these questions do not even involve the frequency or quality of her sexual experiences. The point, of course, is that a tremendous number of things may influence a person's behavior. What we are doing here is pointing to some of the basic social factors that influence most people in our society.

REFERENCES

BEE, LAWRENCE S. 1959. *Marriage and Family Relations,* New York: Harper.

BELL, ROBERT R. 1962. "Some Factors Related to Coed Marital Aspirations," *Family Life Coordinator,* XI, 91–94.

BERNARD, JESSIE. 1964. *Academic Women,* University Park: Pennsylvania State University Press.

BLOOD, ROBERT O., JR. 1956. "Uniformities and Diversities in Campus Dating Preferences," *Marriage and Family Living,* XVIII, 37–45.

BREED, WARREN. 1956. "Sex, Class, and Socialization in Dating," *Marriage and Family Living,* XVIII, 137–144.

BRODERICK, CARLFRED B., and STANLEY E. FOWLER. 1961. "New Patterns of Relationships Between the Sexes Among Preadolescents," *Marriage and Family Living,* XXIII, 27–30.

BURCHINAL, LEE G. 1964. "Premarital Dyad and Love Involvement," in Harold T. Christensen, ed., *Handbook of Marriage and the Family,* Chicago: Rand McNally.

CAMERON, WILLIAM J., and WILLIAM F. KENKEL. 1960. "High School Dating: A Study in Variation," *Marriage and Family Living*, XXII, 74–76.

CHRISTENSEN, HAROLD T., and GEORGE R. CARPENTER. 1962. "Timing Patterns in the Development of Sexual Intimacy," *Marriage and Family Living*, XXIV, 30–35.

COLEMAN, JAMES S. 1961. (With John W. C. Johnstone, and Kurt Jonassohn.) *The Adolescent Society*, New York: Free Press of Glencoe.

DEGLER, CARL N. 1964. "Revolution Without Ideology: The Changing Place of Women in America," *Daedalus*, XCIII, 653–670.

DONNELLY, MARGARET E. 1963. "Toward a Theory of Courtship," *Marriage and Family Living*, XXV, 290–293.

DOUVAN, ELIZABETH. 1960. "Sex Differences in Adolescent Character Process," *Merrill-Palmer Quarterly*, VI, 203–211.

EHRMANN, WINSTON W. 1955. "Influence of Comparative Social Class of Companion upon Premarital Heterosexual Behavior," *Marriage and Family Living*, XVII, 48–53.

ELLIS, ALBERT. 1951. *The Folklore of Sex*, New York: Boni.

EMPEY, LaMAR T. 1958. "Role Expectations of Young Women Regarding Marriage and a Career," *Marriage and Family Living*, XX, 152–155.

HARPER, ROBERT A. 1961. "Petting," in Albert Ellis, and Albert Abarbanel, eds., *The Encyclopedia of Sexual Behavior*, Vol. II, New York: Hawthorn, pp. 812–818.

HEISS, JEROLD S. 1960. "Variations in Courtship Progress Among High School Students," *Marriage and Family Living*, XXII, 165–170.

———. 1962. "Degree of Intimacy and Male-Female Interaction," *Sociometry*, XXV, 197–208.

HERMAN, ROBERT D. 1955. "The 'Going Steady' Complex: A Re-Examination," *Marriage and Family Living*, XVII, 36–40.

HILL, REUBEN. 1955. "Courtship in Puerto Rico: An Institution in Transition," *Marriage and Family Living*, XVII, 26–35.

KAGAN, JEROME. 1964. "Acquisition and Significance of Sex Typing and Sex Role Identity," in Martin L. Hoffman, and Lois W. Hoffman, eds., *Review of Child Development Research*, Vol. I, New York: Russell Sage Foundation.

KAMMEYER, KENNETH. 1964. "The Feminine Role: An Analysis of Attitude Consistency," *Journal of Marriage and the Family*, XXVI, 295–305.

KANIN, EUGENE J. 1957. "Male Aggression in Dating–Courtship Relations," *American Journal of Sociology*, LXIII, 197–204.

KAVOLIS, VYTAUTAS. 1962. "Church Involvement and Marital Status as a Restraint on Nonconforming Sexual Behavior," *Journal of Human Relations*, XI, 132–139.

KINSEY, ALFRED C., *et al.* 1953. *Sexual Behavior in the Human Female*, Philadelphia: W. B. Saunders.

KIRKENDALL, LESTER A. 1961. *Premarital Intercourse and Interpersonal Relationships*, New York: Julian Press.

KIRKPATRICK, CLIFFORD, and EUGENE J. KANIN. 1957. "Male Sex Aggression on a University Campus," *American Sociological Review*, XXII, 52–58.

KOMAROVSKY, MIRRA. 1953. *Women in the Modern World*, Boston: Little, Brown.

LEMASTERS, E. E. 1957. *Modern Courtship and Marriage*, New York: Macmillan.

LEUBA, CLARENCE. 1948. *Ethics in Sex Conduct*, New York: Association Press.

LINDSEY, BEN B., and WAINWRIGHT EVANS. 1927. *The Companionate Marriage*, New York: Boni and Liveright.

LOWRIE, SAMUEL H. 1951. "Dating Theories and Student Responses," *American Sociological Review*, XVI, 334–340.

———. 1952. "Sex Differences and Age of Initial Dating," *Social Forces*, XXX, 456–461.

MANNES, MARYA. 1963. "The Problems of Creative Women," pp. 116–130 in Seymour M. Farber, and Roger H. L. Wilson, eds., *The Potential of Women*, New York: McGraw-Hill.

MEAD, MARGARET. 1955. *Male and Female*, New York: Mentor.

MYRDAL, ALVA, and VIOLA KLEIN. 1956. *Women's Two Roles: Home and Work*, London: Routledge & Kegan Paul.

NYE, F. IVAN, and LOIS W. HOFFMAN, eds. 1963. *The Employed Mother in America*, Chicago: Rand McNally.

POFFENBERGER, THOMAS. 1961. "Sex–Courting Concerns of a Class of Twelfth Grade Girls," *Family Life Coordinator*, X, 75–81.

POPE, HALLOWELL, and DEAN D. KNUDSEN. 1965. "Premarital Sexual Norms, the Family, and Social Change," *Journal of Marriage and the Family*, XXVII, 314–323.

REISS, IRA L. 1960. *Premarital Sexual Standards in America*, New York: Free Press of Glencoe.

———. 1964. "Premarital Sexual Permissiveness Among Negroes and Whites," *American Sociological Review*, XXIX, 688–698.

RIESMAN, DAVID. 1964. "Two Generations," *Daedalus*, XCIII, 711–735.

RILEY, MATILDA WHITE, MARILYN E. JOHNSON, and SARANE S. BOOCOCK. 1963. "Women's Changing Occupational Role—A Research Report," *American Behavioral Scientist*, VI, 33–37.

ROSSI, ALICE S. 1964. "Equality Between the Sexes: An Immodest Proposal," *Daedalus*, XCIII, 607–652.

RUSSELL, BERTRAND. 1929. *Marriage and Morals*, New York: Liveright.

SCHNEPP, GERALD J. 1960. "Survey of Going Steady and Other Dating Practices," *American Catholic Sociological Review*, XX, 238–250.

STRATTON, DOROTHY C. 1957. "Interpretations of the Findings of the National Study of Adolescent Girls," *Journal of the National Association of Women Deans and Counselors*, XXI, 18–20.

TEBOR, IRVING B. 1961. "Male Virgins: Conflicts and Group Support in American Culture," *Family Life Coordinator*, IX, 40–42.

TURNER, RALPH H. 1964. "Some Aspects of Women's Ambition," *American Journal of Sociology,* LXX, 271–285.

WALLER, WILLARD. 1937. "The Rating and Dating Complex," *American Sociological Review,* II, 727–734.

WALLIN, PAUL. 1950. "Cultural Contradictions and Sex Roles: A Repeat Study," *American Sociological Review,* XV, 288–293.

WEIL, MILDRED W. 1962. "The Career-Homemaker Role," *Journal of Home Economics,* LIV, 294–296.

WINCH, ROBERT F. 1962. "The Functions of Dating in Middle-Class America," pp. 506–509 in Robert F. Winch, Robert McGinnis, and Herbert R. Barringer, eds., *Selected Studies in Marriage and the Family,* rev. ed., New York: Holt, Rinehart and Winston.

❧ 1 ❧   Being in Love, Going Steady, and Sexual Intimacy

by WINSTON W. EHRMANN

In the study of premarital sexual behavior there is an absence of precise evidence on the extent to which sexual activities are related (1) to being or not being in love, (2) to going steady or not going steady, and (3) to varying codes of sexual morality.[1]

Two partially contradictory popular ideas concerning being in love and sexual behavior exist: (1) males are more restrained in their sexual activities with girls whom they love; and (2) males and females who are in love are more intimate sexually than those who are not.

The first idea was more prevalent in the past, and it points to the existence of a double standard of sexual morality wherein the male is permissive and the female is restrictive in sexual conduct. The second idea is presently more prevalent; it points to a single standard for members of both sexes, a more restrictive or conservative standard for those who are not in love, and a more permissive or liberal standard for those who are in love.

Some studies of sexual behavior supply findings which have an immediate bearing on the problem under consideration, but they give only partial and indirect answers. One of the major findings of Kinsey and associates[2] is that premarital petting and coitus are correlated with nearness to marriage among the females, but that

Adapted by the editor from Winston W. Ehrmann, "Premarital Sexual Behavior and Sex Codes of Conduct with Acquaintances, Friends, and Lovers," *Social Forces,* XXXVIII, 1959, 158–164; and Winston W. Ehrmann, *Premarital Dating Behavior,* New York: Holt, Rinehart and Winston, 1959, pp. 134, 140, 175, 181–182, 269, 279. Copyright © 1959 by Holt, Rinehart and Winston, Inc. By permission of the author, the University of North Carolina Press, and Holt, Rinehart and Winston, Inc.

this relationship is relatively insignificant among the males in their
sample. These findings suggest, but do not confirm, that since a
greater proportion of the premarital sexual behavior of the female
than of the male is with the future spouse and with nearness to
marriage, the sexual behavior of the female is more closely correlated with being in love than is the sexual behavior of the male.
But these data do not offer any definite clues to the relationship
between being in love, going steady, and sex codes of conduct.

Sexual Behavior and Personal Codes with Acquaintances, Friends, and Lovers

First we shall report on the sexual behavior and personal codes
of a sample of college students with acquaintances, friends, and
lovers.* All of the subjects in this sample† had had dates with
acquaintances and friends; 45 (90 per cent) of the males and 42
(84 per cent) of the females had been in love. The reported sexual
experience and personal code of sex conduct with acquaintances,
friends, and lovers is given in Table 1.

More males had had sexual intercourse with nonlovers than with
lovers. The personal code shows the same relationship in that more
males considered that coitus was permissible with a nonlover than
with a lover. A significant fact is that the males were consistent
in their codes and behavior with nonlovers, but inconsistent with
lovers in that only half of those who considered coitus permissible
with a lover had engaged in such behavior (47 per cent as compared to 24 per cent).

Only 2 per cent of the females had had premarital intercourse
with an acquaintance and 6 per cent with a friend, but 17 per cent
with a lover. The personal code and lifetime behavior of the girls
in our sample are essentially identical for each class of companions,
indicating the extent to which it is the girls who determine "how
far" a relationship goes. The degree of physical intimacy which

* "Lover" is used here to indicate the loved one, and not necessarily one
with whom one is having a sexual relationship.
† This sample consists of 100 students, 50 males and 50 females, who
were randomly selected by sex from an original sample population of over
1000 unmarried students. The original sample was drawn at random over a
period of several years from students in a university course in marriage and
the family.

TABLE 1

Sexual Behavior and Personal Codes with Acquaintances, Friends, and Lovers (Lifetime Behavior)*

Number	Light Petting	Heavy Petting	Coitus	Total
		Stages of Behavior and Codes (Per cent)		
MALES				
With Acquaintances				
(50) Lifetime Behavior	28	16	56	100
(50) Personal Code	28	12	60	100
With Friends				
(50) Lifetime Behavior	22	18	60	100
(50) Personal Code	20	8	72	100
With Lovers				
(45) Lifetime Behavior	36	40	24	100
(45) Personal Code	24	29	47	100
FEMALES				
With Acquaintances				
(50) Lifetime Behavior	92	6	2	100
(50) Personal Code	92	4	4	100
With Friends				
(50) Lifetime Behavior	82	12	6	100
(50) Personal Code	84	10	6	100
With Lovers				
(42) Lifetime Behavior	42	41	17	100
(42) Personal Code	46	40	14	100

* "Lifetime behavior" refers to the most advanced stage of sexual behavior ever experienced. "Personal code" refers to the most advanced stage that the individual considered permissible. Those classified under "light petting" had engaged in kissing and hugging and/or the male caressing the female's covered breast, but had not gone farther; those under "heavy petting" had experienced more intimate fondling without sexual intercourse; and those under "coitus" had experienced sexual intercourse with the indicated category of companion.

the females had experienced or had considered permissible for themselves is *directly related* to the intimacy of the boy-girl relationship. There is a marked difference between the code and behavior for nonlovers and lovers: the girls are far more liberal in personal behavior and code with lovers than with nonlovers.

There are a number of reasons why males and females differ in their sexual behavior with lovers and nonlovers. Females are subjected to much stronger social taboos which limit their sexual activity. They do not have to seek males who are willing sexual partners. In fact, the converse is true: more often than not, girls have to evade sexual advances, particularly if there is an attempt to go beyond light petting. Being in love for them means both a greater desire for heterosexual activities and a greater, though still limited, willingness to flout the folkways and mores which limit petting activities to kissing and hugging. Boys, however, are more consistently motivated toward sexual activities by their ideas of manhood. They tend to seek and to find girls who, as friends or acquaintances, are willing sex partners. In addition, among some couples who are in love, the female either willingly or reluctantly engages in sexual intercourse for the first time. Among many others, the male ceases to have intercourse either because the female refuses or because he considers the girl too innocent or too respectable.

Although in general the girls are more conservative than the men, it should be noted (even though this material is not included in the tables) that the group with the highest incidence of premarital coitus with lovers is a female group. This is the small group of females (6 out of 50) who have been in love and who have a liberal personal code. All of these females, in their lifetime behavior, have had coitus with a loved one.

Sexual Behavior in Steady and Non-steady Dating

Although "being in love" and "going steady" are not synonymous, they are overlapping phenomena. With rare exception, people who are in love are also going steady. On the other hand, although not all who are going steady are in love, the great majority are. In fact, these two phenomena are so closely related that an analysis of behavior patterns in terms of going steady and not going steady or of being in love and not being in love yields much the same results.

It is evident from Table 2 on the current sexual behavior of males and females who are or are not going steady that these sexual patterns are comparable to the sexual behavior of lovers and nonlovers. More females were having coitus with their steadies

TABLE 2

Sexual Behavior in Steady and Non-steady Dating (Current Behavior)*

Number		Light Petting	Heavy Petting	Coitus	Total
			Stages (Per cent)		
	MALES				
	Going with:				
(88)	1. Steady only	43	37	20	100
(52)	2. Steady and others	25	19	56	100
(216)	3. Others only	44	16	40	100
	FEMALES				
	Going with:				
(68)	1. Steady only	48	33	19	100
(23)	2. Steady and others	60	31	9	100
(99)	3. Others only	79	15	6	100

* "Current behavior" refers to the most advanced stage of sexual activity to which the individual was going at the time of the study. These data are based on the responses of 356 males and 190 females from the original sample of more than 1000 students.

The category of "steady and others" was included because it was discovered that a substantial percentage of males (15 per cent) and females (12 per cent) were dating others even though they had a steady dating partner.

(19 per cent) than with "others" (6 per cent), and more males were having coitus with "others" (40 per cent) than with their steadies (20 per cent). Many, or perhaps most, of these males believed in the double standard of sexual morality. For example, some of those going steady dated "others" in order to have sexual intercourse, sometimes without the knowledge of their female steady, a "good girl," but sometimes with the tacit consent of the female steady.

Conclusion

The relationship between love and premarital sexual behavior, as indicated by the findings of this research, depends to a large extent upon the sex codes of conduct. Although these matters must be viewed in a somewhat simplified way for the purposes of analysis, it is evident that the sexual codes are a highly complex set of attitudes which the individual has about his own sexual adjustment and by which he accepts or rejects the behavior of others. It was correctly assumed that sex codes of conduct as manifested in expressed attitudes and actual behavior would vary according to the "intimacy relationship" existing between the person and the one dated.

From the data of this study, we can generally conclude that males are more conservative and females are more liberal (both in expressed personal codes of sex conduct and in actual behavior) with lovers than with nonlovers. In other words, the degree of physical intimacy actually experienced or considered permissible is, among males, *inversely* related, and among females *directly* related to the intensity of familiarity and affection in the male-female relationship. Probably the single most important empirical finding of this research is that female sexual expression is primarily and profoundly related to being in love and to going steady; male sexuality is more indirectly and less exclusively associated with being in love and going steady.

NOTES

1. See IRA L. REISS, "The Double Standard in Premarital Sexual Inter-course," *Social Forces*, XXXIV, 1956, 224–230.
2. ALFRED C. KINSEY *et al.*, *Sexual Behavior in the Human Female*, Philadelphia: W. B. Saunders, 1953, pp. 239–241, 293, 296.

✌§ 2 §✭ Cultural Contradictions and Sex Roles

by M I R R A K O M A R O V S K Y

Profound changes in the roles of women during the past century have been accompanied by innumerable contradictions and inconsistencies. With our rapidly changing and highly differentiated culture, with migrations and multiplied social contacts, the stage is set for many combinations of incongruous elements. Cultural norms are often unsuited to the social situations to which they apply. Thus they may deter an individual from a course of action which would serve his own, and society's, interests best. Or, if behavior contrary to the norm is engaged in, the individual may suffer from guilt over violating mores which no longer serve any socially useful end. Sometimes culturally defined roles are adhered to in the face of new conditions without a conscious realization of the discrepancies involved. The reciprocal actions dictated by the roles may be at variance with those demanded by the actual situation. This may result in an imbalance of privileges and obligations[1] or in some frustration of basic interests.

Again, problems arise because changes in the mode of life have created new situations which have not as yet been defined by culture. Individuals left thus without social guidance tend to act in terms of egotistic or "short-run hedonistic" motives which at times defeat their own long-term interests or create conflict with others. The precise obligation of a gainfully employed wife toward the support of the family is one such undefined situation.

Finally, a third mode of discrepancy arises in the existence of incompatible cultural definitions of the same social situation, such

Adapted from "Cultural Contradictions and Sex Roles," *American Journal of Sociology*, LII, Nov., 1946, 184–189. By permission of the author and The University of Chicago Press. Copyright, 1946, The University of Chicago.

as the clash of "old-fashioned" and "radical" mores, of religion and law, of norms of economic and familial institutions.

The problems raised by these discrepancies are social problems in the sense that they engender mental conflict or social conflict or otherwise frustrate some basic interest of large segments of the population.

This article sets forth in detail the nature of certain incompatible sex roles imposed by our society upon the college woman. It is based on data collected in 1942 and 1943. Members of an undergraduate course on the family were asked for two successive years to submit autobiographical documents focused on the topic; 73 were collected. In addition, 80 interviews, lasting about an hour each, were conducted with every member of a course in social psychology of the same institution—making a total of 153 documents ranging from a minimum of five to a maximum of thirty typewritten pages.

The generalization emerging from these documents is the existence of serious contradictions between two roles present in the social environment of the college woman. The goals set by each role are mutually exclusive, and the fundamental personality traits each evokes are at points diametrically opposed, so that what are assets for one become liabilities for the other, and the full realization of one role threatens defeat in the other.

One of these roles may be termed the "feminine" role. While there are a number of permissive variants of the feminine role for women of college age (the "good sport," the "glamour girl," the "young lady," the domestic "home girl," etc.), they have a common core of attributes defining the proper attitudes to men, family, work, love, etc., and a set of personality traits often described with reference to the male sex role as "not as dominant, or aggressive as men" or "more emotional, sympathetic."

The other and more recent role is, in a sense, no *sex* role at all, because it partly obliterates the differentiation in sex. It demands of the woman much the same virtues, patterns of behavior, and attitude that it does of the men of a corresponding age. We shall refer to this as the "modern" role.

Both roles are present in the social environment of these women throughout their lives, though, as the precise content of each sex role varies with age, so does the nature of their clashes change from one stage to another. In the period under discussion the conflict between the two roles apparently centers about dating, social life, academic work, vocational plans, excellence in specific fields of endeavor, and a number of personality traits.

One manifestation of the problem is in the inconsistency of the goals set for the girl by her family.

Forty, or 26 per cent, of the respondents expressed some grievance against their families for failure to confront them with clearcut and consistent goals. The majority, 74 per cent, denied having had such experiences. One student writes:

> How am I to pursue any course singlemindedly when some way along the line a person I respect is sure to say, "You are on the wrong track and are wasting your time." Uncle John telephones every Sunday morning. His first question is: "Did you go out last night?" He would think me a "grind" if I were to stay home Saturday night to finish a term paper. My father expects me to get an "A" in every subject and is disappointed by a "B." He says I have plenty of time for social life. Mother says, "That 'A' in Philosophy is very nice dear. But please don't become so deep that no man will be good enough for you." And, finally, Aunt Mary's line is careers for women. "Prepare yourself for some profession. This is the only way to insure yourself independence and an interesting life. You have plenty of time to marry."

A student reminisces:

> All through high school my family urged me to work hard because they wished me to enter a first-rate college. At the same time they were always raving about a girl schoolmate who lived next door to us. How pretty and sweet she was, how popular, and what taste in clothes! Couldn't I also pay more attention to my appearance and to social life? They were overlooking the fact that this carefree friend of mine had little time left for school work and had failed several subjects. It seemed that my family had expected me to become Eve Curie and Hedy Lamarr wrapped up in one.

Another comments:

> My mother thinks that it is very nice to be smart in college but only if it doesn't take too much effort. She always tells me not to be too intellectual on dates, to be clever in a light sort of way. My father, on the other hand, wants me to study law. He thinks that if I applied myself I could make an excellent lawyer and keeps telling me that I am better fitted for this profession than my brother.

Another writes:

> One of my two brothers writes: "Cover up that high forehead
> and act a little dumb once in a while"; while the other always urges
> upon me the importance of rigorous scholarship.

The students testified to a certain bewilderment and confusion
caused by the failure on the part of the family to smooth the passage from one role to another, especially when the roles involved
were contradictory. It seemed to some of them that they had
awakened one morning to find their world upside down: what had
hitherto evoked praise and rewards from relatives, now suddenly
aroused censure. Once during her freshman year in college, after a
delightful date, a student wrote her brother with great elation:

> "What a wonderful evening at the fraternity house! You would
> be proud of me, Johnny! I won all ping-pong games but one!"
> "For heaven's sake," came the reply, "when will you grow up?
> Don't you know that a boy likes to think he is better than a girl?
> Give him a little competition, sure, but miss a few serves in the
> end. Should you join the Debate Club? By all means, but don't
> practice too much on the boys." Believe me I was stunned by this
> letter, but then I saw that he was right. To be a success in the
> dorms one must date, to date one must not win too many ping-
> pong games. At first I resented this bitterly. But now I am more
> or less used to it and live in hope of one day meeting a man who
> is my superior so that I may be my natural self.

It is the parents and not the older sibling who reversed their
expectations in the following excerpt:

> All through grammar school and high school my parents led me
> to feel that to do well in school was my chief responsibility. A
> good report card, an election to student office, these were the
> news Mother bragged about in telephone conversations with her
> friends. But recently they suddenly got worried about me: I don't
> pay enough attention to social life, a woman needs *some* education
> but not that much. They are disturbed by my determination to
> go to the School of Social Work. Why my ambitions should sur-
> prise them after they have exposed me for four years to some of
> the most inspired and stimulating social scientists in the country,
> I can't imagine. They have some mighty strong arguments on their
> side. What is the use, they say, of investing years in training for a
> profession, only to drop it in a few years? Chances of meeting
> men are slim in this profession. Besides, I may become so pre-
> occupied with it as to sacrifice social life. The next few years are,
> after all, the proper time to find a mate. But the urge to apply what
> I have learned, and the challenge of this profession is so strong
> that I shall go on despite the family opposition.

Sixty-one, or 40 per cent, of the students indicated that they have occasionally "played dumb" on dates, that is, concealed some academic honor, pretended ignorance of some subject, or allowed the man the last word in an intellectual discussion. Among these were women who "threw games" and in general played down certain skills in obedience to the unwritten law that men must possess these skills to a superior degree. At the same time, in other areas of life, social pressures were being exerted upon these women to "play to win," to compete to the utmost of their abilities for intellectual distinction and academic honors. One student writes:

I was glad to transfer to a women's college. The two years at the co-ed university produced a constant strain. I am a good student; my family expects me to get good marks. At the same time I am normal enough to want to be invited to the Saturday night dance. Well, everyone knew that on that campus a reputation of a "brain" killed a girl socially. I was always fearful lest I say too much in class or answer a question which the boys I dated couldn't answer.

Here are some significant remarks made from the interviews:

When a girl asks me what marks I got last semester I answer, "Not so good—only one 'A'." When a boy asks the same question, I say very brightly with a note of surprise, "Imagine, I got an 'A!' "

I am engaged to a southern boy who doesn't think too much of the woman's intellect. In spite of myself, I play up to his theories because the less one knows and does, the more he does for you and thinks you "cute" into the bargain. . . . I allow him to explain things to me in great detail and to treat me as a child in financial matters.

One of the nicest techniques is to spell long words incorrectly once in a while. My boyfriend seems to get a great kick out of it and writes back, "Honey, you certainly don't know how to spell."

When my date said that he considers Ravel's *Bolero* the greatest piece of music ever written, I changed the subject because I knew I would talk down to him.

Once I went sailing with a man who so obviously enjoyed the role of protector that I told him I didn't know how to sail. As it turned out he didn't either. We got into a tough spot, and I was torn between a desire to get a hold of the boat and a fear to reveal that I had lied to him.

It embarrassed me that my "steady" in high school got worse marks than I. A boy should naturally do better in school. I would never tell him my marks and would often ask him to help me with my homework.

I am better in math than my fiancé. But while I let him explain politics to me, we never talk about math even though, being a math major, I could tell him some interesting things.

Mother used to tell me to lay off the brains on dates because glasses make me look too intellectual anyhow.

On dates I always go through the "I-don't-care-anything-you-want-to-do" routine. It gets monotonous but boys fear girls who make decisions. They think such girls would make nagging wives.

I am a natural leader and, when in the company of girls, usually take the lead. That is why I am so active in college activities. But I know that men fear bossy women, and I always have to watch myself on dates not to assume the "executive" role. Once a boy walking to the theater with me took the wrong street. I knew a short cut but kept quiet.

I let my fiancé make most of the decisions when we are out. It annoys me, but he prefers it.

I sometimes "play dumb" on dates, but it leaves a bad taste. The emotions are complicated. Part of me enjoys "putting something over" on the unsuspecting male. But this sense of superiority over him is mixed with feelings of guilt for my hypocrisy. Toward the "date" I feel some contempt because he is "taken in" by my technique, or if I like the boy, a kind of a maternal condescension. At times I resent him! Why isn't he my superior in all ways in which a man should excel so that I could be my natural self? What am I doing here with him, anyhow? Slumming?

And the funny part of it is that the man, I think, is not always so unsuspecting. He may sense the truth and become uneasy in the relation. "Where do I stand? Is she laughing up her sleeve or did she mean this praise? Was she really impressed with that little speech of mine or did she only pretend to know nothing about politics?" And once or twice I felt that the joke was on me: the boy saw through my wiles and felt contempt for me for stooping to such tricks.

Another aspect of the problem is the conflict between the psychogenetic personality of the girl and the cultural role foisted upon her by the milieu.[2] At times it is the girl with "masculine" interests and personality traits who chafes under the pressure to conform to the "feminine" pattern. At other times it is the family and the college that thrust upon the reluctant girl the "modern" role.

While, historically, the "modern" role is the most recent one, ontogenetically it is the one emphasized earlier in the education of the college girl, if these 153 documents are representative. Society confronts the girl with powerful challenges and strong pressure to excel in certain competitive lines of endeavor and to develop certain techniques of adaptations very similar to those expected of her brothers. But, then, quite suddenly as it appears to these girls, the very success in meeting these challenges begins to cause anxiety. It is precisely those most successful in the earlier role who are now penalized.

It is not only the passage from age to age but the moving to another region or type of campus which may create for the girl similar problems. The precise content of sex roles, or, to put it in another way, the degree of their differentiation, varies with regional, class, nativity, and other subcultures.

Whenever individuals show differences in response to some social situation, as have our 153 respondents, the question naturally arises as to the causes. It will be remembered that 40 per cent admitted some difficulties in personal relations with men due to conflicting sex roles but that 60 per cent said that they had no such problems. Inconsistency of parental expectations troubled 26 per cent of the students.

To account for individual differences would require another study, involving a classification of personalities in relation to the peculiar social environments of each. Generally speaking, it would seem that it is the girl with a "middle-of-the-road personality" who is most happily adjusted to the present historical moment. She is not a perfect incarnation of either role but is flexible enough to play both. She is a girl who is intelligent enough to do well in school but not so brilliant as to "get all 'A' 's"; informed and alert but not consumed by an intellectual passion; capable but not talented in areas relatively new to women; able to stand on her own feet and to earn a living but not so good a living as to compete with men; capable of doing some job well (in case she does not marry or, otherwise, has to work) but not so identified with a profession as to need it for her happiness.

A search for less immediate causes of individual reactions would lead us further back to the study of genesis of the personality differences found relevant to the problem. One of the clues will certainly be provided by the relation of the child to the parent of the same and of the opposite sex. This relation affects the conception of self and the inclination for a particular sex role.

The problems set forth in this article will persist, in the opinion

of the writer, until the adult sex roles of women are redefined in
greater harmony with the socioeconomic and ideological character
of modern society.[3] Until then neither the formal education nor
the unverbalized sex roles of the adolescent woman can be cleared
of intrinsic contradictions.

NOTES

1. CLIFFORD KIRKPATRICK, "The Measurement of Ethical Inconsistency in
   Marriage," *International Journal of Ethics,* XLVI (1936), 444–60.
2. MARGARET MEAD, *Sex and Temperament in Three Primitive Societies*
   (New York: Morrow & Co., 1935).
3. See excellent discussions in Talcott Parsons, "Age and Sex in the Social
   Structure of the United States," *American Sociological Review,* VII
   (1942), 604–16, and in the same issue, Ralph Linton, "Age and Sex
   Categories," pp. 589–603, and Leonard S. Cottrell, Jr., "The Adjustment
   of the Individual to His Age and Sex Roles," pp. 617–20. [See also "The
   Changing American Family," below, pp. 248 ff.—Ed.]

ᵉ§ 3 §ᵉ   Permissiveness and Sex Roles

by D A V I D   R I E S M A N

Cross-generational misunderstandings are, of course, no new
thing in America, nor are conflicts about permissiveness and
sex. Indeed, foreign observers visiting this country a hundred years
ago commented about the tolerance shown children, and, while
some admired the children's poise and independence, others were

Adapted from "Permissiveness and Sex Roles," *Marriage and Family Living,*
XXI, Aug., 1959, 211–217.

horrified by their insolence or bad manners. Tocqueville was greatly impressed by the fact that American young women went around what was still a rude country without chaperones, and he and his fellow traveller, Beaumont, wrote home that American girls, while very attractive and appealing, were protected, not as on the continent by ignorance, but by what we might today call know-how. He was not quite sure how he felt about these emancipated women, with whom gallantry was no longer a sport for passing the time and asserting one's superiority.

Something like his complaint is echoed in the tendency for men of my own generation and older to look with dismay on the practice of going steady among young people in high school and college. This older generation compares going steady unfavorably with its own romantic and nostalgic images of "playing the field"; correspondingly, it sees young marriages as a too early captivity avoiding frivolity and flirtation.*

We should note at the outset that early dating and early sex life in general is characteristic of the working class, as Kinsey documented, and of the rural population in many peasant countries. What seems to have happened in this as in so many other ways, is that the middle class has been losing its traditional orientation towards the future and inhibitions in the present, and that the permissiveness which arises from inconsistency and indifference in the lower strata has now become a matter of principle and only an occasionally unprincipled tolerance in the educated strata. Thus, even debutantes and students at the elite colleges go steady, whereas they would once have thought such practices "common."

In an article in *Science,* Margaret Mead and Rhoda Métraux have called attention to a hitherto unnoticed consequence of this change in values.[1] They were investigating (not by means of a national sample, but rather by careful selections here and there) the attitude of high school students towards science and scientists and they made the discovery that the career choice of boys was being increasingly influenced by the judgments of girls as to what

* Some critics, however, speak from the point of view of an older morality. Thus, Catholic priests at some parochial schools and colleges have forbidden steady dating on the ground that it is an occasion for sin. In this they reveal the protective bias the Church has always had towards women, for it could be argued that steady dating, while slightly increasing sin among young women, substantially reduces it among young men.

were good careers for their boyfriends to be in. That is, if girls thought scientists would make poor husbands, this helped shape the image of the scientist that prevailed in high school—and helped, perhaps imperceptibly, to push boys towards careers that were considered compatible with decent domesticity. Of course girls were not wholly responsible for the image of the scientist which the researchers discovered: a person who is remote and sexless, who has too much or too little hair, wrapped up in the laboratory and not quite human—indeed, sometimes quite inhuman like a science fiction monster. But their article suggests that in an earlier day, when boys in the upper strata became aware of girls at a later point in life, when the boys were already themselves committed to a career, the judgment by girls would be less influential: the girls would have to take the men as they had become.

Now, however, both boys and girls are talking with each other about such serious matters as career choice, and not merely handing out a "line" with which to impress each other in the rating-dating game. The very fact that boys as well as girls are willing to go steady and to marry earlier indicates a general cultural change of emphasis towards the affective and non-work side of life, and makes it possible for boys and girls together to decide the kind of domestic life they will jointly seek and the sorts of careers that will further and not interfere with that ideal.

If one talks to the faculties of medical schools, one finds them sometimes quite concerned with these developments. For one thing, there is evidence of a general decline of applications to medical school in the last several years, and it has been suggested that this is partly due to dislike of the postponement medical education requires. At the University of Kansas Medical School, three-quarters of the students are married, and this affects how they conduct themselves as students.[2] The married students are not eager for night duty, for example, or for the surgical residencies that involve night duty; nor do they yearn to sit around talking about science, ethics, and women with their fellow students. Rather, they are quickly off after their stint in the hospital to give their spouses a hand with the children and to relax with them in the evening. Faculties of medical schools under these altered conditions tend to recall their own student days as those of bachelor asceticism (modulated by an occasional binge), and readily feel out

of touch with these new men who are on the one hand so mature
(in being well started on family life and choice of specialty), and
on the other hand, so "mature" as not to care to talk shop. And
the students, in turn, eager to end the long period in which they
must be supported by their wives and families, resent the pro-
tracted training necessary for certain specialties and the arduous
isolation which, if not inherently "necessary," has traditionally
been considered part of the folkways of that specialty.

What men have lost in willingness to undertake arduous and
highly specialized careers has not, of course, marked any com-
mensurate gain for women. Thus, although it is a good deal easier
today than a generation ago for women to enter medical school,
and although they probably suffer less hazing in school from their
professors and from male students, they are still a tiny proportion
of the students—10 per cent or less. (The situation is very different in many countries in Europe and in the Soviet Union where
women play a very large role in medicine.) The same emphasis
on the affective side of life, on the family as the most important
element in the good life, which has influenced the career decisions
of men, has also led even the most brilliant and energetic college
women to decide that they do not want to undertake long preparation for careers which might cut them off from the chance of
marriage or in some subtle way defeminize them. And while that
has always been true of American women, college women today
seem both more universally ready to hold a job than they once
were (there are fewer playgirls) and less ready to risk, on behalf
of greatly ambitious career aims, the possibility of a stable marriage.

These developments are occurring at the same time that there
has been a great hue and cry, stimulated by Sputnik, that we need
more doctors, more scientists, more engineers, more highly trained
people generally. Most of this hue and cry is based on what I regard as an exploitative concern for the state of the national labor
force in the Cold War; it assumes that it is inconceivable that we
might end the Cold War, and that, in a society of abundance, we
might regard the talents of our young people as an opportunity
to develop new sorts of careers and new relations towards work.
Among some of the most sensitive and gifted young people, there
has developed the tendency to withdraw altogether from the great
and overriding political concerns of their elders, sometimes by

choosing fields such as the humanities or the ministry which could not have a conceivable Cold War or big-project relevance, and sometimes by withdrawing any deep involvement from work in large organizations even while going through the motions.[3] As a result of these developments, there would seem to be building up an often irrational reaction against permissiveness—sometimes in the mild forms in which we see it in the cartoons of *The New Yorker,* and sometimes in the intemperate attacks on the schools by such men as Admiral Rickover.

What is left out in this cross-generational bickering is any understanding of what is happening, of some of the positive values that are emerging, and of some of the problems for the individual as well as for society that these new emancipations bring. There can be no doubt that what many educated young men and women today are looking for in each other is not the rating-dating game of twenty years ago.[4] To be sure, there are still fraternities and sororities on the campus and still an interest in good looks, popularity, good grooming, and smoothness. But all this is more subdued and the relationships increasingly sought for are more searching, more profound, more sincere. There is more desire to share; less desire to impress. There is less desire to dazzle members of one's own sex and more to come to some sort of humane terms with the opposite sex. Moreover, it seems to me that young people are increasingly preoccupied with their capacity to love as well as to be loved. And I have the impression that sexual relations themselves when they do occur come about less frequently from a desire on the part of the boys to present trophies to their own male vanity than to secure themselves against the anxiety that they may not be truly and deeply loved, or capable of love.

Moreover, the increase in going steady that has brought about some diminution of the search for those careers which require arduous preparation has not brought about a lessened level of seriousness among students either in high school or college. In fact, it could even be argued that young people who have made themselves secure in a vital area through the practice of going steady can consequently afford to commit themselves more fully to their studies, becoming more equable if sometimes less frantic students than were many in an earlier day who were constantly preoccupied as to whether or not they had a date or should have a date or what they might be missing if they did not.

At some of the more academically oriented colleges, the rise in the level of demands on students has made many students doubt their own intellectual adequacy—and therefore they seek to prove that they are after all good for something in their relations with the opposite sex. They do not choose to go on dates rather than to study; they do both—and if something has to give way under this pressure, it is their sleep. (There is some evidence that students are staying up later and later and, if evidence from various student health services could be compared, it might shed interesting light on some of these problems.)

The seriousness and depth of some of these steady relationships in high school and college are such as to give young people the feeling that they really know members of the opposite sex well enough to choose a marriage partner much earlier in life than people of equivalent sensitivity would have dared to do with their eyes open in an earlier day. Talcott Parsons argues in his writings that romantic love allows a kind of leap of faith across the impossibility of making a rational choice (much as advertising encourages a similar leap of faith among equally available brand-name items). But in fact many of the young people are not "romantic" in the nineteenth century sense; they believe in love, but not in a starry-eyed way. Indeed, the danger of some of these steady relationships may be exactly like that of some marriages; that a plateau of routinization is too quickly reached, with stability quickly achieved as a platform for competent but unexciting family life and serious, if not totally demanding, work.

In our society, whatever becomes a fashion puts pressure on those whom the fashion does not readily fit. In an earlier day, when it was thought sober in the upper strata to postpone marriage, it took a certain hardihood or impulsivity to marry early, and to have more than two or three children. Today, in contrast, things are often hard on those who do not feel ready to "grow up," to date, to marry young, and to have a sizeable family. Girls, of course, are not chaperoned anymore, either in the Latin way or in the more characteristic Calvinist way in which they carried their invisible chaperone inside. Boys are, therefore, not protected from

having to make advances to girls by the latters' obvious unavailabil-
ity. Indeed, the availability of girls in America is an omnipresent
and inescapable part of our visual esthetic—built into the widths
of our cars, the reels of our movies, into the pages of our advertise-
ments, and built into the girls themselves, I might add, in the way
they carry themselves and dress. The greater, but still not sufficiently psychological, awareness has produced the phenomenon I
have occasionally seen as a teacher: that students feel under pressure from adults to have "experiences" and are ashamed to be
thought dull and not to have any.

Likewise, boys and girls have a new fear, one which a generation earlier was not conscious for most men no matter how sheltered, nor for most women—that is, the fear that they might be
homosexual. This fear is one factor which haunts the campus,
putting pressure on many young men to be guarded in their relations with each other, and also with their male teachers, while at
the same time putting pressure on them to seek out relations with
girls in order to convince themselves and perhaps each other that
they are not.

As a concomitant development, the ribbing of sissies, at least in
the middle class, is much less strong now than it once was, and
in that sense, greater "femininity" is being increasingly permitted to
educated men in this country. While one can still find colleges where
men define themselves as men by being athletic and going in for
engineering, there are many institutions throughout the country
where men can without embarrassment be interested in art, in
English, in dance, and in music. But this very openness, which
permits men to do things which they would once (and in many
parts of the country today would still) reject, has also had the
curious consequence that they cannot clearly and unequivocally
define themselves as men by their roles. They have to define themselves as men, therefore, in other ways, and especially in the one
physiological way which appears irrefutable; and the girls are under
somewhat analogous pressure, possibly less out of a fear of homo-
sexuality, but hardly less out of a fear of not being really a woman
and responding to men as a woman should. Whereas, in the days
of the double standard, nice boys would not molest good girls,
that is college girls, now they often use Freud to persuade the
latter, and their steady dates, that to be inhibited is bad, likely

to harm the boy, if not produce or symbolize frigidity in the girl. Thus, we see that permissiveness in some areas, like any movement of liberation, produces unpermissiveness in others. Boys and girls, for instance, have *less* permission than they once did to proceed in their relations to each other and to themselves at idiosyncratic rates.

We can see what this means when we look at high schools in the way that Coleman has recently been doing.[5] He has asked high school students what they are interested in; and when boys are asked this question they volunteer a great many concerns; they are interested in automobiles, in hi-fi, in sports and ham radios, and even occasionally in the curriculum. They are interested in girls, too, but in rather a secondary way. In contrast, the girls are interested in boys and in each other, and even their interest in each other I suspect is sometimes secondary or resonant to their interest in boys. Girls in high school are natural sociometrists; even in the fourth grade this is true. The boys have many defenses against being interested in girls, but the girls have very few comparable defenses against an interest in boys, and this is a pressure on boys as well as on girls. We know something of what this means in terms of age disparities. At Vassar the entering freshman girl is already date-conscious and is likely to be picked up, let us say at Yale, by upper classmen.[6] But the senior girl in high school is too old for the comparable boys now and is perhaps cut off by physical or psychological distance from college boys, whereas the freshman and sophomore boys in high school are thrown with girls who are not able to respond to them, or they to the girls, as our popular culture tells them that they should. If William James were to look at this situation, he would say that girls need a moral substitute for boys; and, indeed, for their own development, I think they need an alternative to sociometry as their major field of research in high school and college.

One reason why it seems to me that some people can profit from non-coeducation at some stages in their lives is that girls can be given in this way an alternative—at least a partial one—that allows them to cultivate, free from the pressure of boys and boy-minded girls, including the boy-minded parts of themselves, interests that might otherwise be thought of as unfeminine. And, by the same token, it may allow boys to cultivate an interest in such things as the student newspaper, or ballet, which are occasionally monopolized by girls in a co-ed school (to be sure, as I have already mentioned, most girls in a co-ed school will be less active and pluralistic in their interests than boys of similar background, but there may be a few who will take over certain artistic activities and thus define them in such a way that boys will feel excluded). We see here a paradox: the influence of girls on boys in high school and college can be a broadening one in that it saves the boys from a narrow vocationalism and over-intellectual or over-ambitious or over-technocratic preoccupation with getting ahead in conventional terms. So, too, girls can be saved by the presence of boys from the kinds of artful stuffiness and female "accomplishment" that some of the more fashionable and less intellectual junior colleges for women still advertise as their stock in trade. But at the margin, the presence of each limits rather than expands the potentialities of the other—and again permissiveness imposes subtle restraints of its own.[7]

These changes in the awareness each sex has of the role of the other have a bearing on our ways of handling education of both sexes in the social sciences and in the other sciences. Every curriculum contains many implicit statements about ideas as "feminine" or "masculine"—statements which are carried in the language or texture of the discipline, and in the tone and attitudes of its professors. For instance, there are many teachers of psychology in college who resent the fact that women who are "interested in people" come into their courses, and these teachers react by turning their subject into a branch of engineering—an aggressively "male" subject from which all concrete and humane concerns of both men and women are excluded in the name of rigor. Then, too, as already indicated, in many good colleges, the more sensitive students of both sexes feel themselves shut out from mathematics, physics, chemistry, and technology generally. This may, in a few cases, be because they associate these fields, understandably enough in our time, with missiles and war maneuvers, with all that they find oppressive and intractable in the modern world. But it is also because these subjects are often taught in such a way that the subtlety of their ideas is not conveyed, but only the "hardware." As I think of the great physicists and mathematicians of recent times, it seems to me that their ideas (consider

Einstein, Oppenheimer, Bohr) have a quality which should not alienate sensitive and very feminine women or sensitive and very intraceptive men. But both in high school and college, these fields are often taught, mainly by men, for whom the text is a kind of cook book—an old-style cook book at that. Conversely, English and art are taught in many secondary schools and some colleges as very much prissy, traditionally female and snob-tainted subjects.

As a result, certain compartmentalizations remain very important in our culture in spite of greater freedom and permissiveness. Women, for instance, remain shut out, by one set of snobberies and self-imposed restrictions, from college and university teaching, while men remain shut out by another set of constrictions from elementary school teaching and from the teaching of music in secondary school. Women in this country are decreasingly charged with carrying the burdens of culture alone, including the burden of human and humane understanding, but there is still much that needs to be done before men are permitted to share more equally in these tasks, and women in the tasks of the outside world of politics and work.[8] Our ideal here would be a culture in which the interests of each would be developed on behalf of the interests of all, on the no doubt utopian assumption that the work of the world would get done through genuine relatedness (in Erich Fromm's sense) and not through the captivity of either sex or the psychological compulsions of a class.

In a way, this is already happening: the liberation of women from traditional and conventional bondages both accompanies industrialization and brings it in its wake. In these respects American women are the envy of the whole world, so that American movies, for instance, are a force for radical emancipation in Moslem countries, and men try to prevent their womenfolk from seeing them lest they become restless and dissatisfied.[9] Women in America are not, as some people claim to think, the dominant sex, but having escaped from traditional bondages they are beginning to face the problems of freedom.

NOTES

1. "Image of the Scientist among High-School Students: A Pilot Study," *Science*, 126 (August 30, 1957), pp. 384–390.

2. I am drawing here on unpublished materials prepared by Howard S. Becker and Blanche Geer, under the direction of Professor Everett C. Hughes. [Cf. Becker, *et al.* (1961), *Boys in White*, University of Chicago Press.—ED.]

3. Compare the interesting article, "Beatniks in Business," *Mademoiselle* (March, 1959), pp. 74–75 and 142–145, and see, more generally, my article, "Work and Leisure in the Post-Industrial World," in Eric Larrabee and Rolf Meyersohn, Editors, *Mass Leisure,* Glencoe, Illinois: The Free Press, 1958.

4. Compare the study by Robert Blood, Jr., "Uniformities and Diversities in Campus Dating Preferences," *Marriage and Family Living,* 18 (February, 1956), pp. 37–45.

5. See James S. Coleman, with John W. C. Johnstone and Kurt Jonassohn, *The Adolescent Society,* New York: Free Press of Glencoe, 1961.—Ed.

6. Compare on the general developmental sequence of college girls at Vassar, Nevitt Sanford, *et al.,* "Personality Development in the College Years," *Journal of Social Issues,* 12, no. 4 (1956), pp. 1–72. [See James S. Coleman (1961), *The Adolescent Society,* New York: Free Press.—ED.]

7. Compare, for further discussion, Riesman, *Some Continuities and Discontinuities in the Education of Women,* John Dewey Memorial Lecture, Bennington College, 1956.

8. I suppose some social scientists would argue that the division of labor here is both a good and a necessary thing. One could draw such an implication from the work of Parsons and Bales, linking the division of labor in small laboratory groups to the division of labor in the family. See Talcott Parsons and R. F. Bales, *Family, Socialization and Interaction Process,* Glencoe, Ill.: The Free Press, 1955.

9. Compare Daniel Lerner, with the collaboration of Lucille W. Pevsner, *The Passing of Traditional Society: Modernizing the Middle East,* Glencoe, Ill.: The Free Press, 1958.

Two

MATE
SELECTION

❧ INTRODUCTION ❧

The elaboration of the dating relationship and the idea of love as a preliminary to marriage are conspicuously middle-class American phenomena. American-style dating and the notion that love and marriage necessarily go together are unknown in many other societies. In some societies the major burden of mate selection falls upon one's family and kin, and the choice is based upon pragmatic considerations such as family prestige, respectability, and financial status. In American society, however, an individual selects his own mate within certain fairly broad limits (see Rodman, 4), and the choice is based upon the romantic consideration of love and affection. The ideal American sequence is the development of mutual love by dating partners, followed by marriage. What happens in actual fact, of course, is usually a good deal more complicated.

Americans do, of course, marry for love. But they also marry for a variety of other reasons—premarital pregnancy, sexual satisfaction, economic security, societal expectations, family pressures, and prestige considerations. Hollingshead (5), for example, points out the importance of a proper marriage to upper-class Protestant males and shows the lengths to which their families will go to enforce compliance. It is an excellent illustration of how pragmatic factors may intrude upon the mate selection process. Christensen (1953, 1963) shows that premarital pregnancy hastens marriage in the United States, in contrast to Denmark, which is more permissive. He estimates that about 20 per cent of all first births within marriage are conceived before marriage in representative areas of the United States. In these, as in other marriages, marriage may result from a variety of other considerations, including love.

The question of who is especially eligible as a mate is explored in some detail in the following selection. We see that a person usually selects a mate who is similar to himself in certain important characteristics—but people vary in what they regard as the important characteristics that should be shared by marriage partners. Religion, race, and social class are probably among the most important limiting factors in the mate selection process, but marriages that are mixed on these characteristics do take place. As a result, there is much interest in the outcome of such mixed marriages—in how successful they are as compared to marriages that are not mixed. Vernon's article (6) indicates, on the basis of three much-quoted studies, that interfaith marriages are less successful when judged in terms of the proportion ending in divorce. But he points out that such results may be reported in different ways—and that they are often reported in a way that seems to exaggerate the divorce-proneness of mixed marriages. It is possible to report a 10 per cent difference or a 300 per cent difference between mixed and non-mixed religious marriages. Both these figures are based upon the same data, and both are correct. Vernon's suggestion is that the usual way of reporting the data, emphasizing the higher percentage, may reflect a bias against mixed religious marriages. At any rate, the reader should be on the alert to read statistical information carefully at all times, lest he be hoodwinked by a skillful statistical liar (cf. Huff, 1954). He should also pay special attention to the interpretations given to statistical information. On this point, the following comment by Rossi (1964) nicely complements Vernon's article:

> When the sociologist finds . . . that the incidence of divorce is higher for those who marry outside their religion than for those who do not, he concludes that intermarriage is "bad" or "risky"; he does not say that such marital failures may reflect the relative newness of the social pattern of intermarriage, much less suggest that such failures may decline once this pattern is more prevalent (p. 612 n.).

A recent report by Burchinal and Chancellor (1963) provides information on "marital survival rates" of Iowa marriages that casts great doubt upon the tremendous increase in the divorce rate that is sometimes said to occur in interfaith marriages. They report a survival rate of 96.2 per cent for Catholic-Catholic marriages, 86.2 per cent for Protestant-Protestant marriages, and 77.6 per cent for Catholic-Protestant marriages. But they also report a survival rate that runs from 89.8 to 94.6 per cent for Lutherans,

Methodists, Presbyterians, and Baptists, regardless of whether the marriage is within their own denomination or another Protestant denomination. Finally, they report survival rates of 90.5 per cent for Catholic-Lutheran marriages, 89.8 per cent for Catholic-Presbyterian marriages, 83.8 per cent for Catholic-Methodist marriages, and 81.6 per cent for Catholic-Baptist marriages. These figures indicate virtually no differences between same-denomination Protestant and interdenominational Protestant survival rates. They also indicate that although the survival rates tend to be lower for Catholic-Protestant marriages, yet the differences are often minimal.*

A recent study by Lind (1964) also "calls into serious question the commonly quoted generalization that interracial marriages always involve greater risks of failure than intraracial marriages." Lind's figures are from Hawaii, where a tradition of greater acceptance of interracial marriages is an important factor. According to the divorce rate he uses, those in a mixed racial marriage have a slightly higher overall divorce rate (29.0 per cent) than couples of the same racial groups (26.8 per cent). For Hawaiians, Koreans, Puerto Ricans, Filipinos, and Caucasians, however, those who were in *mixed* marriages had *lower* divorce rates. This clearly indicates that mixed marriages *per se* do not produce higher divorce rates— the attitudes within the community to the mixed marriages are of great importance.

People of widely different backgrounds often meet on the college campus, and campus life may therefore be an important factor in encouraging mixed marriages. This is particularly true because of the strong liberal and democratic ethic existing on many college campuses (Newcomb, 1957). Leslie and Richardson (1956) show that students who meet and marry on the campus are likelier to enter a mixed marriage than students whose initial meeting was in their home environment. They point out, however, that they are dealing with students of a restricted range of (social class) differences—under such circumstances the degree of difference be-

---

* Some of the "marital survival rates" reported above for Lutherans, Methodists, Presbyterians, and Baptists are probably somewhat higher than they should be because "some persons who reported themselves to be members of a [specific] Protestant denomination at the time of marriage reported themselves as unaffiliated Protestants at the time of divorce." (Burchinal and Chancellor, 1963.)

tween the mates is ordinarily not very great.* Moreover, even within this narrow range of differences there may be a tendency to pay attention to prestige factors at all stages of the mate selection process, from dating to pinning to engagement (Rogers and Havens, 1960). Where the differences between students are greater there may be fewer mixed marriages taking place, but nevertheless a good deal of interaction. Blood and Nicholson (1962a), for example, point out that almost half of the University of Michigan coeds in their sample have dated at least one foreign student by the time they are in their senior year; and that of those coeds who have dated foreign students, there is a tendency to find such dating more enjoyable than American dating—40 per cent find it more enjoyable, 46 per cent find it equally enjoyable, and 14 per cent less enjoyable than dating American students (Blood and Nicholson, 1962b). The authors suggest that one reason for this preference is that foreign students make an extra effort to please their American dates, and that dating foreign students provides a "built-in protection against the likelihood of serious emotional involvement." Some of these dating relationships do, nevertheless, lead to marriage.

The United States was once characterized as a melting pot in which all peoples would become assimilated. Kennedy (1944; n.d.), however, suggested that there was a "triple melting pot" rather than a "single melting pot," because Protestants, Catholics, and Jews tended to marry within their own religious groups. Although the figures on the extent of interfaith marriages have been much disputed—there is, after all, much regional variation in the rates (see Rodman, 4)—it is nevertheless fairly clear that a large majority of Americans marry within their own religion. Gordon (1961) suggests, however, that we have more than "three melting pots" because other groups in the United States, such as Negroes, Mexican-Americans, Puerto Ricans, and American Indians, also tend to marry within their own groups and to retain their own social structure. At the same time he also suggests that among some individuals we do have a "single melting pot"—these are "the intellectuals in America in which true structural intermixture

* For additional data on social class intermarriage see Dinitz et al., 1960. For a case where social class intermarriage is officially supported and where political homogamy is encouraged, see Huang (1962).

among persons of various ethnic backgrounds, including the religions, has markedly taken place."

REFERENCES

BLOOD, ROBERT O., JR., and SAMUEL O. NICHOLSON. 1962a. "The Attitudes of American Men and Women Students Toward International Dating," *Marriage and Family Living*, XXIV, 35–41.

———. 1962b. "International Dating Experiences of American Women Students," *Marriage and Family Living*, XXIV, 129–136.

BURCHINAL, LEE G., and LOREN E. CHANCELLOR. 1963. "Survival Rates Among Religiously Homogamous and Interreligious Marriages," *Social Forces*, XLI, 353–362.

CHRISTENSEN, HAROLD T. 1953. "Studies in Child Spacing: Premarital Pregnancy as Measured by the Spacing of the First Birth From Marriage," *American Sociological Review*, XVIII, 53–59.

———. 1963. "Child Spacing Analysis Via Record Linkage: New Data Plus a Summing Up from Earlier Reports," *Marriage and Family Living*, XXV, 272–280.

DINITZ, SIMON, FRANKLIN BANKS, and BENJAMIN PASAMANICK. 1960. "Mate Selection and Social Class: Changes During the Past Quarter Century," *Marriage and Family Living*, XXII, 348–351.

GORDON, MILTON M. 1961. "Assimilation in America: Theory and Reality," *Daedalus*, XC, 263–285.

HUANG, LUCY JEN. 1962. "Attitude of the Communist Chinese Toward Inter-Class Marriage," *Marriage and Family Living*, XXIV, 389–392.

HUFF, DARRELL. 1954. *How to Lie with Statistics*, New York: Norton.

KENNEDY, RUBY JO REEVES. 1944. "Single or Triple Melting Pot? Intermarriage Trends in New Haven, 1870–1940," *American Journal of Sociology*, XLIX, 331–339.

———. n.d. "Single or Triple Melting Pot? Intermarriage in New Haven, 1870–1955," mimeographed.

LESLIE, GERALD R., and ARTHUR H. RICHARDSON. 1956. "Family Versus Campus Influences in Relation to Mate Selection," *Social Problems*, IV, 117–121.

LIND, ANDREW W. 1964. "Interracial Marriage as Affecting Divorce in Hawaii," *Sociology and Social Research*, XLIX, 17–26.

NEWCOMB, THEODORE M. 1957. *Personality and Social Change*, New York: Holt, Rinehart & Winston.

ROGERS, EVERETT M., and EUGENE HAVENS. 1960. "Prestige Rating and Mate Selection on a College Campus," *Marriage and Family Living*, XXII, 55–59.

ROSSI, ALICE S. 1964. "Equality Between the Sexes: An Immodest Proposal," *Daedalus*, XCIII, 607–652.

~§ 4 §~ Mate Selection: Incest Taboos, Homogamy, and Mixed Marriages

by HYMAN RODMAN

Who marries whom? How is the choice made? In very general terms a person tends to marry someone like himself socially. The choice may be made by the marital partners or by their families, or jointly, and this will depend upon the particular society involved, or upon the particular individuals in the society.

Incest Taboos

Those who are most like each other socially—and also genetically—are the members of the same nuclear family. They usually belong to the same nationality, religious group, economic level, and racial group and would thus be ideal mates, insofar as homogeneity in such background factors is thought to be desirable. The incest taboo, however, almost universally precludes sexual relations or marriages between mother and son, father and daughter, or brother and sister. In addition, these taboos always are extended to at least some other relatives in all societies. In this respect an individual practices exogamy—that is, he must marry outside the group of relatives to which the incest taboo applies.

Written especially for this reader, the paper summarizes much of what is known about mate selection, highlights some of the major points and problems, and presents some recent statistics on mixed religious marriages. It is based upon many sources, but special acknowledgment must be made to the following summary statements on intermarriage and mate selection: Kingsley Davis, 1941; Robert K. Merton, 1941; George P. Murdock, 1949; Manford H. Kuhn, 1955; Robert F. Winch, 1958; Linton C. Freeman, 1958; John E. Mayer, 1961; Jacobsohn and Matheny, 1962; and Bernard Farber, 1964.

He therefore does not ordinarily mate with those who are most like him in their social characteristics.

The incest taboo has not applied to all members of the nuclear family in all societies without exception. The nobility or royalty in certain societies—Azande, Calusa, Hawaiian, Inca, Egyptian— once permitted, or even preferred, father-daughter or brother-sister marriage. There is also evidence that at one time in Egyptian history brother-sister marriage was practiced by commoners with some frequency (Middleton, 1962). In all these instances, however, including the ancient Egyptian commoners, brother-sister marriages (or father-daughter marriages among the Azande) were a means of maintaining wealth and property within a narrowly limited family group (Goggin and Sturtevant, 1964). Functionally, such a practice is not unlike the tendency for members of the upper class to mate with each other in all societies. This serves to maintain privilege and property within a narrow social group. It is therefore not surprising that more effort goes into controlling the marriage of upper-class members—there is, after all, more at stake in these marriages (Goode, 1959; Hollingshead, 5; Pope and Knudsen, 1965).

The incest taboo is not based upon "natural" or instinctive drives, but it is a learned, "cultural" rule of behavior. This is obvious, of course; if it were instinctive there would not be any need for a rule, and there would not be any instances of incestuous behavior. Considering the fantastic variety of cultural patterns that are possible, it is rather remarkable that the incest taboo should be found on a nearly universal basis. It suggests that the incest taboo must play a crucial role within the nuclear family for it to have developed, or to have been adopted, by all societies (the exceptions typically involve only a small group of people within a society).

Many attempts have been made to explain the near-universality of the incest taboo. Westermarck (1922) explained it on the basis of the long association between members of the household, which dulled the sexual appetite and eliminated sexual attraction. Such an explanation, however, is not in accord with anthropological evidence that marriage with a member of the same household may be preferred; and it is contradicted by much clinical evidence which suggests that "incestuous desires are regularly engendered within the nuclear family and are kept in restraint only through persistent social pressure and individual repression" (Murdock, 1949, p. 291).

Other important explanations of the incest taboo have been offered by Freud (1924), Murdock (1949), Slater (1959), Aberle *et al.* (1963), and Cohen (1964). Although we cannot go into these different explanations without turning the book into a study of the incest taboo, a number of sociological points about which there is fairly general current agreement can be made. The incest taboo serves an important sociological function by eliminating sexual jealousy and rivalry within the nuclear family, and within the larger kinship group to which it might be extended. It prevents ingrown sentiments and family ethnocentrism by requiring members of one family to take an interest in other families with which they exchange mates, and in this way it helps to maintain a degree of solidarity within the larger community. It also helps to keep different families in contact with each other, and in this way promotes an exchange of useful new ideas and techniques. As a result, we can see that there are advantages to the family, as well as to the community, in having an incest taboo. Although this does not provide us with an explanation of how the incest taboo developed in the first place—perhaps it developed in different ways in different societies—it does provide us with some good reasons as to why the incest taboo is maintained once it has developed.

The Principle of Homogamy

The existence of the incest taboo means that exogamy is practiced with regard to a person's nuclear family and perhaps with regard to a more extended kinship group. At the same time, however, endogamy is usually practiced with regard to one's larger social group. This means that a person usually marries someone from within his own society, tribal group, or social group. Another way of putting it is to say that a person usually marries homogamously. Homogamy refers to a principle of marriage whereby one selects a mate who is like oneself on a variety of characteristics thought to be important. In American society, for example, people usually marry someone from their own racial group. Less markedly, but still usually, they marry someone from their own religious group. Although no longer so important, there still remains a slight trend toward marriage within one's own "nationality" group (for example, Italian-Americans marrying other Italian-Americans).

Selecting a mate from within one's own group (however that may be defined) is related to a variety of factors: (1) an ethnocentric attitude, such that members of other groups are thought to be inferior or odd; (2) greater opportunity to meet and interact with members of one's own group (Katz and Hill, 1958); and (3) greater compatibility with members of one's own group due to similar attitudes and values (Burgess and Wallin, 1943; Schellenberg, 1960; Coombs, 1961). In a sense all of these factors are part of the principle of homogamy because people who belong to the same group are likelier to interact, and in interaction to develop similar values and attitudes, including ethnocentric attitudes toward outsiders.

The homogamy principle is found in most societies (Murdock, 1949), and a great deal of data has been accumulated that shows that this principle holds good in the United States. This homogamous tendency is reflected by a large number of studies showing that members of similar occupations tend to marry each other (Centers, 1949; Warner and Abegglen, 1955); that people who live close together—and presumably share certain social characteristics—tend to marry each other (Kennedy, 1943; Abrams, 1943; Clarke, 1952; Schnepp and Roberts, 1952; Marches and Turbeville, 1953; Coffee, 1962); and that people of the same racial, social class, educational, age, and religious groups tend to marry each other (Hollingshead, 1950). In most cases, individuals who share these various social background characteristics are likelier to have had similar social experiences and to have more values in common. As Hollingshead (1950) puts it in summary form: "In a highly significant number of cases the person one marries is very similar culturally to one's self." Or as Trost (1964) puts it, citing the work of Torgny T. Segerstedt: "One tends to choose a spouse belonging to the same symbolic environment as . . . oneself."

As a result, it is possible to say that there are limits that operate upon the process of mate selection—and this applies even within American society where theoretically there is a free choice of mates. On the one hand the incest taboo rules out a certain group

of individuals as being ineligible because they are too closely related; and on the other hand the principle of homogamy rules out
many individuals as being ineligible because they are too different
from oneself. With respect to the latter consideration, however, it
must be remembered that there are many exceptions—fathers,
that is, do not knowingly marry daughters, but Negroes do marry
whites, Catholics do marry Protestants, Polish-Americans do marry
Italian-Americans, and college graduates do marry high school
graduates.

In talking about homogamy—the marrying of like to like—it is
necessary to note the changing nature of the social characteristics
that are thought to be important. At one time in the United States,
for example, national background was much more important, while
it is now considerably less important, although this varies from
one nationality group to another (Kennedy, 1944, 1952). In addition, there has been somewhat less emphasis placed upon religious
and racial differences. As a consequence, the rate of religious
intermarriage has been increasing (Thomas, 1951; Heer, 1962;
Rosenberg, 1963), and the rate of interracial marriage—although
the data are spotty and show no long-run trend (Myrdal, 1944;
Barron, 1948; Simpson and Yinger, 1958)—may also be increasing in very recent years (Barnett, 1963; Burma, 1963; Heer, 1965).
In Hawaii, there has been a steady increase in interracial marriages,
and the situation there indicates the permeability of the so-called
racial barrier (Adams, 1937; Cheng and Yamamura, 1957). A
definitive statement on whether the rate of interfaith and interracial marriages in the United States as a whole is increasing,
however, must await the availability of more adequate nationwide
data.

Mixed Marriages

To say that a marriage is homogamous with respect to certain
characteristics like race and religion is to tell only a small part of
the story. Each person can be characterized in many different ways
—as to political attitudes, rural versus urban background, intellectual interests, and so on*—and in this sense every marriage

---

* For a review of some literature dealing with homogamy on traits that
sociologists pay little attention to, such as a variety of demographic and
anthropometric traits, see Beckman (1962).

TABLE 1

Percentage of Individuals in Interfaith Marriages:
Roman Catholic, Protestant, and Jewish[a]

a	Time	Per Cent	Reference
	ROMAN CATHOLIC		
ral Pennsylvania[b]	1957	39.1	Willits-Bealer-Bender (1963)
ral Pennsylvania[c]	1957	34.5	Willits-Bealer-Bender (1963)
va (diocese records)	1953–57	14.7	Burchinal-Kenkel-Chancellor (1962)
va (state records)	1953–57	27.6	Burchinal-Kenkel-Chancellor (1962)
annah-Atlanta diocese	1940–50	54.2	Thomas (1951)
vidence (R.I.) diocese	1940–50	9.3	Thomas (1951)
v Mexico	1955	7.0	Locke-Sabagh-Thomes (1957)
nnecticut	1955	13.6	Locke-Sabagh-Thomes (1957)
ted States (church-sanctioned)	1940–50	15.1	Thomas (1951)
ted States	1957	12.1	*Current Population Reports* (1958)
ada	1926–30	8.4	Rosenberg (1963)
ada	1936–40	8.8	Rosenberg (1963)
ada	1946–50	10.8	Rosenberg (1963)
ada	1956–60	11.7	Rosenberg (1963)
	PROTESTANT		
ted States	1957	4.5	*Current Population Reports* (1958)
heran, U.S. & Canada[d]	1946–50	41.0	Bossard-Letts (1956)
heran, U.S. & Canada[e]	1946–50	17.6	Bossard-Letts (1956)
heran, U.S. & Canada[c]	1946–50	9.8	Bossard-Letts (1956)
istian Reformed Church, U.S.[f]	1957–58	25.7	Bouma (1963)
istian Reformed Church, U.S.[g]	1957–58	16.7	Bouma (1963)
istian Reformed Church, U.S.[e]	1957–58	8.7	Bouma (1963)
al Pennsylvania[c]	1957	9.9	Willits-Bealer-Bender (1963)
al Pennsylvania[b]	1957	21.0	Willits-Bealer-Bender (1963)
ada	1926–30	5.3	Rosenberg (1963)
ada	1936–40	6.9	Rosenberg (1963)
ada	1946–50	8.9	Rosenberg (1963)
ada	1956–60	11.1	Rosenberg (1963)
	JEWISH		
ted States	1957	3.7	*Current Population Reports* (1958)
shington D.C. Metropolitan area	1956	7.0	Bigman (1957); Rosenthal (1963)
vince of Quebec (males)	1956–60	5.6	Rosenberg (1963)
atchewan-Alberta (males)	1956–60	34.8	Rosenberg (1963)
ada	1926–30	2.5	Rosenberg (1963)
ada	1936–40	3.2	Rosenberg (1963)
ada	1946–50	4.8	Rosenberg (1963)
ada	1956–60	7.6	Rosenberg (1963)

[a] In order to make the percentages comparable, they are not always the same percentages reported in the original articles. The major change is that those percentages pertaining to the proportion that mixed marriages involving Catholics (or Protestants or Jews) have to all marriages involving Catholics (or Protestants or Jews) have been transformed to the percentage of all Catholics (or Protestants or Jews) entering a mixed marriage. There is a good deal of confusion in the literature that stems from a failure to differentiate

is a mixed marriage (Merton, 1941). Yet, as Vincent (1963) says: "Only certain types of intermarriages are viewed with concern and as social problems; namely, those intermarriages which mirror areas of prejudice and threaten vested interests in our society." Racial and religious intermarriages in the United States are the ones that provoke most discussion and concern because such mixed marriages have their antagonists. It is therefore well to lay special stress on the point that all marriages are mixed. At the same time it must also be recognized that interfaith and interracial marriages involve the crossing of group lines that are among the most firmly drawn in contemporary American life. There is comparatively little data on racial intermarriage (Barnett, 1963), but a good deal of data on religious intermarriage. It is therefore well to look briefly at the extent of religious intermarriage, and at some of the factors that are related to it.

It can be seen in Table 1 that there is a great deal of variation from one area to another in the rates of interfaith marriage for individuals. One reason for this is that the areas vary in the proportions of their population that are Catholic, Jewish, or Protestant. A number of studies have shown that the lower the proportion of a particular group to the total population, the higher its rate of intermarriage (Thomas, 1951; Bossard and Letts, 1956; Locke, Sabagh, and Thomes, 1957; Heer, 1962; Burchinal and Chancellor, 1962). The inference here is that the fewer members, proportion-

---

between these two very different rates of mixed marriage. For example, of 10 marriages involving Catholics, 6 are Catholic-Catholic marriages and 4 are Catholic-Protestant marriages: as a result we can speak of a 40 per cent rate of intermarriage, or a 25 per cent rate. 40 per cent (4 out of 10) of the marriages involving Catholics are mixed, while 25 per cent (4 out of 16) of the Catholics who are marrying are entering a mixed marriage. I refer to the first rate as the *mixed marriage rate for marriages,* and to the second rate as the *mixed marriage rate for individuals,* in order to avoid confusion (cf. Rodman, 1965). It is the mixed marriage rate for individuals that is being used here.

[b] Marriages to a mate listed as having no religious affiliation are considered interfaith marriages.

[c] Marriages to a mate listed as having no religious affiliation are omitted from the tabulation.

[d] Marriages to any non-Lutherans are considered interfaith marriages.

[e] Marriages to non-Protestants only are considered interfaith marriages.

[f] Marriages to any non-Christian Reformed are considered interfaith marriages.

[g] Marriages to Reformed and Protestant Reformed are considered homogamous marriages.

ately, of one's own group, the greater the likelihood that a mate will be chosen outside the group. For example, the Savannah-Atlanta diocese is less than 2 per cent Catholic and the Providence (R.I.) diocese is more than 50 per cent Catholic—and the percentage of Catholics who intermarry is 54.2 and 9.3, respectively (Thomas, 1951). Similarly, the Canadian province of Quebec contains the largest Jewish community of Canada in the metropolitan area of Montreal, and about 98 per cent of Quebec's Jews live in Montreal. By contrast, Saskatchewan and Alberta contain smaller Jewish communities that are much more spread out throughout the whole of these provinces—for example, more than 40 per cent of the Jewish population of Saskatchewan live in towns and villages containing less than one hundred Jews. It is therefore not surprising that the percentage of Jewish men who intermarry is 5.6 in Quebec and 34.8 in Saskatchewan and Alberta (Rosenberg, 1963).

Only part of the variation, however, is due to the sheer proportion of group members in the population. For example, the percentage of Catholics both in New Mexico and Connecticut is 47, and yet in Connecticut the mixed marriage rate for individuals is almost twice the New Mexico rate (13.6 versus 7.0 per cent). This is because the Catholics of New Mexico are largely Mexican-American, and they therefore marry among themselves to a greater extent for ethnic as well as religious reasons (Locke, Sabagh, and Thomes, 1957). Attention must also be paid to the cohesiveness and tradition of a group—thus, Jews in the United States and Canada intermarry less than Catholics or Protestants despite their fewer numbers, and Rosenthal (1963) reports that rural Jews in Germany, despite a lower population density, intermarried less than urban Jews because of their stricter Orthodox tradition (cf. Barron, 1946; Shanks, 1953). Demographic factors that favor a high rate of intermarriage may, in Merton's terms (1941), "be more than counterbalanced by in-group sentiments."

Another factor to consider in dealing with interfaith marriages is the definition of an interfaith marriage. Is it an interfaith marriage when an Orthodox Jew marries a Reform Jew, or when a Protestant of one denomination marries a Protestant of another denomination? For the most part these are considered to be religiously homogamous. Varying definitions of what is homogamous and what is mixed can lead to very different rates. The possibilities for generating highly variable rates can be seen by examining Bouma's study (1963) and Bossard and Letts' study (1956). For example, Bouma found that 25.7 per cent of Christian Reformed Church members intermarry, if marriage to any other denomination or church is considered intermarriage; that 16.7 per cent intermarry, if marriage to a member of one of two closely related denominations is considered homogamous; and the percentage drops to 8.7 if we consider a marriage to a member of any Protestant denomination to be homogamous.

Finally, one should also note that there are differences between men and women in the extent of interfaith marriages. The Jewish male intermarries far more frequently than the Jewish female; among Protestants and Catholics it is not clear whether there is such a sex difference, and different studies report contrasting results (Barnett, 1962). In Canada, where comprehensive data are available, we find that Jewish men intermarry more than twice as frequently as Jewish women. From 1956 to 1960, the percentage of men who intermarried was 10.0; of women, 4.8. For Ontario and British Columbia the percentages for 1956–1960 were 11.7 and 32.2 respectively, for men; and 6.1 and 20.4 respectively, for women (Rosenberg, 1963). A similar differential is reported for many European countries by Ruppin (1940, p. 128). This is part of the tendency for men of minority groups to intermarry to a greater extent than minority group women—and the data we have also indicate that most Negro-white marriages are between Negro men and white women (Simpson and Yinger, 1958; Barnett, 1963).

One reason that has been offered for the sex difference in intermarriage rates is that an "exchange" takes place between the minority group male and the female of the dominant group—the male's "higher economic position" is exchanged for the female's "higher caste [or ethnic] status" (Merton, 1941; Davis, 1941). The data on which this generalization is based, however, were gathered in the early decades of the present century. More recently, Golden (1953) and Pavela (1964) have challenged the "exchange" explanation, and have reported roughly equal economic status for the spouses in Negro-white marriages. It may be that in the early 1900's some of the intermarrying white females were first-generation immigrants who were likelier to be low in economic status and in anti-Negro prejudice. This may have contributed to the tendency for some economically successful Negro males to marry economically inferior white females. At the present time, however, lower-status American individuals are the ones with a higher degree of prejudice against Negroes. In addition, there is a growing acceptance, in many quarters, of the democratic values which stress individualistic rather than racial (or ethnic) factors in the selection of a mate. As a result, a white female is less likely to become available as a potential spouse because she is economically inferior, and she is more likely to become available as a potential spouse because she has a liberal attitude regarding racial intermarriage. In almost all of these cases, of course, regardless of whether the social scientist can point to an "exchange" or to "liberal attitudes," the spouses see themselves as marrying for love, as do most Americans (Barron, 1951; Pavela, 1964).

Another reason that has often been offered in the past to explain racial or religious intermarriage, and that is no longer so popular, "involved the imputation of some defect in the contracting parties" (Sklare, 1964). Thus, it was thought that there must be something wrong with the Gentile girl who agreed to marry a Jew, or the white girl who agreed to marry a Negro. And there was also something wrong with the Jew or the Negro in the match—perhaps he was expressing self-hatred (and hatred of his own group), or perhaps he was a social climber. The prevalence of such ideas naturally served to keep the rate of intermarriage down. However, "from the evidence that has begun to accumulate, it is becoming impossible to view intermarriage as an indication either of personal aberration or of social persecution," and Sklare (1964) cites evidence from studies by Maria and Daniel Levinson and by Jerold Heiss to support this statement. As a result, the idea that one must be inferior or deviant to intermarry is on the wane, and the rate of intermarriage is on the rise.

What can be said about the rate of interfaith marriage for the United States as a whole? On the basis of comprehensive data, we can see that the following percentages of Catholics, Protestants, and Jews in Canada entered a mixed marriage between 1956 and

1960: 11.7, 11.1, and 7.6. For the United States as a whole, however, comparable data are not available. The best source of information is *Current Population Reports* (1958), which reports individual mixed marriage rates of 12.1 per cent, 4.5 per cent, and 3.7 per cent for Catholics, Protestants, and Jews. These rates, based upon a survey carried out in 1957, underestimate the percentage of individuals entering mixed marriages for at least the following reasons: (1) they do not report data on mixed marriages involving a person who reported himself as having no religious affiliation or an affiliation other than Catholic, Protestant, or Jewish; (2) they do not report on mixed marriages in which one partner changed his religion to that of his spouse after the marriage but before the survey; and (3) they probably underestimate the percentage of mixed religious marriages because some enumerators may have assumed, without asking, that both spouses were of the same religion as the respondent (cf. *Current Population Reports,* 1958; Glick, 1960).

There is no way of knowing the extent to which *Current Population Reports* (1958) underestimates the rate of interfaith marriages. We might guess, however, that the percentage of individuals entering an interfaith marriage is at least twice the rate reported in that survey. This would be at least 24 per cent for Catholics, 9 per cent for Protestants, and 7 per cent for Jews.

Some support for the estimated Catholic rate is provided by Thomas (1951), who reports that 15.1 percent of Catholics entered a church-sanctioned interfaith marriage between 1940 and 1950. This rate changes to approximately 25 per cent if we use Thomas's (1956, p. 160) tentative estimate that about 40 per cent of all Catholic interfaith marriages are not sanctioned by the Church. A similar change, from 14.7 to 27.6 per cent, is shown by comparing diocese and state records in Iowa (Burchinal *et al.,* 1962). Some support for the estimated Jewish rate is provided by Bigman (1957) and Rosenthal (1963). Besanceney's (1962; personal correspondence) data for Detroit suggest that a survey study on currently mixed marriages misses at least half of the marriages that were initially mixed. As a result, the estimates we have come up with for Catholics, Protestants, and Jews—24, 9, and 7 per cent—based upon a doubling of the *Current Population Reports* (1958) survey, are on the conservative side. This is

particularly true if we want an estimate of the present rates of interfaith marriage because of the general upward trend that has been
observed.

Heterogamy: Complementary Needs

What about the theory that people of unlike characteristics
marry each other—that "opposites attract"? This would be a
marriage that follows the principle of heterogamy, and Winch
(1958) and Ktsanes (1955) have presented some evidence showing a tendency for such marriages to take place. The characteristics involved here, however, are not social characteristics, but
psychological needs. According to Winch, individuals tend to
marry others of a complementary need structure (for example, a
nurturant person marries a succorant person, or a dominant
person marries a deferential person) because they are better able
to fulfill each other's needs. Where there is a degree of individual
choice (as opposed to a situation where an individual does not
select his own mate) it is possible that personality factors enter
into the situation in such a way that people of opposite need structures tend to marry. Insofar as this may be so, we could then
say that the principle of homogamy operates with respect to social
characteristics (and also on certain psychological characteristics
like I.Q. and a variety of attitudes) and that the principle of
heterogamy operates with respect to psychological needs. A number of attempts have been made to replicate Winch's findings
(Bowerman and Day, 1956; Schellenberg and Bee, 1960; Murstein,
1961), but without success, so that we presently cannot say
whether the principle of heterogamy actually is involved in the
process of mate selection.* An interesting study by Kerckhoff and
Davis (1962) suggests that a developmental sequence may take
place—homogamy in social characteristics may be characteristic
of the early stages of courtship, consensus on values may become
important somewhat later, and need complementarity comes into
operation later still. The authors see these as "filtering factors,"
and suggest that they operate to sift out prospective mates at dif-

* For additional commentary and references on attempts to replicate
Winch's research, see Winch (1963, pp. 592–593) and Burchinal (1964, pp.
665–670).

ferent stages of the mate selection process.* If this is so then newly-
wed couples should exhibit a considerable degree of complementarity, but Murstein (1961) finds that this is not so. Kerckhoff and
Davis (1962), Murstein (1961), and Udry (1963) all indicate
that many problems and difficulties remain to be worked out before
we can say definitively what sort of complementarity, if any, is a
factor in mate selection.

Summary

By way of a summary of the material presented here, I have
attempted to indicate, in Figure 1, some of the major points made
about mate selection. On one side, we can see that, because of

FIGURE 1

Mate Selection:
The Incest Taboo, Homogamy, and Heterogamy

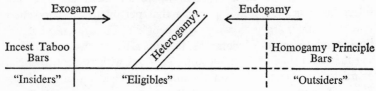

the incest taboo, marriage is forbidden to a group of "insiders,"
and this means that exogamy is practiced with regard to the group
of "insiders" to whom the incest taboo applies. On the other
side, we can see that, because of the principle of homogamy,
marriage is forbidden, or at least unusual, to a group of "outsiders," and this means that endogamy is practiced such that
marriage takes place among people of the same society who are
alike with respect to important social and cultural characteristics.
This leaves a group of "eligibles" in the middle, and it is from

* Some of the findings on complementary need patterns may be explained as a result of a developing relationship between the spouses—
through time, they accommodate to each other (and this may lead to complementary patterns of relationship) regardless of initial "needs" (see Turner,
1958; and Farber, 1964). The same explanation may also hold for findings
of homogamy with respect to attitudes—through time, the married pair may
develop similar attitudes (Snyder, 1964).

within this pool of eligibles that a mate is usually selected. The broken lines at the border between the "outsiders" and the "eligibles" indicates that the criteria according to which people are defined as "eligibles" or "outsiders" may vary from society to society, from group to group within the society, or even from individual to individual. For example, what is statistically recorded as a religious intermarriage between a Catholic and a Protestant may not be a mixed marriage at all from the point of view of the individuals involved if religion plays no part in their lives. The broken lines on the horizontal axis indicate that changes may take place through time such that fewer groups, or more groups, come to be defined as "outsiders." Finally, insofar as Winch's hypothesis may be viable, the principle of heterogamy with regard to personality needs would point to a band of people from among the pool of eligibles who are likelier to be chosen as mates because their needs complement the needs of the person who is selecting a mate.

REFERENCES

ABERLE, DAVID F., U. BRONFENBRENNER, E. H. HESS, D. R. MILLER, D. M. SCHNEIDER, and J. N. SPUHLER. 1963. "The Incest Taboo and the Mating Patterns of Animals," *American Anthropologist,* LXV, 253–265.

ABRAMS, RAY H. 1943. "Residential Propinquity as a Factor in Marriage Selection: Fifty Year Trends in Philadelphia," *American Sociological Review,* VIII, 288–294.

ADAMS, ROMANZO. 1937. *Interracial Marriage in Hawaii,* New York: Macmillan.

BARNETT, LARRY D. 1962. "Research in Interreligious Dating and Marriage," *Marriage and Family Living,* XXIV, 191–194.

———. 1963. "Interracial Marriage in California," *Marriage and Family Living,* XXV, 424–427.

BARRON, MILTON L. 1946. "The Incidence of Jewish Intermarriage in Europe and America," *American Sociological Review,* XI, 6–13.

———. 1948. *People Who Intermarry,* Syracuse: Syracuse University Press.

———. 1951. "Research on Intermarriage: A Survey of Accomplishments and Prospects," *American Journal of Sociology,* LVII, 249–255.

BECKMAN, LARS. 1962. "Assortative Mating in Man," *Eugenics Review,* LIV, 63–67.

BESANCENEY, PAUL H. 1962. "Unbroken Protestant–Catholic Marriages Among Whites in the Detroit Area," *American Catholic Sociological Review*, XXIII, 3–20.

BIGMAN, STANLEY K. 1957. *The Jewish Population of Greater Washington in 1956*, Washington, D.C.: Jewish Community Council.

BOSSARD, JAMES H. S., and HAROLD C. LETTS. 1956. "Mixed Marriages Involving Lutherans—A Research Report," *Marriage and Family Living*, XVIII, 308–310.

BOUMA, DONALD H. 1963. "Religiously Mixed Marriages: Denominational Consequences in the Christian Reformed Church," *Marriage and Family Living*, XXV, 428–432.

BOWERMAN, CHARLES E., and BARBARA R. DAY. 1956. "A Test of the Theory of Complementary Needs as Applied to Couples during Courtship," *American Sociological Review*, XXI, 602–605.

BURCHINAL, LEE G. 1964. "The Premarital Dyad and Love Involvement," in Harold T. Christensen, ed., *Handbook of Marriage and the Family*, Chicago: Rand McNally.

BURCHINAL, LEE G., and LOREN CHANCELLOR. 1962. "Proportions of Catholics, Urbanism, and Mixed-Catholic Marriage Rates Among Iowa Counties," *Social Problems*, IX, 359–365.

BURCHINAL, LEE G., WILLIAM F. KENKEL, and LOREN E. CHANCELLOR. 1962. "Comparisons of State- and Diocese-Reported Marriage Data for Iowa, 1953–1957," *American Catholic Sociological Review*, XXIII, 21–29.

BURGESS, ERNEST, and PAUL WALLIN. 1943. "Homogamy in Social Characteristics," *American Journal of Sociology*, XLIX, 117–124.

BURMA, JOHN H. 1963. "Interethnic Marriage in Los Angeles, 1948–1959," *Social Forces*, XLII, 156–165.

CENTERS, RICHARD. 1949. "Marital Selection and Occupational Strata," *American Journal of Sociology*, LIV, 530–535.

CHENG, C. K., and DOUGLAS S. YAMAMURA. 1957. "Interracial Marriage and Divorce in Hawaii," *Social Forces*, XXXVI, 77–84.

CLARKE, A. C. 1952. "An Examination of the Operation of Residential Propinquity as a Factor in Mate Selection," *American Sociological Review*, XVII, 17–22.

COFFEE, THOMAS M. 1962. "An Empirical Study of Residential Propinquity and Marital Selection," *Dissertation Abstracts*, XXIII, 1450–1451.

COHEN, YEHUDI A. 1964. *The Transition from Childhood to Adolescence*, Chicago: Aldine.

COOMBS, ROBERT H. 1961. "A Value Theory of Mate Selection," *Family Life Coordinator*, X, 51–54.

Current Population Reports. 1958. "Religion Reported by the Civilian Population of the United States: March 1957," P–20, No. 79, Washington, D.C.: Bureau of the Census.

DAVIS, KINGSLEY. 1941. "Intermarriage in Caste Societies," *American Anthropologist*, XLIII, 376–395.

FARBER, BERNARD. 1964. *Family: Organization and Interaction*, San Francisco: Chandler.

FREEMAN, LINTON C. 1958. "Marriage Without Love: Mate–Selection in Non-Western Societies," pp. 19–39 in Robert F. Winch, *Mate Selection,* New York: Harper.

FREUD, SIGMUND. 1924. *A General Introduction to Psychoanalysis,* New York: Boni and Liveright.

GLICK, PAUL C. 1960. "Intermarriage and Fertility Patterns Among Persons in Major Religious Groups," *Eugenics Quarterly,* VII, 31–38.

GOGGIN, JOHN M., and WILLIAM C. STURTEVANT. 1964. "The Calusa: A Stratified, Nonagricultural Society," in Ward H. Goodenough, ed., *Explorations in Cultural Anthropology,* New York: McGraw-Hill.

GOLDEN, JOSEPH. 1953. "Characteristics of the Negro–White Intermarried in Philadelphia," *American Sociological Review,* XVIII, 177–183.

GOODE, WILLIAM J. 1959. "The Theoretical Importance of Love," *American Sociological Review,* XXIV, 38–47.

HEER, DAVID M. 1962. "The Trend of Interfaith Marriages in Canada: 1922–1957," *American Sociological Review,* XXVII, 245–250.

————. 1965. "Negro–White Marriage in the United States," *New Society,* Aug. 26, 1965, pp. 7–9.

HOLLINGSHEAD, AUGUST B. 1950. "Cultural Factors in the Selection of Marriage Mates," *American Sociological Review,* XV, 619–627.

JACOBSOHN, PETER, and ADAM P. MATHENY, JR. 1962. "Mate Selection in Open Marriage Systems," *International Journal of Comparative Sociology,* III, 98–123.

KATZ, ALVIN M., and REUBEN HILL. 1958. "Residential Propinquity and Marital Selection: A Review of Theory, Method, and Fact," *Marriage and Family Living,* XX, 27–35.

KENNEDY, RUBY JO REEVES. 1943. "Premarital Residential Propinquity and Ethnic Endogamy," *American Journal of Sociology,* XLVIII, 580–584.

————. 1944. "Single or Triple Melting-Pot? Intermarriage Trends in New Haven, 1870–1940," *American Journal of Sociology,* XLIX, 331–339.

————. 1952. "Single or Triple Melting-Pot? Intermarriage in New Haven, 1870–1950," *American Journal of Sociology,* LVIII, 56–59.

KERCKHOFF, ALAN C., and KEITH E. DAVIS. 1962. "Value Consensus and Need Complementarity in Mate Selection," *American Sociological Review,* XXVII, 295–303.

KTSANES, THOMAS. 1955. "Mate Selection on the Basis of Personality Type," *American Sociological Review,* XX, 547–551.

KUHN, MANFORD H. 1955. "How Mates are Sorted," in Howard Becker, and Reuben Hill, eds., *Family, Marriage and Parenthood,* 2d ed., Boston: D. C. Heath.

LOCKE, HARVEY J., GEORGES SABAGH, and MARY M. THOMES. 1957. "Interfaith Marriages," *Social Problems,* IV, 333–340.

MARCHES, JOSEPH R., and GUS TURBEVILLE. 1953. "The Effect of Residential Propinquity on Marriage Selection," *American Journal of Sociology,* LVIII, 592–595.

MAYER, JOHN E. 1961. *Jewish–Gentile Courtships,* New York: Free Press of Glencoe, 1–11.

MERTON, ROBERT K. 1941. "Intermarriage and the Social Structure: Fact and Theory," *Psychiatry*, IV, 361–374.

MIDDLETON, RUSSELL. 1962. "Brother–Sister and Father–Daughter Marriage in Ancient Egypt," *American Sociological Review*, XXVII, 603–611.

MURDOCK, GEORGE P. 1949. *Social Structure*, New York: Macmillan, 284–322.

MURSTEIN, BERNARD I. 1961. "The Complementary Need Hypothesis in Newlyweds and Middle-Aged Married Couples," *Journal of Abnormal and Social Psychology*, LXIII, 194–197.

MYRDAL, GUNNAR. 1944. (With Richard Sterner and Arnold Rose.) *An American Dilemma*, New York: Harper.

PAVELA, TODD H. 1964. "An Exploratory Study of Negro–White Intermarriage in Indiana," *Journal of Marriage and the Family*, XXVI, 209–211.

POPE, HALLOWELL, and DEAN D. KNUDSEN. 1965. "Premarital Sexual Norms, the Family, and Social Change," *Journal of Marriage and the Family*, XXVII, 314–323.

RODMAN, HYMAN. 1965. "The Textbook World of Family Sociology," *Social Problems*, XII, 445–457.

ROSENBERG, LOUIS. 1963. "Intermarriage in Canada: 1921–1960," pp. 57–81 in Werner J. Cahnman, ed., *Intermarriage and Jewish Life*, New York: Herzl Press and Jewish Reconstructionist Press.

ROSENTHAL, ERICH. 1963. "Studies of Jewish Intermarriage in the United States," *American Jewish Year Book, 1963*, LXIV, 3–53.

RUPPIN, ARTHUR. 1940. *The Jewish Fate and Future*, London: Macmillan.

SCHELLENBERG, JAMES A. 1960. "Homogamy in Personal Values and the 'Field of Eligibles,'" *Social Forces*, XXXIX, 157–162.

SCHELLENBERG, JAMES A., and LAWRENCE S. BEE. 1960. "A Re-Examination of the Theory of Complementary Needs in Mate Selection," *Marriage and Family Living*, XXII, 227–232.

SCHNEPP, G. J., and LOUIS A. ROBERTS. 1952. "Residential Propinquity and Mate Selection on a Parish Basis," *American Journal of Sociology*, LVIII, 45–50.

SHANKS, HERSHEL, 1953. "Jewish–Gentile Intermarriage: Facts and Trends," *Commentary*, XVI, No. 4, 370–375.

SIMPSON, GEORGE E., and J. MILTON YINGER. 1958. *Racial and Cultural Minorities*, rev. ed., New York: Harper.

SKLARE, MARSHALL. 1964. "Intermarriage and the Jewish Future," *Commentary*, XXXVII, No. 4, 46–52.

SLATER, MARIAM K. 1959. "Ecological Factors in the Origin of Incest," *American Anthropologist*, LXI, 1042–1059.

SNYDER, ELOISE C. 1964. "Attitudes: A Study of Homogamy and Marital Selectivity," *Journal of Marriage and the Family*, XXVI, 332–336.

THOMAS, JOHN L. 1951. "The Factor of Religion in the Selection of Marriage Mates," *American Sociological Review*, XVI, 487–491.

———. 1956. *The American Catholic Family*, Englewood Cliffs, N.J.: Prentice-Hall.

Trost, Jan. 1964. "Mate Selection, Marital Adjustment, and Symbolic Environment," *Acta Sociologica*, VIII, 27–35.

Turner, Ralph H. 1958. Review of R. F. Winch, *Mate Selection*, in *Social Forces*, XXXVII, 175–176.

Udry, J. Richard. 1963. "Complementarity in Mate Selection: A Perceptual Approach," *Marriage and Family Living*, XXV, 281–289.

Vincent, Clark E. 1963. "Interfaith Marriages: Problem or Symptom?" pp. 349–359 in Marvin B. Sussman, ed., *Sourcebook in Marriage and the Family*, 2d ed., Boston: Houghton Mifflin.

Warner, W. Lloyd, and James C. Abegglen. 1955. *Big Business Leaders in America*, New York: Harper.

Westermarck, Edward. 1922. *The History of Human Marriage*, 5th ed., Vol. 2, New York: Allerton Book Co.

Willits, Fern K., Robert C. Bealer, and Gerald W. Bender. 1963. "Interreligious Marriage Among Pennsylvania Rural Youth," *Marriage and Family Living*, XXV, 433–438.

Winch, Robert F. 1958. *Mate Selection*, New York: Harper, 3–18.

————. 1963. *The Modern Family*, rev. ed., New York: Holt, Rinehart and Winston.

❧ 5 ❧ In-Group Marriage in the Upper Class

by A U G U S T   B .   H O L L I N G S H E A D

Families in the upper class may be divided into two categories on the basis of the length of time they have occupied upper-class position: (1) *established* families, which have been in the upper class for two or more generations; and (2) *new* families, which have achieved their position through the success of the present adult generation.

Selection from August B. Hollingshead, "Class Differences in Family Stability," *The Annals of the American Academy of Political and Social Science*, CCLXXII, Nov., 1950, 39–46. With permission.

Who one's ancestors were, and who one's relatives are, count for more in the established family group than what one has achieved in one's own lifetime. "Background" is stressed most heavily when it comes to the crucial question of whom a member may or may not marry, for marriage is the institution that determines membership in the family group. Indeed, one of the perennial problems of the established family is the control of the marriage choices of its young men. Young women can be controlled more easily than young men, because of the sheltered life they lead and their passive role in courtship. The passivity of the upper-class female, coupled with sex exploitation of females from lower social positions by upper-class males that sometimes leads to marriage, results in a considerable number of old maids in established upper-class families. Strong emphasis on family background is accompanied by the selection of marriage mates from within the old-family group in an exceptionally high percentage of cases, and if not from the old-family group, then from the new-family segment of the upper class. The degree of kinship solidarity, combined with intraclass marriages, found in this level results in a high order of stability in the upper class, in the extended kin group, and in the nuclear family within it.

The established upper-class family is basically an extended kin group, solidified by lineage and a heritage of common experience in a communal setting. A complicated network of consanguineal and affinal ties unites nuclear families of orientation and procreation into an in-group that rallies when its position is threatened by the behavior of one of its members, particularly where out-marriage is involved; this principle will be illustrated below. Each nuclear family usually maintains a separate household, but it does not conceive of itself as a unit apart from the larger kin group. The nuclear family is viewed as only a part of a broader kin group that includes the consanguineal descendants of a known ancestral pair, plus kin that have been brought into the group by marriage.

An important factor in the extended established family's ability to maintain its position through several generations is its economic security. Usually a number of different nuclear families within a kin group are supported, in part at least, by income from a family estate held in trust. Also, because of the practice of intramarriage it is not unusual for a family to be the beneficiary of two or more estates held in trust. For example, in an eastern community of some 80,000 population, one of these extended family groups is the beneficiary of a trust established a century ago that yields something over $300,000 annually, after taxes. This income is divided among 37 different nuclear families descended from the founder, 28 of whom live in the community; 23 of these families are beneficiaries of one other trust fund, and 14 receive income from two or more other trust funds. These different nuclear families regard themselves as parts of the Scott* family; moreover, they are so regarded by other upper-class families, as well as by persons lower in the status system who know something of the details of the family history.

The Scott family has maintained its upper-class position locally for more than two centuries by a combination of property ownership, educational, legal, and political leadership, and control of marriages generation after generation. Its members are proud that it has never had a non-Protestant marriage in seven generations; only five divorces have been traced, but these are not mentioned; one desertion has been hinted, but not confirmed.

The In-Group Marriage Test

The tradition relative to Protestant intra-upper-class marriages had a severe test in recent years. A son in one family, who had spent four years in the armed services in the late war, asked a middle-class Catholic girl to marry him. The engagement was announced by the girl's family, to the consternation of the Scotts. The Scotts immediately brought pressure on the boy to "break off the affair." His mother "bristled" at the very idea of her son's marriage; his father "had a talk with him"; his 84-year-old paternal grandmother snorted, "A Scott marry a Flaherty, never!" A great-aunt remarked icily, "No Scott is dissolute enough to *have* to marry a Flaherty." After the first shock of indignation had passed, the young man was told he was welcome in "any Scott home" without that "Flaherty flip." A few weeks later his maternal grandfather told him he would be disinherited if he "demeaned" himself by marrying "that girl."

---

* All names are pseudonyms; they are used because some of the quotations have meaning only in terms of them.

After several months of family and class pressure against the marriage, the young man "saw his error" and broke the engagement. A year later he married a family-approved "nice" girl from one of the other "old" families in the city.

This case illustrates a number of characteristics typical of the established upper-class family. It is stable, extended, tends to pull together when its position is threatened—in this instance by an out-marriage—exerts powerful controls on its members to ensure that their behavior conforms to family and class codes, and provides for its members economically by trust funds and appropriate positions.

⊷§ 6 §⊶   Bias in Professional Publications Concerning Interfaith Marriages

by GLENN M. VERNON

The religiously mixed marriage excites the interest of a large number of people today. Many and varied are the reasons back of this interest. The social scientist, particularly the sociologist and the psychologist, shares this interest—especially those who have concerned themselves with the so-called problem areas of human behavior. Of all those mentioned, the social scientist plays a somewhat unique role, in that he attempts to see the situation through scientific eyes. He attempts to see the data objectively. He tries to be unbiased and is only interested in presenting the facts as they are, not in trying to determine what they ought to be.

Adapted from *Religious Education*, LV (July-Aug. 1960), No. 4, 261–264; by permission of the author and the publisher, The Religious Education Association, New York City.

This interest has led to the gathering of facts and figures by the social scientist so that he would not have to rely upon guess-work, hunches, or preconceived conclusions. Since religion is involved in the interfaith marriage issue, there is a possibility that the human tendency for the individual to see what he wants to see may be exaggerated, thus making accurate statistics very necessary.

We are fortunate that some limited statistics are available. This article is concerned with the influence which some of these statistics may have upon our students and the reading public. More specifically, the concern is with the manner in which they have traditionally been presented, at least as evidenced in the current textbooks in the area. This concern also extends to the reflection which this presentation makes upon our profession, in that we profess to be impartial, objective scientists.

The statistics referred to are those which compare the divorce rate of religiously homogeneous and religiously heterogeneous marriages. When the sociologist considers this area, the figures most often quoted are those from the Landis study done in Michigan.[1] The Weeks study[2] and the Bell study[3] are also frequently used. Let us look at the traditional presentation of the results of the Landis study.*

PER CENT DIVORCED

Both Catholic	4.4
Both Jewish	5.2
Both Protestant	6.0
Mixed, Catholic-Protestant	14.1
Both none	17.9

The main emphasis of this chart is that once we begin to cross religious lines in marriage, the likelihood of divorce increases tremendously—about 2 to 3 times, in fact. Speaking in terms of percentages, it suggests that the chances for divorce increase from 200 to 300 per cent in an interfaith marriage as compared to a one-faith marriage. From this, although the figures do not actually say it, it is easy for the student or the reader to leave with the impression that interfaith marriages are almost doomed to failure from the beginning—after all, a difference as high as 200 to 300 per cent is a big one.

* These figures are sometimes presented graphically or pictorially as well as in tabular form.

One wonders whether the effect upon the student would be any different if the reverse set of figures were presented—the per cent of couples staying together. In this case the figures would be as follows.

PER CENT ENDURING

Both Catholic	95.6
Both Jewish	94.8
Both Protestant	94.0
Mixed, Catholic-Protestant	85.9
Both none	82.1

It would seem that quite a different impression would be left with the reader from an analysis of this set of figures. In the first place, all of the figures are high ones—well above 75 per cent, so that even though he may not remember any exact figures, he is left with the impression that the great majority of marriages do endure, including interfaith marriages. There is a differential rate of success to be sure, but in this case the difference is not from 200 to 300 per cent, but rather the difference is around 10 per cent.

The whole difficulty is emphasized in a recent book written by a religionist,[4] who states that in the ministry he has been called upon to do a good deal of counseling, and that he has yet "to deal with a problem or discern a solution which was not at root religious." In discussing interfaith marriages, he states:

Suppose you wanted to fly the Atlantic and asked the agent: "Is it a safe trip?" and he answered, "Oh, yes, every once in a while a plane gets through," I doubt if you would book passage. What you would want to know—if you still had the courage to pursue the matter further—is "What are the chances?" What is important to a young couple contemplating the matter is not that this or that couple seem to have worked it out all right, but rather, what by and large is the success of mixed marriages? Fortunately this is a question we are able to answer—in a rough and ready way to be sure, because the answer is in terms of divorce and separation—which is only a partial reflection of the scope of unhappiness and dissatisfaction which it suggests.

From what is called the "Maryland Study" we learn about the religious connections of the parents of twelve thousand young people and whether their parents were living together or not. . . . The figures show that where both parents were Protestant . . . 6.8 per cent of the parents were separated. . . . Where both parents were Roman Catholic 6.4 per cent of the parents were separated. In the case of mixed marriages 15.2 per cent represented broken homes. . . . In short, there was in the case of mixed marriages 2¼ times as much separation and divorce as in the families where there was religious homogeneity.

The author starts his discussion by suggesting that what we really want to know is how many "get through," and indicates that he has some rough answers. However, he does not present them, but reverses his field, and presents figures as to how many did not get through, thus permitting him the telling point that the difference was about 2¼ times greater that the interfaith marriage would fail, rather than about 10 per cent less that an interfaith marriage would get through.

It would seem possible that our concentration upon the one set of figures with the 200 to 300 per cent difference may have contributed to religious scapegoating as far as religiously mixed marriages are concerned not only on the part of the parents and friends, but on the part of the individual participants in such marriages. Thus, we may unintentionally be creating additional hazards for the interfaith marriage.

It would seem that this whole issue is a particularly pertinent one in light of the large number of interfaith marriages being contracted today. This is true whether we take the approach of the strict scientist who is merely presenting the facts, where his selection of one set of figures to the exclusion of another equally valid set may evidence possible unintentional biases, or whether the interest is more that of a social actionist interested in trying to help young couples make a go of their marriage.

It is certainly not the intent of this article to minimize the problems which frequently accompany a religiously mixed marriage, but neither does it seem proper to over-emphasize potential difficulties, and thus help make these predictions somewhat self-fulfilling. It would seem that we have an obligation to our students and readers to point up the chances for such marriages staying together as well as the chances for breaking up. It is further suggested that the fact that the reverse statistics are implicit in either presentation does not relieve us of this obligation. If the text or the professor emphasizes but one set, the chances are good that this is the emphasis which will be retained by the student or reader.

This article should not be construed as an endorsement of interfaith marriages. Neither is it an indictment of such marriages. The scientist is not concerned with either of these approaches. The question is being raised as to whether intentionally or unintentionally our biases are showing in the set of statistics which we seem to consistently select for presentation to our readers and students.

NOTES

1. J. T. LANDIS, "Marriages of Mixed and Non-Mixed Religious Faiths," *American Sociological Review*, XIV (1949), p. 403.
2. H. ASHLEY WEEKS, "Differential Divorce Rates by Occupation," *Social Forces*, XXI (1943), p. 336.
3. HOWARD M. BELL, *Youth Tell Their Story*, Washington, D.C.: American Council on Education, 1938, p. 21.
4. JAMES A. PIKE, *If You Marry Outside Your Faith*, New York: Harper and Brothers, 1954, pp. 26–28.

Three

HUSBAND-WIFE
RELATIONS

❧ INTRODUCTION ❧

The nature of husband-wife relations is importantly influenced by cultural factors. This becomes very clear if we examine the different cultural rules that are to be found regarding such matters as the preferred number of spouses a person should have, or the degree to which sexual relations are confined to spouses. Murdock (1949) characterizes 193 societies in his sample as practicing polygyny (where the preferred form of marriage is for one man to have two or more wives); 43 societies as practicing monogamy (one man—one woman); and 2 societies as practicing polyandry (one woman—two or more husbands). Murdock also points out that of the societies in his sample for which he has information, "65 allow unmarried and unrelated persons complete freedom in sexual matters, and 20 others give qualified consent, while only 54 forbid or disapprove premarital liaisons between non-relatives, and many of these allow sex relations between specified relatives such as cross-cousins" (p. 5). In addition he notes that in a majority of the societies in his sample "a married man may legitimately carry on an affair with one or more of his female relatives" (p. 6). Such information indicates something of the range of cultural rules to be found, and should make it clear that middle-class American husband-wife relations represent only a small band within the range of cultural variability.

It has already been pointed out that Americans marry for many reasons besides love (pp. 43 ff.) We can add here that they also marry for many reasons besides sex, even though the official prohibition of all sexual intercourse except between husband and wife makes sex a powerful marriage-producing factor in American society. Sex is obviously a much less powerful marriage-producing factor in those societies where premarital sexual relations are not forbidden. "The attribution of marriage primarily to the factor of sex must be recognized as reflecting a bias derived from our own very aberrant sexual customs." (Murdock, 1949, p. 6.)

The Roles of Husband and Wife

In American society husbands and wives are expected to contribute differently and unequally to the marital relationship, although some of these role differences are gradually changing. There is still considerable evidence of an American pattern of male dominance and superiority. R. L. Coser (1960), for example, points out that women on the staff of a mental hospital she studied, although perfectly "capable of telling good jokes or making witty remarks in informal situations," seldom did this at formal staff meetings because of the expectation that such remarks were more fitting for a man. Kenkel (1963) points out that 48 per cent of the spouses in his sample expected the husband to have greater influence in decision-making, and 10 per cent expected the wife to have greater influence. In actual fact, however, 28 per cent of the husbands had more influence and 16 per cent of the wives. This suggests that expressed expectations may be substantially influenced by traditional American values, even while these values are changing. The current situation is perhaps best expressed in terms of a gradual movement toward greater equality between the sexes, even though there is still a good deal of variation from group to group within American society (Strodtbeck, 1951; Komarovsky, 1953; Lovejoy, 1961; *Marriage and Family Living*, 1961; Nye and Hoffman, 1963; Madsen, 1964).

Husbands and wives also specialize in certain roles that do not directly involve the question of dominance or equality. For example, even though much variation is to be found, there are still certain household tasks that are generally done by men and others that are generally done by women. Blood and Wolfe (1960, p. 50) point out that the husband always or usually shovels the sidewalk, mows the lawn, and repairs things around the house (more than 70 per cent of the couples in each case); and that the wife always or usually does the evening dishes, gets the husband's breakfast on work days, and straightens up the living room when company is coming (also more than 70 per cent of the couples in each case). Grocery shopping, and especially keeping track of the money and bills, are a bit more spread out: 56 per cent of the wives and 14 per cent of the husbands always or usually shop for groceries, while husband and wife shop equally in 29 per cent of the cases; 41 per cent of the wives and 25 per cent of the husbands always or usually keep track of the money and bills, while they share this equally in 34 per cent of the cases. When it comes to the influence over decisions that affect both husband and wife, there is a good deal more equality in the marital roles. In two areas, for example—where to go on a vacation and what house or apartment to take—Blood and Wolfe (1960, p. 21) point out that in more than one-half of the cases the husband and wife have an equal say in the decision.

Mutual Development

From the first time that prospective mates meet they begin to influence each other and to develop patterns of behavior between themselves and with others. There is mutual influence and development throughout the dating relationship and all stages of married life. The points of transition from one stage to another are usually the most critical times—for example, the first date, first being married, or first meeting after a long period of separation. It is at such points that the pattern of mutual adjustment and development begins to take shape, and this can have far-reaching consequences for the future. The selection by Waller and Hill (7) is an interesting illustration of mutual adjustment and the development of habits in married life, and also of the reaction to the loss of this habit system at the time of bereavement. Cuber and Haroff (8) also indicate the nature of certain patterns of adjustment and development in married life, and the way these may be part of a larger system in which each of the spouses may have outside relationships.

The selections by Waller and Hill and by Cuber and Harroff show something of the complexity of married life. One way of emphasizing this complexity is to point out the oversimplification involved in the notion that a good marriage is made by matching up the husband and wife according to a number of key traits, such as leisure-time preferences, political preference, or religious preference. One problem here is that people may be characterized by an infinite number of traits, and in matching them on several important traits they may still be mismatched on other important traits. Another problem is that we have only meager evidence on what a good matching of traits would be—it is the question of homogamy versus heterogamy once again (see Rodman, *4*). Finally, regardless of how a couple is matched or mismatched on a variety of traits, there is the whole question of how they interact and develop together as a couple. As Foote (1956) says: "Matching is a continual process." He further states:

> One of the less helpful influences of psychology upon the study of the family has been the example of treating physiological maturity as the end-point of personality development. This means that the development of children within the family has gotten attention almost to the exclusion of the continuous development of husband and wife as a product of their interaction with each other.

During a long separation between husband and wife each has been interacting and developing social relationships with others. In a sense, husband and wife have been growing apart, and this may threaten their marital relationship. Enforced separation during the war years led to severe problems of adjustment for many families (Hill, 1949). The problem is aptly stated by Foote (1956)—after a long separation "reunion requires reweaving the skein of interconnection between the hundreds or thousands of events in the life of one and the life of the other, through conversation and non-verbal communication." If husband and wife have, however, developed in very different directions with very different interests and attitudes, the reweaving of their relationship may not be possible.

Even without separation a husband and wife may develop in very different directions. If the husband is at college or at an interesting job while the wife has no important interests except her housework, the couple may grow apart; or, as it is often said, the husband may "outgrow" his wife. At the point that the husband receives his promotion to an executive position he may discover that the girl he married from back home no longer fits into the life he is now expected and prepared to live along with his fellow executives (Whyte, 1951). It is therefore important to pay attention to the mutual development of husband and wife as a way of understanding the nature of their relationship and the reasons for its success or breakdown.

If the marital relationship does break down and if a divorce and subsequent remarriage take place, the individuals involved go through new stages of development requiring a variety of adjustments and adaptations (Bernard, 1956; Goode, 1956). Most individuals who divorce and remarry share at least some problems with one another. It is necessary to break the once-strong bonds of attachment to the first spouse and to begin to build new bonds of attachment to the second. It is therefore understandable that people of similar marital status tend to marry each other, widows tending to marry widowers and divorcés tending to marry divorcées (Bowerman, 1953; Bernard, 1956, p. 9). As Foote (1956) sees it, such mates are matched "in terms of similar developmental tasks," and in this sense they share problems and interests that stem from their marital status and that therefore help them to establish a relationship between themselves.

Marriage: Romance or Routine?

There is a strong romantic notion associated with courtship and marriage in Western society, and especially in American society. But there is also a strong tendency to deplore romantic love as the basis for marriage. The romantic notion is said to build up expectations that cannot be fulfilled in the day-to-day routine of married life. Rougemont (1948; 1956; 1963) is the most eloquent spokesman for this point of view. According to him, romantic love is a temporary state that is based upon an imaginary link between a man and a woman who have no real communication between them. There is "a double make-believe" to romance, in which each partner builds up an image of the other that has no basis in reality. Romantic love thrives upon obstacles that keep the man and woman apart, and it withers in the cold light of marriage:

> Romance is by its very nature incompatible with marriage even if the one has led to the other, for it is the very essence of romance to thrive on obstacles, delays, separations, and dreams, whereas it is the basic function of marriage daily to reduce and obliterate

these obstacles. Marriage succeeds only in constant physical proximity to the monotonous present. . . . Romance is . . . incapable of establishing a durable marriage, and it is not an act of courage but one of absurdity to marry someone forever because of a fever that endures for two months. (Rougemont, 1948.)

Johnson's (1946) description of the "IFD disease," which he regards as an ailment that is especially common among university students, can be exemplified by Rougemont's ideas about romance and marriage. The IFD disease refers to the movement from idealism to frustration to demoralization—or from romance and marriage to frustration to divorce, in Rougemont's example. In a close look at American popular songs, Hayakawa (1955) has also illustrated the way in which they demonstrate the IFD disease in their lyrics. The transformation from romance to the routine of marriage is put more caustically by Wylie (1959), who refers to the girl who is Cinderella but briefly, after which, like a butterfly turning into a moth, she turns into Mom and becomes "all tongue and teat and razzmatazz" (p. 189).

Other writers look upon romantic love favorably, and do not see it as producing frustration but as assisting "in the adjustment to frustrating experiences" that stem from the many changes taking place in industrialized societies. According to this view, "it has saved monogamous marriage from complete disorganization." It is a mutually affectionate and supportive relationship within which the individual finds peace from "the high tensions of the modern workday" (Beigel, 1951). It is true that "sexual cravings are easily mistaken for love" and that "the desire to escape depressing home restrictions" is also easily mistaken for love. "But such immature ideas cannot be blamed on love itself" (Beigel, 1951). In other words, as Goode (1959) and Knight (1959) have pointed out, we have here differences of opinion and value—"whether or not successful marriage can be based on romance is a question upon which we should suspend judgment until the disagreement can be shown to be more factual than we see it at present." (Knight, 1959.)

The disagreement about whether romantic love is a good basis for marriage is semantic as well as evaluational. Rougemont (1963, pp. 51, 61) refers to love through characters in Robert Musil's *The Man Without Qualities:* it requires a partner "who would be absolutely inaccessible"; "one really loves only an unreal person."

Beigel (1951) defines love as "understanding and mutual assistance in emotional conflicts, . . . moral support and common interests, . . . mutual confirmation and emotional security." There are thousands of other definitions of romantic love,* and it is to be expected that those who stress unreality, immaturity, and irresponsibility in their defintion would not see it as a good basis for marriage, while those who stress reality, maturity, and mutuality in their definition *would* see it as a good basis for marriage.

One line of evidence that throws some indirect light upon the possible adequacy of romance as a basis for marriage is the data that we have on changes in marital satisfaction. Hobart (1960) has shown that couples do become increasingly romantic as marriage approaches. What happens to their marital satisfaction after marriage? Generally speaking, there is a steady decline in marital satisfaction through time, although this may differ by social class (cf. Komarovsky, 1964, p. 329). Blood and Wolfe (1960, p. 264) report the following average marital satisfaction scores: under 2 years of marriage, 5.36; 3–9 years of marriage, 5.02; 10–19 years, 4.77; 20–29 years, 4.20; 30 or more years, 4.10. The French Institute of Public Opinion (1961, p. 168) reports the following percentages of women who describe their married life as a routine or a great disappointment: under 5 years of marriage, 16 per cent; 5–10 years of marriage, 24 per cent; 11–15 years, 28 per cent; more than 15 years, 33 per cent. Terman (1938) reports a downward trend in marital happiness, but the changes he reports are more cyclical and show an upward trend in the later years of marriage. Dennis *et al.* (1956) report that in the English mining town they studied it is

> a common feature for no development or deepening of the husband-wife relationship to take place after the initial intensive sex-life of early marriage. Indeed those couples which seemed happiest were in the first year or two of marriage, when most problems were solved by going to bed (p. 228).

Bowerman (1957), Hobart (1958), and Pineo (1961) all report a decline in marital adjustment or satisfaction, and Pineo refers to this as indicating a process of disenchantment—"this is a process which appears to be generally an inescapable conse-

* See Fromm (1956) for an account of various forms of love. See Kolb (1950) for a clear picture of contrasting definitions of the romantic complex.

quence of the passage of time in a marriage." Blood and Wolfe
(1960, p. 263) similarly refer to "the corrosive influence of time."
It should be clear that the above findings of a gradual decline
in marital satisfaction do not apply to all couples—yet enough
couples are affected to give us pause. Is there too high an expectation on the part of many people getting married (regardless of
whether or not this is conceptualized as "romantic love" or "lack
of realism"*), and is this expectation bound to be disappointed?

The paper by Cuber and Harroff (8) is an important contribution toward a more realistic understanding of the husband-wife
relationship, and of man-woman relationships generally. They
point out that there are very few husband-wife pairs in their
sample who have a rich, vital, highly satisfying relationship. In a
large majority of the cases the husband-wife relationship is passive,
devitalized, and highly routinized. In some of these cases there is a
degree of congeniality and contentment to the relationship; in
others there is not, and the relationship is "devoid of vital meaning by comparison to what it was when the mating began and what
was then considered to be its *raison d'être*." In many instances
adjustments have taken place through the years, including the
avoidance of communication about sensitive areas (see *11*), and
the establishment of relationships with third persons. Such a study
is valuable in its own right, and doubly valuable because of the
needed corrective it provides to the rosy picture that is so often
painted about marriage and the family.

REFERENCES

BEIGEL, HUGO G. 1951. "Romantic Love," *American Sociological Review,*
XVI, 326–334.

BERNARD, JESSIE. 1956. *Remarriage: A Study of Marriage,* New York:
Dryden.

BLOOD, ROBERT O., JR., and DONALD M. WOLFE. 1960. *Husbands and
Wives,* New York: Free Press of Glencoe.

* Romanticism is not highly related to disillusionment (Hobart, 1958); it
is apparently not at all related to immaturity, perhaps because the romantic
love complex "may be so all-pervasive in American youth culture" that its
presence or absence does not distinguish between the more or less mature
(Dean, 1961; 1964).

BOWERMAN, CHARLES E. 1953. "Assortative Mating by Previous Marital Status: Seattle, 1939–1946," *American Sociological Review*, XVIII, 170–177.

———. 1957. "Adjustment in Marriage: Over-All and in Specific Areas," *Sociology and Social Research*, XLI, 257–263.

COSER, ROSE L. 1960. "Laughter Among Colleagues," *Psychiatry*, XXIII, 81–95.

DEAN, DWIGHT G. 1961. "Romanticism and Emotional Maturity: A Preliminary Study," *Marriage and Family Living*, XXIII, 44–45.

———. 1964. "Romanticism and Emotional Maturity: A Further Exploration," *Social Forces*, LXII, 298–303.

DENNIS, NORMAN, FERNANDO HENRIQUES, and CLIFFORD SLAUGHTER. 1956. *Coal Is Our Life*, London: Eyre & Spottiswoode.

FOOTE, NELSON N. 1956. "Matching of Husband and Wife in Phases of Development," *Transactions of the Third World Congress of Sociology*, London: International Sociological Association, IX, 24–34.

French Institute of Public Opinion. 1961. *Patterns of Sex and Love*, New York: Crown.

FROMM, ERICH. 1956. *The Art of Loving*, New York: Harper.

GOODE, WILLIAM J. 1956. *After Divorce*, Glencoe, Ill.: Free Press.

———. 1959. "The Theoretical Importance of Love," *American Sociological Review*, XXIV, 38–47.

HAYAKAWA, S. I. 1955. "Popular Songs vs. the Facts of Life," *Etc.*, XII, 83–95.

HILL, REUBEN. 1949. (With Elise Boulding.) *Families Under Stress*, New York: Harper.

HOBART, CHARLES W. 1958. "Disillusionment in Marriage, and Romanticism," *Marriage and Family Living*, XX, 156–162.

———. 1960. "Attitude Changes During Courtship and Marriage," *Marriage and Family Living*, XXII, 352–359.

JOHNSON, WENDELL. 1946. *People in Quandaries*, New York: Harper.

KENKEL, WILLIAM F. 1963. "Observational Studies of Husband–Wife Interaction in Family Decision-Making," pp. 144–156, in Marvin B. Sussman, ed., *Sourcebook in Marriage and the Family*, 2d ed., Boston: Houghton Mifflin.

KNIGHT, THOMAS S. 1959. "In Defense of Romance," *Marriage and Family Living*, XXI, 107–110.

KOLB, WILLIAM L. 1950. "Family Sociology, Marriage Education, and the Romantic Complex: A Critique," *Social Forces*, XXIX, 65–72.

KOMAROVSKY, MIRRA. 1953. *Women in the Modern World*, Boston: Little, Brown.

———. 1964. *Blue-Collar Marriage*, New York: Random House.

LOVEJOY, DEBI D. 1961. "College Student Conceptions of the Roles of the Husband and Wife in Family Decision-Making," *Family Life Coordinator*, IX, 43–46.

MADSEN, WILLIAM. 1964. *Mexican-Americans of South Texas*, New York: Holt, Rinehart and Winston.

Marriage and Family Living. 1961. XXIII, November, entire issue.

MURDOCK, GEORGE P. 1949. *Social Structure,* New York: Macmillan.

NYE, F. IVAN, and LOIS W. HOFFMAN, eds. 1963. *The Employed Mother in America,* Chicago: Rand McNally.

PINEO, PETER C. 1961. "Disenchantment in the Later Years of Marriage," *Marriage and Family Living,* XXII, 3–11.

ROUGEMONT, DENIS DE. 1948. "The Romantic Route to Divorce," *Saturday Review of Literature,* Nov. 13, 1948, 9–10, 59.

———. 1956. *Love in the Western World,* rev. ed., New York: Pantheon.

———. 1963. *Love Declared,* New York: Pantheon.

STRODTBECK, FRED L. 1951. "Husband-Wife Interaction over Revealed Differences," *American Sociological Review,* XVI, 468–473.

TERMAN, LEWIS M. 1938. *Psychological Factors in Marital Happiness,* New York: McGraw-Hill.

WHYTE, WILLIAM H. 1951. "The Wives of Management," *Fortune,* XLIV, 86 ff.

WYLIE, PHILIP. 1959. *Generation of Vipers,* New York: Pocket Books.

✌ 7 ʕ✎   Habit Systems in Married Life

by W I L L A R D   W A L L E R   *and*

R E U B E N   H I L L

The early months of marriage are usually characterized by a high degree of euphoria, a continuation of the ecstasy of the honeymoon period, when the whole of life tends to be suffused with erotic pleasure. The newly married individuals continue to widen the range of their personal contacts; during this time of exploration (which began in the engagement period), the habit systems of the two individuals must adjust to new situations arising out of the fact that they are now a dyad. The euphoria of the early months subsides, for the sound reason that people cannot continue indefinitely to live on a high emotional pitch. But the type of solidarity peculiar to the honeymoon period also breaks down, once its accompanying euphoria has faded. Conflict inevitably emerges, its intensity depending upon several factors in the personalities involved. Since the processes of married living also produce solidarity, in the usual case conflict is arrested at some point and is limited by accords. The adjustment of personality to the routine of marriage involves far-reaching changes and usually some frustration; patterns of release and escape therefore make their appearance. After a time marriage interaction tends to slow down to a more tolerable interplay characteristic of settled married folk.

Marriage as an Undefined Situation

"Lay the law down to her the first day and you'll never have any trouble with your wife." So ran the advice which in other days the experienced patriarch gave to the young husband. If we grant the premises, the saying expresses a sound understanding of the realities of marriage interaction. For the start is all-important. Actually, as we have already pointed out in discussing engagement, processes have been unleashed in the engagement which the wedding merely ceremonializes. Not with the words "I now pronounce you," but early in the functioning engagement did the dyadic processes begin which will go on "till death us do part." Once married, however, the man and the woman have started on a journey from which it is difficult to turn back. The words "husband" and "wife" soon acquire meanings not given in the dictionary definition.

Strictly speaking, engagement or no engagement, every new marriage is an undefined situation, just as every new status involves undefined elements for the neophyte. Each individual begins tentatively to explore the behavior possibilities of the situation. Each tries to find out what he can do and should do and begins to form habits, but neither can stabilize his habits at once, because the other person is also carrying on an exploratory process.

The social form created by marriage must find its way by a rather tentative process, making many false starts but attaining at last a tolerable living pattern. Like a rat in a maze, each member must try out many patterns of behavior in the new situation. Some patterns will appear highly successful; these will tend to stabilize in the form of powerful habits. Other patterns of behavior will be penalized by conflict or other forms of failure; it is thus that the limits of interaction are defined. A man who moves into a new house must go through a period of tension and attention before he is at home; he must find the switches for the lights; he must learn which is the hot and which the cold water faucet; above all, he must be careful of the cellar stairs. In the end one comes to be at home in a new home. So with marriage. . . .

The Interlocking of Habit Systems

The nexus of interaction which is a family may be viewed as a set of intermeshing, mutually facilitating habits. The married pair start with their separate systems of habit, which they formed in their parental families and in some years of life away from the family. After a time they form interlocking habit systems by modifying old habits and forming new ones; the interlocked habit systems are a great deal more stable than the habit system of the individual could ever be and rest upon a different set of psychological mechanisms—certainly not upon mere routinization, but rather upon the habit of adjusting to the situation created by the real or imaginary demands and expectations of others. When a child enters the family there are vast changes, but these result in an increase in stability, for the routine care of the child imposes a great range of new necessities. The child forms his habits in the social setting furnished by the habits of others, and this is true of each successive child. It is significant that the first habit functioning of the child is in this setting, a setting in which the habits of each are adjusted to the satisfactions required by the habits of others, certainly not a situation of mere competition or of like response to like stimulus. When the youngster leaves the family and lives in a college dormitory, he perceives the difference.

The novelist Sigrid Undset, wishing to convey an impression of the solidarity of a marriage, does it by describing the interaction of a single habit. She says that the husband used to laugh when the wife referred to anthills as ants' houses, but now he does not laugh any more; in fact, he sometimes uses the expression himself. Each individual member of a family has made certain habit adjustments to the physical setting in which the family lives; each knows at just what height to insert the key in the lock of the front door and each has acquired the knack of giving a little twist to the key which makes the door open easily; each one is able to enter any of the rooms in the darkness and to find the switches for the lights without any difficulty; each knows where to sit on hot afternoons in August, and how to descend the rickety cellar stairs. And each one, likewise, has made a multitude of adjustments to the presence of others in the house. In the morning the father of the family gets up and tends the furnace. He walks carefully in order not to disturb the others, but there is no need of this, for the others have adjusted to his early morning noise and do not hear him. A little later the mother gets up and calls the children, perhaps a number of times, for they may have made an adjustment to her habitual technique and have shifted the responsibility entirely upon her; they have, perhaps, developed "mother deafness." She then prepares breakfast, sets the table, and calls the family. Father has been reading the paper, which is now split into sections. Each one eats his breakfast in his customary way; there is the usual interchange of pleasantries and the usual grumbling and complaining. Then ensues the morning crisis of getting the children off to school and helping father to catch the eight-thirty train: the struggle over the bathroom, the effort to find things, the examination of shirts to see whether they will do for another day, and all the myriad adjustments which arise from a civilization which demands neatness and promptness. Then all the members of the family but one leave the home, pausing a moment to say good-by to mother and to pet the dog. This is a small segment of their habitized day, and we have intentionally overlooked all the more subtle nuances of conversation and gestural interplay.

As to the sense of time, not only is time of the essence of these interwoven habits of family life; they are the essence of time. Time is always relevant to a social situation.[1] (Thomas Mann's *The Magic Mountain* shows very clearly what happens to the sense of time when daily tasks and the intermeshed habits of life are destroyed.) Time is important in the modern family; haste enters into it and murders peace. The "long arm of the job" reaches in; the motion picture snatches certain ones at appointed hours and the radio and television programs make others impatient; the school, the bridge club, and the market place make everybody watch the clock. So the habits of family life are a part of the great rhythm of civilization and the whole is the slave of the pendulum. Society is founded on clocks.*

* Social theory has never quite done justice to the solidity of such masses of social habits. In discarding instincts as causes of human behavior, we have had recourse to social habits as explanatory factors, but it is possible that social change would be no more difficult if it involved changing the heredity of mankind. The habits of each member of the family are intermeshed with the habits of all the others, and with highly stable elements of the outside world, and the whole persists because there is no social technique by which all the members of the family can make changes in all their habits at the same time. Dewey has discussed the interdependence of each habit of the individual with every other habit, and this furnishes an additional complexity. Dewey uses the telling illustration of a man who decides to remedy his standing posture, but succeeds only in standing a "different kind of badly." Each habit of the individual family member has its roots in his own personality and is interlinked with habits of others which likewise are entrenched in the systems of habit of the others. One becomes convinced that Sumner was almost right in his remarks on the folly of trying to make the world over. The mother tries to stop giving her child money every time he

Fundamental to the formation of a system of collective habits, there is an interchange of tastes, likes and dislikes, and disgusts in the married state. This ranges from the interaction of quite simple, almost reflex patterns to the mutual pressure of highly complex attitudes. One mate introduces the other to a number of new food objects, and the setting for the reaction of the one is furnished by the established liking of the other. A strong avoidance by one of the mates may exclude an article of food completely from the diet of the couple, or the aversion may be transferred to the other mate by conditioning. Such an attitude as a dislike for lengthy telephone conversations is easily transmitted in the marriage situation, and it is then, of course, asserted outside the relationship. In a certain marriage one of the mates was extremely sensitive to any form of ego gloat, and very keen in detecting such an attitude beneath its possible disguises; the other mate had previously been tolerant of such assertions of the feeling of self but now came to experience toward them a qualified dislike. A taste for such forms of entertainment as dancing and the theater and for social groups which center around such diversions is likewise easily transmissible.

The interaction of judgments of people is a much more subtle but probably inevitable part of marriage interaction. In one typical marriage, the husband had a habit of making highly analytical but balanced judgments of people; he liked no one to excess and hated no one. The wife had a pattern of association which consisted of liking people very much for a time, excluding from consciousness everything contrary to this attitude, and then at long last turning completely and finally against those who had imposed upon her too much. The effect upon her personality of the husband's analytical attitude was at first to cause her to reject nearly everybody; later

---

asks for it, and for a few days follows the rules laid down for her by the bright young psychologist, but the old norms are implicit in all that she does and in the whole pattern of life in the family, and before long she returns to the old ways because it was easier, after all, to put up with a demanding child than to stop indulging him. Pleasant and unpleasant experiences are alike powerless to change these collective habits, though perhaps we should not overlook the disorganizing effect of financial success, which operates to destroy masses of habits by breaking the physical basis of family interdependence, making it possible for members of the family to travel, to make new contacts, and to find amusements in new groups. Callers and visitors demand adjustments of the system of habits, but these adjustments likewise soon become habitual. Charles Lamb has commented on the disorganizing effect of casual droppers-in. This effect is easily understandable in the context of the discussion.

she came a considerable distance toward his system of balanced judgments.

The consensus which married persons work out by their long discussions of other persons is doubtless very important as a phase of their social relations. A great deal has been said about the desirability of common tastes in marriage, and it is doubtless true that married persons get along better if they start with a background of consensus, but all of this would need to be qualified in terms of what we are able to say about the remolding of tastes in marital interaction. . . .

Mourning and the Habit System

In delineating the dynamics of mourning, we may think of the bonds which connect the person to the deceased as strivings, habits, habits with immense propulsive power which ramify into every branch of the individual's existence. When the deceased was alive, this complex of strivings was daily expressed in a multitude of ways. When the person dies, these habits of others are blocked, but they continue as demands for activity. They show themselves first in the attempted persistence of routine, which produces the immediate phenomenon of grief. The earliest experiences of grief are almost muscular, the result of postures, gestures, and muscular sets which can no longer lead to the appropriate actions with reference to the loved person. When they are persistently blocked, these habits express themselves in imagination, perhaps by hallucinatory experiences (the "sense of presence"), by the bereavement dream, or by the reactivation of old experiences in fantasy.

Because of the tensions within himself, the bereaved person is peculiarly sensitive to all that reminds him of his loss, and indeed needs no reminder; his mind is self-activated to recall all the incidents and activities which bound him to the deceased. There ensues the process of mourning. Under the terrific impulsion of frustrated love, one relives the past bit by bit; as each old incident is recalled for the first time since the death, it is connected with the new association of death and annihilation, and then there is a fresh expression of grief. A man who has lost his wife sees a dress in a shop window; he thinks, "She liked dresses of that sort," then, "She is dead now," and then he feels the stab of grief. A woman who has lost her husband cannot sit down to a meal without a keen realization that he is not there; she cannot buy a dress without regretting that he will never see it. If one has been deeply attached to the deceased, the process is self-activating and one does not need to be reminded to mourn. If one has not been deeply involved emotionally but is merely reacting to a many-branched change in his life, the process depends somewhat more upon externals.

The entire process is useful, although painful; imagining old experiences expresses the frustrated attitudes which would otherwise certainly become pathogenic; the thought of death furnishes a new connection which aids in the final acceptance of reality; the stab of grief expresses some of the pent-up emotion of loss, and releases it in quantities small enough for the individual to assimilate.

Once a certain memory of the deceased has been recalled and reacted to, it is associated with a psychic pain which may inhibit its further recall. As time goes on, more and more distant associations are awakened and emotionally reacted to, until at length the process is finished. The process of mourning must continue until new associative bonds have been established throughout the whole range of connections, and until the conative trends connected with the deceased have lost their propulsive force—in Freudian terms, until the libido has been freed from the love object.

The pain of the mourning process steadily diminishes. Of course the individual rarely realizes that this is happening. When the process of mourning is nearly complete, new experiences may claim the individual again.* It is submitted that this account of the process is essentially correct whether the bereavement situation represents the loss of a person intensely loved or merely a greatly ramified loss entailing necessary readjustments in a number of phases of life. In the ideal typical case, mourning represents a reaction to both of these things.

* In *The Old Love and the New*, Liveright, 1930, pp. 144–147, Waller discussed the process in which the divorcee breaks the chain of associations which brings the absent mate to mind. The process, described there in some detail, is in many respects similar to mourning. There is in divorce the same frustration, the same reliving of experiences consequent upon frustration, the same process of formation of new association bonds as in mourning. A difference is that the formula "We've separated now," is less final and convincing than "She's dead now." A further difference is that custom does not require of the divorced person a period of mourning or abstention from sex relations, as it does of the one who has been bereaved of his mate. The divorcee may therefore employ a series of affairs (regression to an earlier adjustment) as a means of freeing himself from the mate.

NOTE

1. See R. K. MERTON and P. A. SOROKIN, "Social Time: A Methodological and Functional Analysis," *American Journal of Sociology*, XLII, 615–629. See also A. IRVING HALLOWELL, "Temporal Orientation in Western Civilization and in a Preliterate Society," *American Anthropologist*, XXXIX, 647–670.

≈§ 8 §≈   The More Total View: Relationships Among Men and Women of the Upper Middle Class

by J O H N F. C U B E R *and*

P E G G Y B. H A R R O F F

The "field" of marriage and family now consists of an impressive array of expert findings, theories, and typologies which together purport, by implication at least, to present to the interested student and colleague a composite picture of the bi-sexual world today. A strong accent, not always so stated, in all of this is diagnostic. Within certain limits we profess to *understand* the condition of man, so to speak, in his bi-sexual nature, the traditional and emergent forms which this nature takes and something about the predicaments which he persistently gets into. We have evolved a set

Adapted from *Marriage and Family Living*, XXV, May, 1963, 140–145; and from personal correspondence with the authors. Used with permission of the authors and *Marriage and Family Living*. For additional details, see John F. Cuber and Peggy B. Harroff (1965), *The Significant Americans: A Study of Sexual Behavior among the Affluent*, New York: Appleton-Century.

of concepts like "the child-centered family," "permissive parent-hood," "the family cycle" and have formulated a number of theoretical models and sequences which have become almost professional clichés—"from institution to companionship," "alternative roles for women," "complementary needs"—and a plethora of analyses as to why more and more marriages are apparently impermanent. This all adds up for one who tries to see it as a gestalt to a professional diagnosis as to what "is," what is wrong—or at least troublesome—and to some extent how it might be remedied.

Something additional might presumably be gained by turning to the subjects themselves for *their* concepts and *their* diagnosis of the state of the bisexual world. It might be well, moreover, to find out whether the concepts of professionals are reasonably in line with laymen's own perceptions and whether the imagery of the professionals corresponds to the imagery of the subjects about the same matters. We (the professionals) might, as Bierstedt says in another connection, often be re-enacting the deaf man in Tolstoy, muttering answers to questions that no one has asked.

In the research we have conducted, we have focused upon a select group of subjects for the purpose of securing their conceptions of reality in the man-woman world, their strivings and apathies, and their own evaluation of the success or failure of their own *modus operandi*. In constructing this collective self portrait, we invented, or more accurately, adapted a type of inquiry apparently not much in use by contemporary social scientists, with the exception perhaps of some anthropologists. It could be described tersely as the unstructured, lengthy, and intimate interview. In some respects it resembles a depth interview, because being un-structured, there was no way to avoid subjects' efforts at deeper self-examination, if they so chose. The subjects had wide latitude in their choice of what to discuss, and they had the opportunity to talk at great length. It would be possible in a number of in-stances to write a sizable book on the basis of the information we have about a given person or a given pair.

Such an undertaking, however, presents problems. First of all it presumes that one can find subjects sufficiently self-conscious about their life processes that they have intellectualizations worth talking about and second, that they are sufficiently articulate to be able to communicate such ideas effectively to someone else. Obviously, many potential subjects would be disqualified on one or another of these counts. It is also important to secure a sufficiently homogeneous group so that there would be some comparability relative to their life circumstances in order that even guarded generalization would be possible.

As the best approximation of our objectives, we settled upon a group of subjects whom most sociologists would probably designate as "upper middle class." We interviewed individuals, not couples or families, although in a number of instances both husband and wife came to be included. Since our focus was upon men and women and not upon marriage or family, we also interviewed widowed, divorced and single people in the approximate percentage in which they are found in this population. To insure further homogeneity interviewees were limited to an age span of 35 to 55 because we were more interested in mature reflection than in the immature projections of the very young and yet wanted persons in the vital years, before, as a rule, serious health or disillusionment begin to presage senility. We have interviewed in all 437 such persons. Of these, 406 were married at the time of the study, 76 for the second time; 19 were either widowed or divorced; and 12 were single.

Our rationale for this kind of selection is simply this: Since this segment of the population is highly educated, highly travelled, and widely exposed to allegedly emancipating influences, it could be presumed that they would have had occasion to observe and reflect seriously upon the man-woman world and would be relatively articulate in communicating their perceptions, evaluations and adaptations. These assumptions seemed vindicated by our actual experience in communicating with them. There were virtually no refusals; they had a great deal they wished to talk about, and by and large, were eager to talk about it.

One final criterion for selection of interviewees was observed. So much work in the social sciences has been done with relatively captive samples of people who are caught at some point of crisis in their lives, that a serious bias might thus have been introduced. We sought a non-clinical sample; that is, one limited to people not currently securing any kind of counselling or psychotherapy or having recently had any, or who were, in the opinion of the interviewers, clearly in need thereof. Obviously, such a sample is not normal by every criterion of normality, but it is at least free of some of the manifest distortion-producing influences of a crisis-caught group.

The problem of moving from data gathering to reporting is always ticklish. Many devices for content analysis of interview records have become conventional. These were not functional for us, because such techniques presume comparability of data for each subject. This we did not seek and therefore did not get. Accordingly we resorted to an informal, ideal-typical procedure in which we repeatedly reviewed and analyzed our materials looking for commonalities, generalizations and recurrent syndromes, none of which has at this point any formal statistical validity other than that it is *recurrent*. In other words, idiosyncratic data have been completely ignored in the analysis. We sought generalizable information, even though we knew before we started that generalizing would have to occur in non-statistical language.

Perhaps our most important finding was not in the form of data about men and women or marriage, but a vivid and recurrent reminder that when the professional listens modestly, he can learn a great deal more from the subject than he would have had the wit to ask about, if he had approached the interview with a set of questions or hypotheses derived from prior experience. It seems to us that the most important part of this investigation consists of new concepts and hypotheses which apparently are quite familiar to the persons in this class but which for the most part specialists have not talked about or have touched upon only obliquely.

A Typology of Marriages

One specific and recurrent enlightenment concerns the omnipresent problem of categories. Such familiar categories as marriage, monogamy, divorce have become in the modern world, if they have not always been so, highly diversified—or "contaminated" as some methodologists aptly put it. Persons and pairs who have one common attribute are conventionally placed in some category but often have so little in common otherwise that to hold them in a single category is a serious distortion of reality. One divorce, for example, may grow out of exploitation, irresponsibility and de-

generacy and leave scars of bitterness and pathology on a number
of people. In another instance a divorce may be an orderly, em-
pathetic, cooperative effort on the part of two or more people
simply in order to bring their subjective experience and their legal
status into more reasonable consonance. Similarly, a "stable"
married pair may on the one hand be deeply fulfilled people, living
vibrantly, or at the other extreme entrapped, embittered, resentful
people, living lives of duplicity in an atmosphere of hatred and
despair. And more important perhaps than the extremes are the
wide ranges in between. The use of categories in research and theory
building are, of course, essential and to some extent dissimilarities
of otherwise homogeneous cases may be ignored or presumed to be
randomized out. But there is no license here for the use of traditional legalistic and theological categories merely because they are
convenient stereotypes and reflect comfortable simplitudes about
people. In short, it is a major lesson from our inquiry that more
professional effort should be devoted to establishing more truly
discriminating categories.

The following categories have grown out of an analysis of the
testimony of those persons in our sample who have been married for
at least a decade, indicated that they had never considered separation or divorce, and so far as they knew, no one, including members of the family, thought of them as other than normal American
families.*

Conflict-Habituated Relationships.   In this husband-wife configuration there is much tension and conflict—although largely
"controlled." At worst, there is some private quarreling, nagging,
and "throwing up the past" of which members of the immediate
family, and more rarely even close friends and relatives, have
some awareness. At best, the couple is discreet and polite, "genteel about it" when in the company of others, but rarely succeeds
completely in concealing it from the children—although the illusion is common among them that they do. The essence, however,
is that there is awareness by both husband and wife that incom-
patibility is pervasive, conflict is ever-potential, and an atmosphere

* [A very large majority of the marriages is *passive-congenial* or *devitalized.* Few are *conflict-habituated, vital,* or *total.* Cuber stresses (personal
correspondence) that the proportions here are highly tentative—that he did
not select a representative sample and that the discovery of relative magni-
tudes was not an objective of the study.—ED.]

of equilibrated tension permeates their lives together. These relationships are sometimes said to be "dead" or "gone" but there is a more subtle valence here—a very active one. So central is the necessity for channeling conflict and bridling hostility that these imperatives structure the togetherness. Some psychiatrists have gone so far as to suggest that it is precisely the conflict and the habituated need to do psychological battle with one another which constitutes the cohesive factor which insures continuity of the marriage. Possibly so, but from a less psychiatric point of view, the overt and manifest fact of habituated attention to handling tension, keeping it chained, and concealing it, becomes the overriding life force. And it can, and does for some, last for a lifetime.

"Devitalized" Relationships.   Here the relationship is essentially devoid of zest. There is typically no serious tension or conflict and there may be aspects of the marriage which are actively satisfying, such as mutual interest in children, property, or family tradition. But the interplay between the pair is apathetic, lifeless. There is no serious threat to the marriage. It will likely continue indefinitely, despite its numbness, partly because of the inertia of "the habit cage." Continuity is further insured by the absence of any engaging alternatives, "all things considered." Perpetuation is also reinforced, sometimes rather decisively, by legal and ecclesiastical requirements and expectations. These people quickly explain that "there are other things in life" which are worthy of sustained human effort. But the relationship *between the pair* is essentially devoid of vital meaning by comparison to what it was when the mating began and what was then considered to be its *raison d'être*.

This kind of relationship is exceedingly common. Many persons in this circumstance do not accurately appraise their position because they frequently make comparisons with other pairs, many of whom are similar to themselves. This fosters the illusion that "marriage is like this—except for a few oddballs or pretenders who claim otherwise."

While these relationships lack vitality, there is *"something there."* There are occasional periods of sharing at least of something, if only memory. Formalities can have meanings. Anniversaries can be celebrated, even if a little grimly, for what they once commemorated. As one said, "Tomorrow we are celebrating the anniversary of our anniversary." Even clearly substandard sexual expression is said by some to be better than nothing, or better than a clandestine substitute. A "good man" or "good mother for the kids" may "with a little affection and occasional companionship now and then, get you by."

Passive-Congenial Relationships. This configuration seems roughly about as prevalent as the preceding one. There is little suggestion of disillusionment or compulsion to make believe to anyone. Existing modes of association are comfortably adequate—no stronger words fit the facts. There is little conflict. They tip-toe rather gingerly over and around a residue of subtle resentments and frustrations. In their better moods they remind us that "there are many common interests" which they both enjoy. When they get specific about these common interests it typically comes out that the interests are neither very vital things nor do they involve participation and sharings which could not almost as well be carried out in one-sex associations or with comparative strangers. "We both like classical music"; "We agree completely on religious and political matters"; "We both love the country and our quaint exurban neighbors"; "We are both lawyers."

We get the strong feeling when talking with these people that they would have said the same things when they were first married —or even before. When discussing their decisions to marry, some of them gave the same rationales for that decision that they do now for their present relationship, some twenty or thirty years later. This is why we have said that they seem to be passively content, not disillusioned, even though, as compared to the next type, they show so little vitality and so little evidence that the spouse is important to the satisfactions which they say they enjoy.

Vital Relationships. It is hard to escape the word, vitality, here —vibrant and exciting sharing of some important life experience. Sex immediately comes to mind, but the vitality need not surround the sexual focus or any aspect of it. It may emanate from work, association in some creative enterprise, child rearing, or even hobby participation. The clue that the *relationship is vital* and significant derives from the *feelings of importance about it* and *that that importance is shared.* Other things are readily sacrificed to it. It is apparent, even sometimes to the superficial observer, that these people are living for something which is exciting; it consumes their interest and effort, and the particular man or woman who shares it is the indispensable ingredient in the meaning which it has.

"Total" Relationships. The total relationship is like the vital relationship with the important addition that it is *multi-faceted.* This kind of man-woman relationship is rare in marriage or out, but it does exist and undoubtedly could exist more often than it does were men and women free of various impediments. One will occasionally find relationships in which *all* important aspects of life are mutually and enthusiastically shared. It is as if neither partner had a truly private existence. Cynics and the disillusioned scoff at this, calling it "romance" and usually offering an anecdote or two concerning some such "idyllic" relationship which later lost its totality, if not its vitality too. This should not be taken to mean, however, even if accurately interpreted and reported, that the relationship had not been total at the prior time. Or it may simply be evidence of the failure of the observer to be more discriminating in the first place.

Relationships are not *made* vital, much less total, by asserting them to be so, by striving to make them so, or by deceiving the neighbors that they are so. This is not to deny, however, that the total relationship is particularly precarious; precisely because it is multi-faceted, it is multi-vulnerable as circumstances change.

These five types of marital relationships are not to be considered as stages in some presumed cycle of marital change or disintegration. Some relationships do change, but the preponderant finding of our study is that these relationship types tend to be lasting. People are adjusted and in a certain sense "happy" in each of these relationships. Likewise, disillusionments and divorces occur in each of them.

This typology is offered as an illustration of some needed refinements in thinking about man-woman relationships. People involved in all five of the above relationships are (1) married and (2) stay so. (3) There is no public awareness of conflict. (4) Nor is there any offense to the most genteel standards of propriety. What, however, does one know when he has ascertained that a given pair has been married for a decade, that no one has seen them quarrel? What does he know, that is, about the life essence, the *joie de vivre?* Obviously nothing, until the pair is seen against the backdrop of some sort of taxonomy and more private facts about them are known.

Some Tentative Findings

Partly because our methods and inquiry have been quite unorthodox, it becomes exceedingly difficult to present the findings of the study in the customary format for reports on research. Nevertheless, a few somewhat guarded general ideas, *sans* documentation, will be attempted. It should be remembered that these generalizations apply to that American subculture, the upper middle class, which comprises no more than nine per cent of the American population. Moreover, our sample is completely a metropolitan sample, is white, is non-clinical, and probably oversamples the upper echelons of the nine per cent. Obviously, the empirical base, being what it is, requires us to say that our generalizations should not be trusted beyond the limits of this class.

(1) Our vague hunch at the beginning of the study that marital relationships between men and women of middle age comprised by no means the preponderant part of man-woman *meaningful* interaction was abundantly documented. Partly *sub rosa* and partly with the open knowledge of spouses, numerous kinds and degrees of meaningful non-marital man-woman relationships abound. These are not always frankly sexual, but they are nonetheless meaningful, *important* and *central* in the lives of these people.

If we are going to understand the bisexual world better, we need to cast a larger net when drawing in our specimens for examination. Attention has usually been focused chiefly upon those institutional arrangements known as "marriage and the family." It seems to us that the focus instead should be directly upon men and women—the entire bisexual world. For many students, moreover, marriage has come to be reified as something in and of itself, many times to the rather dismal neglect and devaluation of other intensely important aspects in the total lives of mature men and women. Little has been said or written, for example, concerning the important *constructive* realities regarding divorce or about "third parties" in relationship triangles. There is a continuing preoccupation with predicting divorce and measuring the effects and causes (so-called) of divorce. As any man on the street can tell us, and probably should, the incidence of divorce has little connection with the incidence of breakdown of man-woman relationships in marriage, and deeply fulfilling man-woman relationships exist where there is no marriage at all—and may never be.

We are not maintaining that there is any error necessarily in being concerned in research and thinking with marriage and family relationships *per se*. It is the *preoccupation* and the *reification* which has narrowed the focus. To comprehend adult man-woman relationships as coterminous with marriage and family relationships is like trying to understand, say, the United States Senate simply by watching what goes on on the Senate floor. The result is a colossal naïveté. It is not so much that the existing knowledge is demonstrably wrong so far as it goes, but that it is almost child-like in its self-imposed innocence and isolation from more complete awareness.

(2) Despite the monolithic character of religious and legal sanctions concerning man-woman behavior, *individuation rather than universalism* is a preponderant condition of their man-woman world. Nor are these radical variations from person to person and pair to pair completely idiosyncratic. There are numerous typologies which stand out. The important thing about these, however, is that they do not correspond to the typologies that are conventional in the professional literature, and that presumably deal with the bisexual world in America. We are not asserting that professional opinion is wrong. An alternative possibility is that the upper middle class has been insufficiently studied and may have a more distinct subculture than the professionals have apprehended. More likely, the disjuncture results from the fact that research has been, as we said before, too preoccupied with "marriage" and moralism and not enough with men and women.

(3) There is a manifest, yet at the same time subtle, amorality which forms the backdrop for the behavior of the prevailing groups in this class. Their refusal to be guided by other than pragmatic considerations where important decisions are concerned, is the prevailing weather in their intellectual climate.

There are typically sharp contradictions between their public ver-balisms and their overt conduct in almost every matter in their man-woman worlds.

(4) There is a pronounced tendency to polarize man-woman relationships over against other important valences in their life space. Not many are in-between. Mostly they function with a supremely valued or an equally extremely *de*valued conception of man-woman relationships in the total scheme of things. At the one extreme there is a pronounced asceticism, a devaluation of all aspects of the man-woman world from sex to joint problem solving, which distinctly separates them from the other group for whom all life exigencies are mediated through the inescapable and supremely important nexus of man and woman.

(5) If there is a core problem in the world of men and women, whether married or not, the nub of it is the impasse in communi-cation between them. These impasses persist despite the fact that this is a highly educated, articulate group, highly adept in social skills.

(6) Viewing the matter qualitatively, the evidence forces us to an extremely depressing conclusion: there are very few good man-woman relationships at these ages in this class. We are quite aware that we have not defined the word, "good." Pending more detailed elaboration, we may say here that by "good" we mean simply deeply satisfying man-woman relationships as appraised by the people themselves. This is meant to include the narrowly sexual as well as the more diffuse companionship and intellectual aspects of relationships. The fact of enduring marriage is in nowise to be confused with a satisfying relationship as subjectively experienced by the people in it. Further, of the good relation-ships that do exist, there is a surprisingly high incidence of them outside of marriage—either as enduring, relatively total associa-tions among the unmarried, or, as is more often the case, extra-marital in the sense that one or both in the pair are married to someone else.

To conclude, the overriding generalization of this study is that marriage is often continued out of habit, tradition, practical con-venience, or austere social sanctions, and that what the mental hygienist might call a good man-woman relationship in marriage is the exception rather than the rule.

Four

PARENT-CHILD
RELATIONS

Sears *et al.* (9) point to three questions that can be asked about child rearing. The first is: How *do* parents rear children? Wolfenstein (*10*), as well as the selection by Sears *et al.,* provide some answers to this question. In these selections certain aspects of child rearing are discussed—in particular, weaning, toilet-training, and the handling of thumbsucking and masturbation. This information is presented in historical perspective, and we can see that there has been, over the years, a gradually more permissive orientation toward the handling of these aspects of child rearing in middle-class America.

Another of the questions raised by Sears *et al.* is: Why do parents rear children in certain ways? Some of the changing practices go along with new research findings that have pointed to the inadequacy of former practices; some of them go along with changing ideologies in the social sciences. For example, the finding that it was not only very difficult to toilet-train an infant of a few months old but that there was also a great deal of backsliding on the part of such infants gradually led to substantial changes in the kind of professional advice that was given in this area (Brazelton, 1962). In the early 1900's parents were advised to start toilet-training their infants from the age of 2–3 months; by the 1940's and to the present day, they are advised to start toilet-training between 18 and 24 months.

If we adopt a longer time perspective and a cross-cultural perspective we find a much wider range of variations in child-rearing practices. Mead (1928) indicates that Samoan girls are socialized by many relatives other than their parents, and that if a girl is harshly treated by one set of relatives "she has but to change her residence to the home of some more complacent relative."

Under these circumstances the emotional bond between a girl and her parents is less intense than in the American case, and she may therefore experience less conflict in her relationship with her parents. Other accounts of cultural differences, for example during the ancien régime in France, in contemporary American life, and elsewhere, are to be found in Ariès (1962), Sears et al. (9), and B. Whiting (1963).

Social Class and Child Rearing

A number of researchers have documented the changing nature of certain child-rearing practices in the United States (Wolfenstein, 10; Stendler, 1950; Vincent, 1951; Miller and Swanson, 1958; N. Maccoby, 1961), and it is rather generally accepted that there has been an increasing degree of permissiveness in the present century, with a turn in the direction of somewhat less permissiveness since the 1950's. When the findings are broken down by social class, however, there are several conflicting reports regarding whether the middle classes or the working classes are more permissive in their child-rearing practices. Davis and Havighurst (1946) and Havighurst and Davis (1955) have presented evidence that the working classes are more permissive, while E. Maccoby et al. (1954) and Sears et al. (1957) have presented evidence that the middle classes are more permissive. Many studies have addressed themselves to these contrary findings. White (1957) and especially Bronfenbrenner (1958) have summarized the nature of the controversy and have made sense of the data. Bronfenbrenner points out that it is necessary, first, to look upon the changing professional advice that has been offered through the years regarding child rearing; second, to distinguish between the middle classes and the working classes in the degree to which they are exposed to and follow professional advice; and finally, to specify when the various conflicting researchers gathered their data on child rearing. It turns out, in summary form, that professional advice has gradually emphasized a greater degree of permissiveness; that middle-class parents pay more attention to professional advice; and that the studies in which a greater degree of permissiveness is reported for the working class were carried out before the studies that reported the reverse. In other words, the working classes have remained relatively stable in their degree of permissiveness in child rearing, while the middle classes have become gradually more permissive. In the 1930's, therefore, the middle classes were less permissive than the working classes; by the 1950's they were more permissive. The controversy, as we can see, is clarified by historical knowledge about the practices of the social classes and the extent to which they followed changing professional advice through the years.

What Are the Consequences?

Another question asked by Sears *et al.* is: What effects do particular kinds of child-rearing practices have upon the personality of the child? For example, does it make any difference in the later adjustment of the child whether as an infant he is breast-fed or bottle-fed? Fed on schedule or on demand? Weaned gradually or abruptly? Toilet-trained early or late? Punished or not punished for toilet accidents? Orlansky (1949), Sewell (1952), and Harris (1959) point out that none of these things, singly or taken together, make a difference. Sewell says, in his summary, that "such practices as breast-feeding, gradual weaning, demand schedule, and easy and late induction to bowel and bladder training, which have been so much emphasized in the psychoanalytic literature, were almost barren in terms of relation to personality adjustment as measured in this study." He points out that "it is entirely possible that the significant and crucial matter is not the practices themselves but the whole personal-social situation in which they find their expression, including the attitudes and behavior of the mother." In support of this point, Harris (1959, pp. 29–30) reports that "good mothering" which led to well-adjusted children was not related to such matters as breast versus bottle feeding—"the quality of mothering should not be confused with specific actions in the process of mothering." There are, in other words, many varying influences upon the personality development of the child, including the socio-cultural environment, the parental attitudes, the societal attitudes with regard to specific forms of infant training, and the nature of the total parent-child relationship. It is therefore too much to expect that one form of infant training as specific as that of breast versus bottle feeding is going to make its influence felt in the face of so many other factors that enter into the situation.*

The paper by Vogel and Bell (*11*) focuses upon the impact that parents exert upon the personality development of children as a result of a disturbance in their marital relationship. In this case we are not dealing with the consequences of a specific infant training practice, but rather with the consequences of a total pattern of interaction within the family. One way in which emotional disturbance seems to develop is through the selection of the child as a scapegoat by his parents—parents having severe conflicts in their relationships may use one of their children to act out the conflict. In this way, their marital conflict is kept within bounds, but the personality development of the child suffers. For example, the wife who felt hostile toward her husband for poor work performance channeled this hostility toward her son for his poor school performance. Her husband went along with her in this criticism, and thereby kept the focus of his wife's concerns upon his son rather than upon himself. As a result, the child becomes a scapegoat within the family; in a sense, he is forced into playing a disturbed role. The expectations of the child's parents are exceedingly important in defining the type of role the child plays and the self-conception that the child develops. As Haimowitz (1960, p. 364) says:

> When persons important to the child don't trust him, he may come to distrust himself. The conception of oneself as a law-violator, or just a hateful, worthless, public nuisance does not usually develop full-blown in a few minutes. . . . Little children interact thousands of times with others, thereby learning what is expected of them. . . .
> We have observed eleven-year-old children who could not clear the table or wash a dish ("She might break them," the mother would say); and we have observed other children, five years old, who could clear the table, wash, and dry the dishes. One mother expects the child to break the dishes; the other mother expects the child to do a good job. Both children do what is expected of them, and by doing so, each is developing a self-conception.

* For a careful and comprehensive review of the consequences of infant care practices, see Caldwell (1964); for interesting commentaries upon the complexity of the problems that researchers in this area face, see Hoffman and Lippitt (1960) and Leslie and Johnsen (1963).

A large number of studies have dealt with the various types of parental behavior and their consequences for the child. There are studies, for example, that deal with the impact of various discipline techniques upon the child (Sigel, 1960; Hoffman, 1960); with the impact of maternal employment upon the child (Nye and Hoffman, 1963); with the impact of maternal deprivation upon the child (Casler, 1961; Yarrow, 1961; World Health Organization, 1962); and with the impact of paternal deprivation upon the child (Mischel, 1961; McCord, McCord, and Thurber, 1962). We shall deal briefly with only one set of studies of this type: the impact that various forms of parental practices have upon the moral development of the child. Reviews of the literature by Hoffman (1963a, 1963b) and Kohlberg (1963, 1964) point to the complexity that lies hidden behind the apparently simple question of parental practices and their impact upon the child's moral development. There are many gaps and inadequacies in the research, and yet a number of findings do seem to emerge from the various studies that have been done. Psychological discipline and parental affection foster a moral structure that is internal to the child; the child adopts parental moral standards as his own. Physical punishment (power assertion), on the other hand, fosters a moral structure in the child that is based upon external considerations; the child reacts to fear of detection and punishment. All of these studies make it clear that although many other factors may have an influence, the personality development of a child is importantly influenced by the nature of the parent-child relationship, and by the nature of the relationships within the family as a whole.

REFERENCES

ARIÈS, PHILIPPE. 1962. *Centuries of Childhood,* New York: Knopf.
BRAZELTON, T. BERRY. 1962. "A Child-Oriented Approach to Toilet Training," *Pediatrics,* XXIX, 121–128.
BRONFENBRENNER, URIE. 1958. "Socialization and Social Class Through Time and Space," in Eleanor E. Maccoby, Theodore M. Newcomb, and Eugene L. Hartley, eds., *Readings in Social Psychology,* 3d ed., New York: Holt.

CALDWELL, BETTYE M. 1961. "The Effects of Infant Care," in Martin L. Hoffman, and Lois W. Hoffman, eds., *Review of Child Development Research,* Vol. I, New York: Russell Sage Foundation.

CASLER, LAWRENCE. 1961. "Maternal Deprivation: A Critical Review of the Literature," *Society for Research in Child Development,* Monograph, Vol. XXVI, No. 2.

DAVIS, ALLISON, and ROBERT J. HAVIGHURST. 1946. "Social Class and Color Differences in Child Rearing," *American Sociological Review,* XI, 698–710.

HAIMOWITZ, MORRIS L. 1960. "Criminals Are Made, Not Born," in Morris L. Haimowitz, and Natalie R. Haimowitz, eds., *Human Development,* New York: Crowell.

HARRIS, IRVING D. 1959. *Normal Children and Mothers,* New York: Free Press of Glencoe.

HAVIGHURST, ROBERT J., and ALLISON DAVIS. 1955. "A Comparison of the Chicago and Harvard Studies of Social Class Differences in Child Rearing," *American Sociological Review,* XX, 438–442.

HOFFMAN, LOIS W., and RONALD LIPPITT. 1960. "The Measurement of Family Life Variables," in Paul H. Mussen, ed., *Handbook of Research Methods in Child Development,* New York: Wiley.

HOFFMAN, MARTIN L. 1960. "Power Assertion by the Parent and Its Impact on the Child," *Child Development,* XXXI, 129–143.

————. 1963a. "Child-Rearing Practices and Moral Development: Generalizations from Empirical Research," *Child Development,* XXXIV, 295–318.

————. 1963b. "Early Processes in Moral Development," presented at the Social Science Research Council Conference on Character Development, New York, 1963, mimeographed.

KOHLBERG, LAWRENCE. 1963. "Moral Development and Identification," in Harold Stevenson, Jerome Kagan, and Charles Spiker, eds., *Child Psychology,* Sixty-second Yearbook of the National Society for the Study of Education.

————. 1964. "Development of Moral Character and Moral Ideology," in Martin L. Hoffman, and Lois W. Hoffman, eds., *Review of Child Development Research,* Vol. I, New York: Russell Sage Foundation.

LESLIE, GERALD R., and KATHRYN P. JOHNSEN. 1963. "Changed Perceptions of the Maternal Role," *American Sociological Review,* XXVIII, 919–928.

MACCOBY, ELEANOR E., PATRICIA K. GIBBS, et al. 1954. "Methods of Child-Rearing in Two Social Classes," in William E. Martin, and Celia B. Stendler, eds., *Readings in Child Development,* New York: Harcourt, Brace.

MACCOBY, NATHAN. 1961. "The Communication of Child-Rearing Advice to Parents," *Merrill-Palmer Quarterly,* VII, 199–204.

MCCORD, JOAN, WILLIAM MCCORD, and EMILY THURBER. 1962. "Some Effects of Paternal Absence on Male Children," *Journal of Abnormal and Social Psychology,* LXIV, 361–369.

MEAD, MARGARET. 1928. *Coming of Age in Samoa,* New York: William Morrow.

MILLER, DANIEL R., and GUY E. SWANSON. 1958. *The Changing American Parent,* New York: Wiley.

MISCHEL, WALTER. 1961. "Father-Absence and Delay of Gratification: Cross-cultural Comparisons," *Journal of Abnormal and Social Psychology,* LXIII, 116–124.

NYE, F. IVAN, and LOIS W. HOFFMAN, eds. 1963. *The Employed Mother in America,* Chicago: Rand McNally.

ORLANSKY, HAROLD. 1949. "Infant Care and Personality," *Psychological Bulletin,* XLVI, 1–48.

SEARS, ROBERT R., ELEANOR E. MACCOBY, and HARRY LEVIN. 1957. *Patterns of Child Rearing,* Evanston, Ill.: Row, Peterson.

SEWELL, WILLIAM H. 1952. "Infant Training and the Personality of the Child," *American Journal of Sociology,* LVIII, 150–159.

SIGEL, IRVING E. 1960. "Influence Techniques: A Concept Used to Study Parental Behaviors," *Child Development,* XXXI, 799–806.

STENDLER, CELIA B. 1950. "Sixty Years of Child Training Practices," *Journal of Pediatrics,* XXXVI, 122–134.

VINCENT, CLARK E. 1951. "Trends in Infant Care Ideas," *Child Development,* XXII, 199–209.

WHITE, MARTHA S. 1957. "Social Class, Child Rearing Practices, and Child Behavior," *American Sociological Review,* XXII, 704–712.

WHITING, BEATRICE B., ed. 1963. *Six Cultures: Studies of Child Rearing,* New York: Wiley.

World Health Organization. 1962. *Deprivation of Maternal Care: A Reassessment of Its Effects,* Geneva.

YARROW, LEON J. 1961. "Maternal Deprivation: Toward an Empirical and Conceptual Re-Evaluation," *Psychological Bulletin,* LVIII, 459–490.

⋘§ 9 §⋙ The Three Research Problems

by R O B E R T R. S E A R S , E L E A N O R E.

M A C C O B Y , *and* H A R R Y L E V I N

There are three kinds of questions that can be asked about child-rearing practices and values. The *first,* and simplest, wants a purely descriptive answer: How *do* parents rear children? The *second* goes deeper and asks what effects different kinds of training have on children. The *third* relates to the mothers themselves: What leads a mother to use one method rather than another?

In pursuing the *first* of these questions, we discovered there is surprisingly little information about what American parents believe or what they do with their youngsters. Do most mothers breast-feed their babies? Do they spank them for being sassy? Are chores and responsibilities a part of most children's lives? Do very many mothers let their three-year-olds run around naked in the house? How serious do mothers think it is when a child strikes a parent? Do any mothers ever actually encourage children to fight the neighbor children? The answers to these questions, and to many others like them, are needed not only to give a frame of reference within which a particular practice can be viewed, but to permit any one mother to gain perspective on her own practices by comparing or contrasting her characteristic ways of treating her child with those of other mothers.

Curiously enough, anthropologists have secured more complete information about child rearing in at least seventy other cultures than they have about child rearing in the United States.[1] . . . With the exception of a few recent studies, the source of most of our knowledge about American child-rearing behavior is inferential, deriving in the main from the books, pamphlets, and magazine articles that give advice to parents. These sources are scarcely data, in the sense of being reports about actual practices, but in certain instances their popularity suggests that a good many people may have found them attractive and may have followed the advice.

One series of pamphlets has provided a unique opportunity to observe changes in what may be called the "official" child-rearing culture of the United States. These are the ten successive editions of *Infant Care,* published by the U. S. Children's Bureau; the first appeared in 1914 and the latest in 1955.* This small book provides a great deal of useful information for the young mother. Much of the material is factual, well geared to American economy and conditions of life. But some has to do with methods of child rearing, and it is in this connection that one can see secular changes in attitudes and values.

Wolfenstein (*10*) has studied these variations in advice through the first nine editions (1914–1951) with respect to the handling of five problems: thumb-sucking, weaning, masturbation, bowel and bladder training. We call these "problems" because each refers to a form of child behavior that is *changeworthy,* that is, a kind of action either to be inhibited as much as possible or to be replaced by new behavior of a more mature kind. Such control and training can be done with different degrees of severity. The mother can be highly punitive and refuse to tolerate any lapses whatever, or she can be gentle in her urging of new actions and ignore accidental reversions to the changeworthy ones. Most observers of young children believe this dimension of *severity of training* has important effects on children's personalities, though there is little direct evidence as to just what the effects may be. . . .

These changing patterns of advice are a part of the child rearing values of their times. What relation there may have been between the values—the "what ought to be"—and the actual practices of mothers cannot now be discovered. The practices of forty years ago

---

* [A new edition of *Infant Care* was published in 1963; the selection by Wolfenstein (*10*) has been updated in order to reflect some of the information from this edition and from the 1955 edition.—ED.]

are irretrievably buried in mothers' memories, and their only monuments are the personality structures of children who have grown to middle age themselves.

It would be a mistake, of course, to assume that there is any one pattern of child rearing that can be called "the American pattern." The United States contains a rich variety of subcultures. In spite of thirty-six million distributed copies of *Infant Care,* there is no dread uniformity of child-rearing practices. Differences of religion, of ethnic origin, of socio-economic status, and of family size all contribute to the great variety of values and practices.

As an illustration we may cite some comparative findings from three different communities in which we secured information about child rearing. One, called Homestead, is a small New Mexican village with a population originating mainly in the dust-bowl areas of Texas and Oklahoma. A second, Rimrock, is just a few miles away, but its population is of Old American stock with Mormon traditions. The third is the suburban metropolitan area in New England from which the information for this present book was obtained. Our interviewers secured reports from about twenty mothers in each of the two villages, and from 379 mothers in the New England area.

Three items exemplify the extraordinary differences that can be found within our national borders. The first is the age at which mothers weaned their children. In Homestead, for instance, 50 per cent had completed weaning before the child was eight months old, while in Rimrock none had. In the New England sample, 37 per cent had. A second item relates to who, in the family, had the chief responsibility for deciding on child-rearing policies. In Homestead, 22 per cent of the mothers said the father was the chief policy-maker; in Rimrock, 67 per cent said the father; and in the New England group, only 8 per cent reported the father. Or consider the degree to which physical punishment was used as a frequent and major method of discipline. In Homestead, 39 per cent of the families used it; in Rimrock, only 5 per cent; and in New England, 20 per cent. . . .

The *second* type of question leads to an inquiry about the effects of training on the child. Does self-demand feeding make children more dependent? Does punishment for bed-wetting just make the matter worse? Does early insistence on complete modesty make children more curious than ever about sex? Does spanking insure the development of a good strong conscience? Answers to such cause-and-effect questions as these will eventually provide some help to parents in making decisions about how to rear children. If a mother knows the effect of a particular practice, she can decide whether to use it or not. She can base her judgment on a knowledge of what product she will get.

Clinical observations, and theories developed from them, have suggested a number of hypotheses about the relation between certain kinds of child rearing and the personality qualities produced by them. Ideally, to test these notions, the measures of mother and child behavior should be entirely independent of one another. . . . Relying entirely on the mothers' interview reports for measuring both is not ideal for answering all such cause-and-effect questions. . . .

Third, and finally, one can ask what leads a mother to use one method rather than another. Child-rearing beliefs and values and practices do not just appear out of the blue. They are products of the mother's own personality, her values and attitudes. She may feel, for example, that she has reasoned herself quite objectively to an answer as to how she *should* handle her child's quarreling, but the extent to which she *can* tolerate open fighting influences her decision. All reasoning rests on assumptions that, in turn, rest on the values and attitudes the mother has developed throughout her own life. Her own upbringing has influenced these, and of course the nature of the family situation at any one time helps dictate a decision as to how to treat the children. Hence it will not prove surprising to find that there are substantial differences in mothers' values and practices depending on the satisfactoriness of her relations with her husband, on her self-esteem, and on certain of her own pervasive moral values, such as her attitudes toward sex and aggression.

To put the matter most succinctly, child-rearing practices can be viewed as both causes and effects. They are responsible, in some degree, for the personality characteristics of the child, and they are themselves the products of cultural factors operating in the life of the mother. . . .

NOTE

1. J. W. M. Whiting and I. L. Child, *Child Training and Personality: A Cross-Cultural Study,* New Haven: Yale University Press, 1953; C. Heinicke and B. B. Whiting, *Bibliographies on Personality and Social Development of the Child,* New York: Social Science Research Council, Pamphlet No. 10, 1953.

10 Trends in Infant Care

by MARTHA WOLFENSTEIN

In our culture where we tend to believe persistently that the latest is the best, we often fail to reckon sufficiently with the residues of the past. We behave as if convictions of a year or two ago had been banished without a trace once they have been contradicted by the most recent discovery. This is particularly so with our ideas about child training. We rarely pause to consider the tremendous changes which have taken place in these ideas in the last few decades. But overlooking does not abolish the things that are thus passed over. In all of us—parents, teachers, pediatricians, child psychologists, therapists—there are the accumulated ideas of a number of periods which have passed in rapid succession. And these ideas, insofar as they are not sorted out, cause considerable uncertainty and conflict.

In the fall of 1951, the United States Children's Bureau issued a

Adapted by the editor from "Trends in Infant Care," *American Journal of Orthopsychiatry,* XXIII, Jan., 1953, 120–130; Copyright, the American Orthopsychiatric Association, Inc. Reproduced by permission.

new edition of the bulletin *Infant Care,** which first appeared in 1914 and which subsequently underwent several drastic revisions. This would seem to be a good occasion for surveying the changes which have appeared during these years in this most widely circulated child care publication.

I shall deal here mainly with the trends in severity and mildness in handling the impulses of the child, as manifested in the areas of thumb-sucking, weaning, masturbation, and bowel and bladder training. I shall not undertake to judge the correctness of the procedures recommended at one time or another. Nor shall I attempt to trace the various influences (of behaviorism, Gesell, psychoanalysis, etc.) which may be observed. What I wish to bring out are facts of social history. I should like to show the sharp contrasts between what mothers of the twenties and those of the forties were told about the best way to bring up their babies (for instance, in the twenties bowel training was to be completed by eight months; in the forties it was to be begun at eight months or later). Marked shifts have also occurred in much shorter periods of time (in 1938, the bulletin still showed a stiff cuff that could be bound on the baby's arm so that he could not bend his elbow to get his thumb in his mouth; in 1942, mothers were told that thumb-sucking is a harmless pleasure that should not be interfered with). It would require further research to determine to what extent mothers were influenced by these ideas (from mother to daughter, or the same mother with an older and a younger child). However, we may suppose that a considerable number of mothers have participated in these changing attitudes. I shall try to show that the fluctuations of opinion in this field are related not only to advances in knowledge, but also in part to unresolved conflicts in our feelings about the child's impulses.

Let me indicate first the main trends through time which we may observe in various editions of *Infant Care*. (This account is based on the editions of 1914, 1922, 1929, 1938, 1942, 1945 and 1951. I omit those of 1932 and 1940, which I was unable to obtain.) In the first period, 1914–22, the danger of the child's autoerotic impulses was acutely felt. Thumb-sucking and masturbation, if not promptly and rigorously interfered with, would grow beyond con-

* [Some data from the 1955 and 1963 editions of *Infant Care*, published since Wolfenstein's article first appeared, have been incorporated by the editor in the summary table (Table 1) of this article.—ED.]

trol and permanently damage the child. While he was in bed, he was to be bound down hand and foot so that he could not suck his thumb, touch his genitals, or rub his thighs together.

In the next period, 1929–38, the focus of severity shifts. Auto-erotism seems less dangerous. Now it is bowel training which must be carried out with great determination as early as possible. Severity in this area increases as compared with the previous period. This is accompanied by a pervasive emphasis on regularity, doing every-thing by the clock. Weaning and the introduction of solid foods are also to be accomplished with great firmness, never yielding for a moment to the baby's resistance. The main danger which the baby presented at this time was that of dominating the parents. Successful child training meant winning out against the child in the struggle for domination.

In 1942–45, all this was changed. The child became remarkably harmless, in effect devoid of sexual or dominating impulses. His main active aim was to explore his world; autoerotism was an incidental by-product of such exploration. When not engaged in his exploratory undertakings, the baby needs attention and care; and giving these when he demands them, far from making him a tyrant, will make him less demanding later on. At this time mildness is advocated in all areas: thumb-sucking and masturbation are not to be interfered with; weaning and toilet training are to be accom-plished later and more gently.

In 1951 there is an attempt to continue this mildness, but not without some conflicts and misgivings. Autoerotic activities become even more harmless and negligible. Sucking is a permissible though low-grade pleasure (a poor substitute for being held or fed or talked to) and the pacifier (explicitly taboo, 1914–38; not men-tioned, 1942–45) is now restored. Rocking and head-banging (not masturbation) are the puzzling things which babies may do in bed and from which they seem to get some satisfaction; perhaps they do it out of boredom. Masturbation is mentioned only in con-nection with toilet training. While on the toilet, the baby may touch his genitals. This does not amount to anything (not even pleasure), but if it bothers the mother she may give the child a toy. Here the tolerance for autoerotism seems to require increasing denial of its nature. Requirements in toilet training become even more easy-going than in the preceding period. But the anxiety of 1929 that the child may dominate the parents reappears. If one picks up the child whenever he cries, he may become a tyrant. And in the area of toilet training, gentleness is urged out of the consideration that if the mother tries to be tough she cannot win. If she seems to be fighting the child, he can really hold out against her. Thus we get, if we compare 1929 with 1951, the same anxiety about the child's possible domination combined with extremely polarized approaches toward toilet training, on the one hand very strict, on the other, very mild. Neither the problems of the child's autoerotism nor of his possible domination seem to have been quite solved.

Masturbation. To document the foregoing points: In the 1914 edition of *Infant Care* masturbation is called an "injurious practice"; it "easily grows beyond control . . . children are sometimes wrecked for life." "It must be eradicated . . . treatment consists in mechanical restraints." In the 1922 revision this is already toned down a bit: "a common habit . . . it grows worse if left uncontrolled." The mechanical restraints are slightly moderated; the nightgown sleeves must still be pinned down, but it is no longer specified (as it was in 1914) that the child's legs should be tied to opposite sides of the crib. In 1929, the atmosphere is much more relaxed: this "early period of what may be called sex awareness will pass away unless it is emphasized by unwise treatment on the part of adults." Physical restraints are now considered of little value. "Occupation and diversion" are the best treatment. The baby may be given a toy to hold until he goes to sleep. The 1938 revision anticipates the exploratory theme which subsequently becomes central: children "discover accidentally" that they can get pleasure from touching their genitals. The point about spontaneous recovery is repeated. In 1942, we are told: "Babies want to handle and investigate everything that they can see and reach. When a baby discovers his genital organs he will play with them. . . . A wise mother will not be concerned about this." Also, "see that he has a toy to play with and he will not need to use his body as a plaything." There is no change in 1945. In the 1951 edition we read: "Sometimes a baby handles his genitals when he is sitting on the toilet, or at other times when he is undressed. This is a common thing, and usually will not amount to anything if let alone. But sometimes it is disturbing to mothers, so if you feel uncomfortable about it you can try giving him a toy to hold while he's on the toilet seat. Don't confuse him by saying, 'No, No.' " The increased moderation in handling masturbation in the course of these years is accompanied by an increasingly diluted version of the activity. From expressing an urgent and dangerous impulse of the child, masturbation becomes an act about which the child has no feelings and which is only inexplicably embarrassing to the mother.

Thumb-sucking. The alarm about thumb-sucking is somewhat less extreme than that about masturbation in the beginning, but it persists longer. Thus while mechanical restraints in connection with masturbation are abandoned in 1929, such restraints are still recommended to combat thumb-sucking as late as 1938. In 1914–22, mothers are cautioned that thumb-sucking deforms the mouth and causes constant drooling. "Thumb or finger must be persistently and constantly removed from the mouth and the baby's attention diverted to something else." Thus diversion, a relatively mild technique which is not yet envisaged in the case of masturbation, is considered at least partially effective against thumb-sucking. However, it is not enough; sleeves should also be "pinned or sewed down over the offending hand for several days and nights or the hand put in a cotton mitten." The zeal of the mother to keep the child's hand inaccessible is considered so great that the following caution is added: "The baby's hands should be set free now and then, especially if he is old enough to use his hands for his toys, and at meal times to save as much unnecessary strain on his nerves as possible, but with the approach of sleeping time the hand must be covered" (1914; 1922). At this time also the use of a pacifier is called a "disgusting habit" which the adults are to blame for introducing. The pacifier "must be destroyed." "Thumb and finger sucking babies will rebel fiercely at being deprived of this comfort when they are going to sleep, but this must be done if the habit is to be broken up" (1914; 1922 is about the same). Thus in the period of open struggle against the baby's oral pleasures the ferocity of this drive is fully acknowledged.

In 1929–38, thumb-sucking retains the same hazards and is to be treated by the same methods. However, it is described in a more reassuring way. "When the baby first discovers his finger or thumb he naturally starts sucking it." "It is a natural habit . . .

it should not excite parents unduly." While mechanical restraints are still recommended, there is a greater emphasis on diversion: "The best way to break up the habit is to keep the hands occupied with some toy" (1929). In 1942–45, the exploratory motive becomes central; thumb-sucking like masturbation becomes an incident in the baby's exploration of his world. "A baby explores everything within his reach. He looks at a new object, feels it, squeezes it, and almost always puts it in his mouth." The baby "knows how to suck because he has learned to get food that way, and naturally he sucks on anything he puts in his mouth." No interference with thumb-sucking is required: "Usually children will outgrow the habit unless too much fuss is made . . . as he grows older other interests and pleasures take the place of suck-ing" (1942; 1945). Oral drives have now lost their first tenacity; they are easily outcompeted by other interests. The baby is now much more attracted by things around him than by his own body.

In 1951, thumb-sucking has become even more permissible and even more devalued as a satisfaction. When the baby is "tired or hungry or doesn't have anything interesting to watch or do, he may try to get a little pleasure out of his thumb or fingers. Sucking is a poor substitute for being held, or talked to, or fed; but it is better than nothing." Where the motivation for pleasure sucking had been first a fierce specific urge, later a more bland diffuse exploratory impulse, it is now more apt to arise from "loneliness or boredom." Thus as the attitude toward the child's impulses becomes increasingly permissive these impulses are depicted as increasingly weak and weary. It is now a matter for wonder that thumb-sucking was ever objected to. "Why do so many of us have this strong feeling against what is so perfectly natural for babies to do?" Why such a strong feeling against such a trivial impulse? Even the pacifier is now permitted. The damaging effect of early sucking on jaw formation is denied.

Weaning. In 1914 there seemed to be little anxiety that mothers would wean their babies too soon. However, there was great stress on gradualness in weaning. No precise time schedule was given. A first bottle might be introduced at five months to give the baby plenty of time to get used to it; weaning might be completed by one year. In 1922 the anxiety about too early wean-

ing set in. Where previously mothers were told that the baby might
be weaned by one year, they are now warned that he should not
be weaned before six months. Attention is focused on the minimal
nursing period. After six months a normal baby can be weaned
if necessary, though preferably weaning should be postponed till
about nine months. Once initiated, it "need not take more than
two weeks." The mother is advised to persist in getting the baby
to take the artificial food even if he refuses it at first: "the child
will finally yield." The 1929 and 1938 editions continue and even
elaborate this concern about maintaining dominance over the baby.
Weaning, once the time had come to initiate it, was to be carried
out according to a strict schedule and no backsliding was to be
permitted. The mother was to refuse the breast and later the bottle
with great firmness; the baby would yield and take the proferred
substitutes.

In 1942–45 for the first time the emotional impact of weaning
on the baby is acknowledged. Giving up the breast "is a big step
for the baby in growing up. Later steps will be easier if the baby
finds this one pleasant." If the transition to the bottle is sufficiently
gradual, "he will take the step forward gladly. If the change is
made suddenly he may resist it." Thus instead of firmly overriding
the baby's resistance, the mother should now avoid rousing it.
The tempo of weaning is to be adapted to individual needs rather
than following a preconceived schedule. The transition from the
bottle to the cup is "also a big problem for the baby. . . . Let
him take his time. . . . It makes little difference at exactly what age
bottle feeding is given up for good. It makes a great deal of difference to the baby's mental and emotional health that he does not
feel cheated out of something important to him, but that he does
feel that he is giving up a baby way for a grown-up way" (1945). A
new consideration is introduced in connection with weaning: the
mother may want to wean the baby sooner than she would otherwise in order to return to work. However, she is advised to discuss
this with the father; perhaps they can arrange for her to stay home
and "nurse their baby, especially when they realize what a good
start in life breast feeding will give the baby."

In 1951 the long-term intransigence about breast feeding is
relaxed: the mother should not feel guilty if she prefers to bottle-
feed her baby from the first. It is again stressed, as in the preceding

period, that weaning should be gradual and adapted to the readiness of the individual child to give up the pleasures of sucking. The child should be compensated by "a little extra attention" for the loss of this satisfaction. While there is "no set time at which the baby should be drinking his milk from a cup," there is now some anxiety that the transition to the cup may be too long postponed. The situation may arise where mothers "are at a loss what to do when their baby gets so used to the bottle that at 18 or 20 months, or even later, when he's fast getting beyond seeming like a baby, he still insists on having the bottle." This expresses a conflict which pervades the 1951 edition. The view had been advanced in 1942–45 that early full gratification facilitates later acceptance of limitations. In 1951 doubts about this have rearisen. May not continued gratification lead to addiction and increasingly intensified demands? Thus while on some points (notably thumb-sucking and acceptance of the baby's preferences in solid foods) it is held that indulgence will not spoil the baby but just the reverse, on other points (continued bottle feeding, picking up the baby when he cries) there is the apprehension that gratification will intensify the baby's demands.

Bowel training. Recommended procedures in bowel training have shown sharp fluctuations. In the twenties there was increasing severity. Subsequently there was a trend in the opposite direction; from 1938 through 1951 increasing mildness has been recommended.

In 1914 bowel training was to be begun "by the third month or even earlier." The mother was to use "the utmost gentleness. . . . Scolding and punishment will serve only to frighten the child and to destroy the natural impulses, while laughter will tend to relax the muscles and to promote an easy movement." Increased severity is evidenced in the 1922 revision in demanding an earlier beginning of bowel training: "as early as the end of the first month . . . as soon as the mother takes charge of the baby after her confinement." The time for the completion of bowel training is now specified: almost any baby can be trained so that there are no more soiled diapers after the end of the first year. Gentleness and laughter are no longer mentioned; the warning against scolding and punishment drops out.

In 1929 the demand for bowel control is most rigorous. "Almost any baby can be trained so that there are no more soiled diapers to wash after he is six to eight months old." In 1938, however, there is a reversal in the trend. We hear no more about beginning bowel training at one month. Now it may be begun "as early as six months" (the time when the mother of 1929 might already expect the baby to be completely trained). The time for completion of training is now put at one year.

In 1942–45 bowel training is to commence still later, "usually at eight or ten months," and the time for completing it is left indefinite. The baby cannot really cooperate in the training until his muscles have matured. If one waits until this time training becomes easy. By 1942–45 the handling of the infant in all areas has become very gentle. This tendency is continued and even carried further in 1951. The advocacy of increased leniency is most marked in respect to bowel training. This is also the aspect of the mother-child relation which is seen as most fraught with emotional hazards. "Why do we stress this [bowel training] so much? Because you can so easily make trouble for yourself and the baby if you start training too early. A child can get to feeling that his mother is his enemy if she urges on him things he is not ready for. . . . Let him sit on his toilet chair only a few moments the first few times. . . . As he gets used to his new seat, you can keep him on a little longer, but never more than five minutes. . . . A lot depends on not letting him get to feel this is a hateful bore. . . . What you're after is not having fewer diapers to wash, but having a baby who feels like working with you instead of against you." In view of all this the commencement of bowel training is postponed to a considerably later time. "Most babies are not ready to start learning bowel control by the end of the first year. One and a half or two years is a much more common time for them to learn willingly."

Bladder training. The handling of bladder training is not correlated exactly with that of bowel training. In 1929 when severity in bowel training was at its height, severity in bladder training decreased as compared with the preceding period. Urination here seems to have more a genital than an anal association (we may recall that severity toward masturbation also decreased at this time. Masturbation was explicitly associated with bed-wetting in the 1929 revision as an early habit which would be easily outgrown. Incidentally, masturbation was associated with thumb-sucking in 1942–45, and with defecation in 1951). Intolerance toward wetting was most intense in 1921; from 1929 on the attitude became steadily gentler.

Discussion. The increase or decrease in severity in the various areas which we have considered may be roughly indicated in Table 1.

TABLE 1

Severity in the handling of:	From 1914 to 1921	From 1921 to 1929	From 1929 to 1938	From 1938 to 1942–45	From 1942–45 to 1951–55[a]	From 1951–55 to 1963[a]
Masturbation	Decreases	Decreases	Constant	Decreases	Constant	Constant
Thumb-sucking	Constant	Decreases	Constant	Decreases	Decreases	Constant
Weaning	Increases	Increases	Constant	Decreases	Constant	Constant
Bowel training	Increases	Increases	Decreases	Decreases	Decreases	Increases
Bladder training	Increases	Decreases	Decreases	Decreases	Decreases	Increases

[a] [The material for 1955 and 1963 has been added by the editor, based upon the 1955 and 1963 editions of *Infant Care*.—ED.]

In respect to masturbation and thumb-sucking the curve of severity shows a consistently declining direction. In weaning and bowel training we find a U-curve, rising in the twenties and subsequently declining.* However, this table refers only to the overt procedures which are recommended (when to begin toilet training or weaning, whether to use mechanical restraints against thumb-sucking or masturbation, etc.) It does not indicate the range of conflicting emotional attitudes which are expressed in more subtle ways (as in the altered conception of autoerotic drives, etc.).

The problem of making scientific insight widely accessible is nowhere more pertinent than in child training. The efforts of the authors of the *Infant Care* bulletins illustrate the difficulty of the undertaking. In the last decade, they have been telling mothers to behave with great tolerance toward the child's autoerotic impulses, his urge to suck, his soiling and wetting. But what has become of the feelings which not so long ago were being expressed with a

* [Except for a slight increase in severity for bowel training in 1963.—ED.]

clear conscience in strenuous struggle against these same impulses in the child? These feelings have certainly not been worked through or transformed, but seem much more to be suppressed or repressed. The mother of 1914 or 1922 was supposed to know that children masturbate in bed, and was told to eradicate this wickedness. The mother of 1951, who is told that masturbation does not amount to anything, is not supposed to know that children masturbate in bed, but may only notice that they sometimes touch their genitals while on the toilet. She is permitted to feel uncomfortable when she observes this and may give the child a toy to relieve her own feelings. But the mother who feels uncomfortable and so must distract her baby may convey, albeit covertly and indecisively, considerable disapproval. And so with other things; changes in behavior too quickly superposed on less quickly alterable feelings may fail to obtain the hoped-for results. The problem remains of how to help people to face the realities of human nature and yet to treat it gently.

◄§ 11 §► The Emotionally Disturbed Child:
A Family Scapegoat

by EZRA F. VOGEL *and*

NORMAN W. BELL

F ew studies of factors affecting the personality of children have considered childhood development in the context of the dynamics of the family as a group. The child's internal processes, or his re-

Adapted by the editor with permission of the authors and publisher from Ezra F. Vogel and Norman W. Bell, "The Emotionally Disturbed Child as the Family Scapegoat," in Norman W. Bell and Ezra F. Vogel, eds., *A Modern Introduction to the Family*, pp. 382–397, 667–668, copyright 1960

lationship with his mother and, more recently, with his father have instead been the focus of investigation. The present study examines the dynamics of the effect of one crucial relationship within the family, the marriage relationship, upon the products of this relationship, the children, in order to provide a broader background for considering the personality development of emotionally disturbed children.

Data for this paper are derived from the intensive study of a small group of "disturbed" families, each with an emotionally disturbed child, and a matched group of "well" families without clinically manifest disturbance in any child.[1] The families were seen by a team including psychiatrists, social workers, psychologists, and social scientists. The disturbed families, on which the data in this paper are based, were seen weekly in the offices of a psychiatric clinic and in their homes over periods ranging from one to four years.

Sources of Tension That Lead to Scapegoating

One of the several determinants of the emergence of an emotionally disturbed child appears to be that the child is being used as a means of preserving his parents' marriage. The parents have succeeded in preserving the marital bond, but perhaps at the cost of the impairment of the child's personality development: The child becomes the scapegoat for the tensions of his parents' marriage.

When the parents are ridden by internal conflict and ambivalence, they may reduce the tension, if each spouse acts out only one side of the conflict. Although at a deeper level they share the same fundamental conflicts, in relationship to each other they behave as if they are polar opposites. Together they form a complete system in which each consciously expresses a side of the conflict that the partner does not. This "polarization" is usually accompanied by a marked isolation on the part of each spouse—isolation which results in both the minimization of actual physical contact, and in the

by The Free Press, A Corporation; and adapted also from Ezra F. Vogel, "The Marital Relationship of Parents of Emotionally Disturbed Children: Polarization and Isolation," *Psychiatry*, XXIII, 1960, 1–12, © The William Alanson White Psychiatric Foundation, Inc., and used with their permission and that of the author.

couple's refusal to discuss certain vital problems. That the two processes, polarization and isolation, serve as temporary tension releases is well illustrated by the following material from the case history of one disturbed couple:

> Mr. and Mrs. D. were both ambivalent in the values they held, for example on the importance of dressing smartly, on whether to be independent of their relatives, and generally on whether to follow middle-class or working-class values. And yet they behaved in relation to each other as if they had opposite sets of value-orientations, and by so doing were able to avoid recognizing their own internal conflicts. On the conscious level they both perceived Mr. D. as having working-class values and Mrs. D. as having middle-class values. This afforded them a level of ego integration that permitted them to function.
>
> Although the conflicts were expressed in periodic fights between Mr. and Mrs. D., the prevailing mood was one of silence and discontented resignation. They had actually made an explicit verbal agreement not to discuss certain topics, assuming that any such discussion would certainly end in an explosion. Once during the years of therapy, when Mr. D. was drunk, he did bring up a forbidden topic—Mrs. D.'s premarital affair—and it did lead to a violent argument. Regarding many other topics, Mr. and Mrs. D. had no explicit verbal agreement, but avoided discussion, which they thought would only lead to arguments without improving the situation. This included virtually all the topics about which they had strong feelings, such as Mr. D.'s work, his family, or Mrs. D.'s not spending time at home with the children. Mrs. D. continually repeated that she could not talk to her husband since he simply couldn't understand her; Mr. D.'s conviction about the lack of value in talking was sufficiently generalized so that he felt very reluctant to talk either to his wife or to his therapist about things that really mattered to him.

Although this pattern of conscious polarization, mutual annoyance, and reduction of potentially dangerous interaction to an absolute minimum has considerable stability, tensions may develop to the point where these mechanisms fail to produce a sufficient amount of tension-release. It is at this point in the marital relationship that an appropriate object may be chosen to symbolize the conflicts and thus draw off the tension.

Conceivably, some person or group outside the family could serve in this capacity. However, in these disturbed families, the parents had by and large internalized the standards of the surrounding community sufficiently so that they had great difficulty in finding a legitimate basis for scapegoating outsiders. If at times they were able to manifest antagonism to outsiders, this usually led to many additional complications; hence the family preferred to scapegoat its own child.*

A number of factors made a child the most appropriate object through which to deal with family tensions. First of all, the child was in a relatively powerless position. While he was dependent on the parents and could not leave the family, he was not effectively able to counter the parents' superior power. Because the child's personality is still flexible, he can be molded to adopt the particular role which the family assigns him. When the child does take on many of the characteristics which the parents dislike in themselves and each other, he becomes a symbolically appropriate object on which to focus their own anxieties. Since the person scapegoated often develops such severe tensions that he is unable to perform his usual task roles, it is important that those family members performing essential, irreplaceable functions for the family not be scapegoated. The child has relatively few tasks to perform in the family compared to the parents or other elders, and his disturbance does not ordinarily interfere with the successful performance of the necessary family tasks. The "cost" in dysfunction of the child is low relative to the functional gains for the whole family.

The selecting of a particular child as a scapegoat is not a random matter; one child is the best symbol. Just as a dream condenses a variety of past and present experiences, and a variety of emotional feelings, the scapegoat condenses a variety of social and psychological problems impinging on the family.

Whoever is selected as the scapegoat is intimately related to the sources of tension. Where value orientation conflicts existed the child chosen was the one who best symbolized these conflicts. For example, if the conflicts revolved about achievement, a child who failed to achieve according to expectations could become the symbol of failure.

---

* The one family which did occasionally express antagonism directly to outsiders was the most disturbed family in the sample. The expression of hostility to neighbors was filled with such conflict that it proved inadequate and the family returned to the scapegoating of their child.

While many members of these families did express prejudice towards minority groups, this prejudice did little to drain the severe tensions within the family. Perhaps the minority groups were not symbolically appropriate for the handling of the family conflicts, or perhaps they were not sufficiently available to serve as a continual focus of family tensions.

The position of the child in the sibling group frequently became a focus for the unresolved childhood problems of the parents. If the parents' most serious unresolved problems were with male figures, the child chosen to represent the family conflict was usually a male child. Similarly, sibling order could be a strong factor. If one or both parents had difficulties with older brothers, an older boy in the family might become the scapegoat.

Another pattern revolved about the identification of a child with a parent whom he resembles. In one form or other this was found in all families, sick and well; but in the disturbed families the child was seen as possessing very undesirable traits, and although the parent actually possessed the same traits the focus of attention was the child and not the parent. In one family in particular this pattern was striking. The father and the eldest son had very similar physical characteristics, and not only had the same first name but were called by the same diminutive name by the mother. At times the social worker seeing the mother was not certain whether the mother was talking about her husband or her son. The wife's concerns about the husband's occupational adequacy were not dealt with directly, but the focus for her affect was the child and his school performance. In fact, the son was criticized by his mother for all the characteristics which she disliked in her husband, but she was unable to criticize the latter directly for these characteristics. She channeled all her feelings—especially anxiety and hostility—to the child, although her husband had similar problems. Not only that, but to control her feelings toward her husband she remained very aloof and distant and was not able to express to him either positive or negative feelings. While she channeled many criticisms and anxieties through the child, she also expressed many of her positive feelings to the child, thereby leading to severe Oedipal conflicts. The husband was not happy about his wife's aloofness. Still, he found that by cooperating with her in criticizing the child, he was able to keep the burden of problems away from himself. He thus joined with the wife in projecting his own difficulties and problems onto the child and in dealing with them as the child's problems rather than his own.

General body type as well as certain physical abnormalities could become the symbol to call forth scapegoating. In two families the spouses had many problems in their sexual life. Rather than face these maladjustments directly, the problems were expressed through concern about the masculinity and normality of a slender, graceful son.

When there is a serious family problem and no child is an appropriate symbol of the problem, there must be considerable cognitive distortion in order to permit the most appropriate child available to be used as a scapegoat. For example, in one family which was deeply concerned about the problems of achievement, the focus of the family's problems was the eldest son. Although he was receiving passing grades in school whereas the parents themselves had had poor school records, the parents were very critical of his school performance. Because of this pressure, the child worked hard and was able to get somewhat better marks on his next report card. However, the mother stoutly maintained that her son didn't deserve those grades, that he must have cheated, and she continued to criticize him for his school performance.

Very often the eldest child becomes the scapegoat simply because he is the first available and appropriate object. In the one case in which a child was able to escape the scapegoat role by decreasing his attachment to the home, the next most appropriate child was cast in that role.

Induction of the Child into the Scapegoat Role

If the child is to be a "satisfactory" scapegoat he must carry out his role as a "problem child." The problem behavior must be reinforced strongly enough so that it will continue in spite of the hostility and anxiety it produces in the child. This delicate balance is possible only because the parents have superior powers of sanction over the child, can define what he should or should not do, and control what he does or does not do. The maintenance of this balance necessarily requires a large amount of inconsistency in the ways parents handle the child.

The most common inconsistency our data revealed was between the implicit (or unconscious) role induction and the explicit role induction.[2] In all cases, certain behaviors of the child violated recognized social norms. In some instances stealing, fire-setting, or expressions of hostility or uncooperativeness, affected the child's relationships with persons outside the family. In other instances bed-wetting, resistance to parental orders, or expressions of aggression to siblings affected relationships within the family. But in all instances, while the parents explicitly criticized the child and at times even punished him, they supported in some way—usually implicitly —the persistence of the very behavior which they criticized. This permission took various forms: failure to follow through on threats, delayed punishment, indifference to and acceptance of the symptoms, or unusual interest in the child because of his symptoms.

Another type of inconsistency seen was encouragement by one parent of a certain type of behavior, and encouragement by the other parent of an opposing type of behavior. The result again was that the child was caught in the conflict. The mechanism also permitted one spouse to express annoyance to the other indirectly without endangering the marital relationship. For example, in one case, the father objected to the son's leaving toys lying around and violently exploded at the child for such behavior, implying that the mother was wrong in permitting him to do this. The mother realized that the father exploded at such behavior and did not stop the father since she "knew he was right." Nevertheless she often indicated that the child need not bother picking up the toys, since she felt that he was too young to have to do such things by himself and that the father was too strict. If the mother's encouragement of the behavior annoying to the father had been explicit, the dangerous possibility might arise of the father directing hostility at the mother rather than at the child. By keeping her encouragement implicit, the mother was able to deny that she had encouraged the child. The father was usually willing to accept this denial, even if he did not believe it, rather than risk an explosion with his wife. In some instances, however, one spouse was angered or felt compelled to criticize the other for not handling the child properly. Then the encouragement of the child by one parent to behave in a certain way would have to become more subtle to avoid criticism from the spouse.

In addition to the inconsistent pressures resulting from the difference between explicit and implicit expectations and from the differences between the expectations of the two parents, the child also had to deal with changes in each parent's expectations. From the parents' conscious point of view, this inconsistency resulted from an attempt to reconcile two conflicting desires: teaching the child to behave properly and not being "too hard on the child." When a parent was consciously attempting to teach the child proper behavior, he was extremely aggressive and critical.* At other times the parent felt he had been too critical of the child and permitted him to behave similarly without punishment, and would be extremely affectionate and supportive. While the explanation given for this inconsistency was that he wanted to teach the desired behavior without being "too hard on the child," its latent function was to prevent the child from consistently living up to the ostensibly desired behavior. The phase of not being "too hard on the child" served to reinforce the disapproved behavior and the phase of "being firm" permitted the parents to express their anxieties and hostility.

Since the conflicting expectations existed over a long period of time, it is not surprising that the child internalized these conflicts. Once the child had responded to his parents' implicit wishes and acted in a somewhat disturbed manner, the parents could treat him as if he really were a problem. The child would respond to these expectations and a vicious cycle was set in motion. It is difficult, if not impossible, to distinguish at just what point the parents begin treating the child as a problem and at what point the child actually does have internalized problems. There does not seem to be any sudden development of the child's problems; rather, it is a process occurring over a period of time. The fact that the child becomes disturbed adds stability to the role system, so that once set in motion, scapegoating does not easily pass from one child to another. In the healthy families, when scapegoating did take place, it was less severe and did not become stabilized with one child as the permanent scapegoat.

The Rationalization of Scapegoating

When a scapegoating situation was established, a relatively stable equilibrium of the family was achieved. However, there were diffi-

---

* This was also true in some of the "well" families, but in these families it was ordinarily possible for the child to escape further punishment by behaving in a different, desired way. There were few possibilities for the child to escape this hostility in the disturbed families.

culties in maintaining this equilibrium. Parents frequently had considerable guilt about the way they treated the child, and when the child was identified as disturbed by neighbors, teachers, doctors, or other outside agencies, pressure was brought to bear for some action to be taken. Although parents did not have much difficulty in explaining why they were so concerned about the child, they did have great difficulty in rationalizing their aggressive behavior toward him.

One way in which the parents rationalized their behavior was to define themselves, rather than their child, as victims. They stressed how much difficulty there was coping with all the problems posed by their child. For example, mothers of bed-wetters complained about the problems of keeping sheets clean and the impossibility of the child staying overnight at friends' or relatives' homes. Such rationalizations seemed to relieve some of the guilt for victimizing the child and served as a justification for continued expressions of annoyance toward him.

Another way of rationalizing their behavior was to emphasize how fortunate their children really were. For most of these parents, the standard of living provided for their children was much higher than the standard of living they enjoyed when they were children. One of the central complaints of these parents, particularly the fathers, was that the children wanted too much and got more than the parents ever had when they were children. This was considered a legitimate excuse for depriving their children of toys or privileges and for refusing to recognize the children's complaints that they were not getting things.

These attempts of the parents to rationalize their own behavior had a very defensive quality and showed their difficulty in reconciling their behavior with general social norms about child-rearing. In the more severely disturbed families the pressing nature of problems required serious distortion of social norms, but in the mildly disturbed families more attention was given to the social norms and attempts were made to express emotions in more acceptable ways. In any event much energy was required to maintain the "hostile equilibrium," a state which required coordination of many subtle and inconsistent feelings and behaviors. It was, in effect, an "armed truce," and the danger of explosion was constantly present.

Functions and Dysfunctions of Scapegoating

In addition to providing needed tension release in order to preserve the marital and familial relationships, scapegoating served another function: for the parents, it acted as a personality stabilizing process. Although the parents of these children did have serious internal conflicts, the projection of these difficulties onto the children served to minimize and contain them. Thus, despite their personality difficulties, the parents were able to live up to their commitments to the wider society, expressing a minimum of their difficulties in the external economic and political systems. Most of the parents were able to maintain positions as steady workers and relatively respectable community members.

While the scapegoating of a child is effective in controlling major sources of tensions within the family, the development of emotional disturbance in a child leads to disturbing secondary complications which are, however, generally less severe than the original tensions. One dysfunction of scapegoating is that certain realistic problems and extra tasks are created for the family. The child does require special care and attention. If, for example, the child is a bed-wetter, members of the family must either wake him up regularly, or wash many sheets and take other precautions.

In addition, while the child is responsive to the implicit sanctions of his parents, he, too, may develop mechanisms of fighting back and punishing them for their treatment of him. Often the child becomes very skilled in arousing his parents' anxieties or in consciously bungling something his parents want him to accomplish. The mother, being available most of the day, experiences most of this counter-aggression, which in part accounts for her greater readiness to bring the child in for treatment. (In most of these families it was the mother who took the initiative in seeking treatment.) It would appear that as long as she can carefully control the amount of hostility the child expresses to her, the mother can tolerate this dysfunction, but when his hostility exceeds a certain point she is willing to seek outside help.

The disturbed behavior may lead to some dysfunctions for the family, but it is still the personality of the child which suffers most as

a result of scapegoating. Other groups besides the family may maintain their integration at the expense of a deviant or scapegoat, who
is subject to pressures which create considerable conflict for him.[3]
Within the family, however, a stable integration must be maintained
for a long period of time. This often results in serious personality
impairment of the child assigned the deviant role. The development
of the emotional disturbance is simply part of the process of in-
ternalizing the conflicting demands placed upon the child by his
parents. In the short run, he receives more rewards from the family
for playing this role than for not playing this role. In the long run,
this leads to serious personality impairment. In general, the scapegoating mechanism is functional for the family as a group but
dysfunctional for the emotional health of the child and for his
adjustment outside the family of orientation.

NOTES

1. The data for the present analysis are taken from a larger study directed
   by John P. Spiegel and Florence R. Kluckhohn and supported by the
   National Institute of Mental Health and the Pauline and Louis G. Cowan
   Foundation. For other reports of this research see John P. Spiegel, "The
   Resolution of Role Conflict Within the Family," *Psychiatry*, XX, 1957,
   1–16; Florence R. Kluckhohn, "Family Diagnosis: Variations in the
   Basic Values of Family Systems," *Social Casework*, XXXIX, 1958, 63–72.
2. The way the parent gives the child implicit approval to act out the
   parent's own unconscious wishes has already been well described for
   the relationship between a single parent and child. Adelaide M. Johnson,
   "Sanctions for Superego Lacunae of Adolescents," in Kurt R. Eissler, ed.,
   Searchlights on Delinquency, New York: International Universities Press,
   1949; Melita Sperling, "The Neurotic Child and his Mother: A Psychoanalytic Study," *American Journal of Orthopsychiatry*, XXI, 1951, 351–
   364. For a more detailed account of family role induction methods, see
   Spiegel, *op. cit.*
3. See, for example, the analysis of the case of Long John's nightmares in
   William F. Whyte, *Street Corner Society*, University of Chicago Press,
   1943; and the report of Asch's experiments in Solomon E. Asch, *Social
   Psychology*, New York: Prentice-Hall, 1952.

Five

ADOLESCENTS, SIBLINGS, AND PEERS

⊰ INTRODUCTION* ⊱

A dolescence is often looked upon as a difficult period. One hears about the "problems," "growing pains," "awkwardness," and "storm and stress" of adolescence. Is the period of adolescence universally a difficult one, or is it difficult only in certain types of societies?

Adolescence is generally seen as a difficult period because of the pronounced physiological changes that take place at that time: changes, for example, in the hormone secretions and in the rate of physical growth. It is a short step from the recognition that such physiological changes take place during adolescence and that adolescence is a difficult period in the United States, to the conclusion that adolescence is a difficult period generally. In other words, the reasoning is that the apparently universal physiological changes of adolescence are universally accompanied by problems, awkwardness, and storm and stress.† This point of view is still current in certain quarters—Kiell (1964), for example, provides a recent statement of adolescence as a period of "turmoil" and "turbulence," using autobiographical material predominantly from writers of Western societies to illustrate his thesis. The best evidence that we presently have, however, suggests that such a viewpoint is

* For a more extended treatment of adolescents, siblings, or peers see Stone and Church (1957); Remmers and Radler (1957); Polsky (1959); Smith (1962); Gottlieb and Reeves (1963); Campbell (1964); Irish (1964); Ritchie and Koller (1964); Douvan and Gold (1966).

† G. Stanley Hall (1904) has been viewed as an early proponent of this view, but his position was more complicated than is usually acknowledged. His primary concern was with "recapitulation" theory, and it was his belief that the developing person recapitulates the evolutionary development of man. As a result he saw childhood as a period that was determined by physiological and genetic factors, while adolescence was the period during which there was much flexibility as a result of possible cultural influences. (See Grinder and Strickland, 1963, for an elaboration of this view.)

incorrect, and underemphasizes social and cultural factors (see Cohen, 1964, p. 100; Rodman, 1965).

If the physiological changes of adolescence lead to adolescent problems, then such problems should be found universally. Margaret Mead (1928; cf. Davis, *12*), however, in an important study, has shown that such is not the case. Samoan adolescents do not experience the kind of strains that are attributed to American adolescents, and Mead suggests that there are certain features of American society—such as the lack of a clear definition of the adolescent's role—that are responsible for the adolescent's problems. The problems, in other words, are not a universal product of physiological changes, but a product only of certain kinds of sociocultural settings. As Davis (*12*) points out, there are certain features of American and Western society that lead to strains and conflicts in the adolescent's relations with his parents: a rapid rate of social change; a complex social structure with competing spheres of authority; and conflicting pressures, especially in the area of sexual behavior.

There are at least two sharply contrasting definitions of adolescence. One is physiological: adolescence is the period between the onset of puberty and the development of complete sexual maturity (Ford and Beach, 1951). The second is sociological: adolescence is the period during which one is no longer regarded as a child but not yet regarded as an adult (Davis, 1948; Hollingshead, 1949). Neither definition is inherently superior—each is useful in its own way. One danger that the sociologist sees in the physiological definition, however, is that it may lead to the conclusion that the physiological changes alone account for the changes in the adolescent's behavior. The physiological changes, of course, do make a difference. But the sociologist is also interested in the different ways the "physiological" adolescent is treated in different groups and societies, and in the consequences for the adolescent of such differential treatment. In American society, for example, the adolescent is not expected to participate in adult sexual or economic roles, while in many other societies the "physiological" adolescent is accorded full adult status. Physiological factors clearly do not explain such differences—one must turn to social and cultural factors for the explanation.

The process of socialization never ends, but as Davis (*12*) points out it does decelerate. Most learning, in other words, takes place when a person is young, and the time of adolescence is perhaps "the last period of intense socialization" (Davis, 1948). What are the major sources of influence upon the person in his transition from childhood to adulthood? From whom does learning take place, in addition to the parents? An answer to these questions would include teachers and perhaps other professional people such as counselors and clergymen; other adults, such as family friends, neighbors, or relatives; the mass media; siblings; and peers. We shall here pay attention to the way in which siblings, and especially peers, are influential in the American adolescent's transition from childhood to adulthood.

The Decline of Parental Influence

One area of research interest has to do with the reaction of adolescents to conflicting pressures from peers and parents: do adolescents follow the expectations of their peers or their parents? To answer such a question it is necessary to know the nature of the conflict between peers and parents. Brittain (1963), for example, reports that parents and peers are seen as "competent guides in different areas of judgments." In a conflict situation, adolescent girls reported they would follow parental advice on whether or not to report someone who damaged public property and on which part-time job to take. Peers were seen as the guides regarding which course to take in school, which dress to buy, and how to dress for a football game and party. On many questions, such as decisions about joining a club, adolescents divide more equally on whether they would follow peers or parents (*A Study of Adolescent Boys,* 1955; Coleman, 1961). Brittain suggests that parents tend to be followed on matters of more general importance to adult society, while peers are followed on matters of special importance to adolescents. Of special interest is Brittain's finding that questionnaire data may overestimate the degree of conformity to parents, and he suggests that one way in which an adolescent copes with potential parent-peer cross-pressures is to avoid communicating with parents about certain matters they would object to.

Coleman (1961) has indicated that urban and suburban high

school students in the United States are more peer-oriented, and that "in general, the adolescent elites tend to be less oriented to parental demands than are their followers." The wave of the future therefore seems to lie with a still greater degree of orientation to peers and a lesser degree of orientation to parents.

It is evident that as American adolescents grow older they become less parent-oriented and more peer-oriented (Neiman, 1954). In a study by Bowerman and Kinch (1959), for example, 87 per cent of 4th graders are reported to be parent-oriented, 50 per cent of 8th graders, and 32 per cent of 10th graders. In the United States in particular, the shift away from dependence upon parents takes place at a comparatively early age—Boehm (1957) reports this in comparison to Swiss children, Vogel and Vogel (1961) report it with respect to Japanese children, and Guthrie and Jacobs (1966) also report it with respect to Filipino children. It is the high value upon independence from the parents in American society that results in this shift to early and strong peer-group ties and relationships. Rosen (1955) and Bell and Buerkle (1962) document the shift away from parental expectations on the part of high school and college adolescents, and their greater reliance upon peer-group expectations, as among Jewish adolescents who tend to follow peer-group expectations regarding sexual and dietary patterns.

Although one can point to the declining influence of parents, the degree to which there is actually conflict between parents and their adolescent children is another matter. Adelson (1964) has suggested that parent-adolescent conflict, which is so often said to occur, is exaggerated. He indicates that both parents and their adolescent children are aware of the long period of the latter's dependence, and that adaptations to this are worked out in such a way that conflict is minimized.

Siblings and Peers

Many things are learned from siblings or peers, rather than from parents. In part, this is a matter of changing patterns of behavior and values, so that an older peer or sibling may be a more knowledgeable source of information. In part it is a matter of certain areas—such as the sexual area—being left to siblings and peers through parental default. And in part it is a matter of the very strong ties that develop among siblings or peers who face the same developmental problems, sharing their experiences and learning from each other. (It should also be noted that Harlow (1962) has demonstrated that infant-infant interaction among monkeys is more important than mother-child interaction for normal social development with appropriate sexual behavior and affectional interaction in maturity.)

One way in which learning takes place is through role-playing. The child who plays at "mother" or "father," "nurse" or "doctor," is learning something about these roles as he plays. In similar fashion, we all "play at" being the person we are interacting with—this takes place internally, however, rather than externally as in child's play. A girl interacting with her brother, for example, may have no desire to be a boy like her brother; yet she must learn something about his role in order to be able to interact effectively with him. In this sense she is learning something about the boy's role, and may even adopt some features of the boy's role as a result of her interaction with her brother. This is precisely what the selection by Brim (*13*) brings out: that children with a sibling of the opposite sex come to adopt some of the features of the role of the opposite sex, and that this is especially true if their opposite sex sibling is older. In other words, to cite an example, a girl with a brother comes to adopt certain masculine characteristics to a greater extent than a girl with a sister, and this is especially true if she has an older brother. We must note, of course, that Brim is discussing a tendency for certain patterns to develop under certain conditions; learning one's sex role does not depend upon the sex of one's sibling alone, and neither does the sex of one's sibling operate in any simple way to produce set patterns of sex role learning. What this means, in other words, is that the *tendency* that Brim points to is not incompatible with exceptions to that tendency. Findings similar to Brim's are also reported by Sutton-Smith *et al.* (1964) and by Kammeyer (1965).

Siblings and peers are both members of one's own generation, and in this sense there are many similarities between them. However, there is far from complete equivalence between the two. For example, it may be possible to discuss certain things with one's siblings that one cannot discuss with one's peers because they are "family matters" that are not supposed to become public information. Similarly, it may be possible to discuss certain things with one's peers that one cannot discuss with one's siblings because the siblings may represent the family and its more conservative and traditional values. There are differences in these matters from society to society, and from group to group within the same society. There are also differences in the extent to which the peer group is accepted in the society as a legitimate group. American parents, for example, may become the stage managers for peer-group interaction from the time their children are two or three years old (cf. Riesman, *14*). They arrange visits to playgrounds and to friends' houses, and they organize birthday parties, toddler schools, and nursery schools because of the importance that is placed upon peer-group interaction. By contrast, Pitts (1960) points out that the French family is not interested in peer-group interaction; a child is discouraged from playing with other children or from making advances to other children. "Very little spontaneity is allowed young French boys (and girls) in the choice of their playmates. . . . They find their playmates more frequently among their siblings." When French children become older and, on their own, develop peer-group ties, these ties are not seen by adults as having a legitimate function. As a consequence, reference is seldom made within the family to the peer-group ties of its adolescents.

Peer-group relationships may clearly be of significance during adulthood and childhood as well as during the adolescent years. Clubs, lodges, recreational groups, and work groups all give evidence of much peer-group contact among adults. Good examples of such contact, in which there is a relationship of strong emotional support, can be found within certain sectarian groups (Wilson, 1961), informal street groups (Whyte, 1955), military groups (Janowitz, 1959), and working-class groups (Gans, 1962). The importance of such support is illustrated by Whyte (1955; 1964), who points out that when certain members of the gang lost the support of their peers they developed neurotic symptoms; these symptoms disappeared once their position in the group was again established.

During childhood there are also many important and satisfying peer-group relationships. Opie and Opie (1959), for example, have referred to the oral tradition that is passed on from one childhood generation to another, consisting of epithets, jeers, riddles, secret languages, counting rhymes, and so on: "The modern schoolchild, when out of sight and on his own, appears to be rich in language, well-versed in custom, a respecter of the details of his own code, and a practising authority on traditional self-amusements" (p. ix). And Ausubel (1958, p. 461) suggests that for many children the peer group "serves as a corrective influence counteracting the undesirable social effects of . . . extreme parental attitudes." In this sense it is necessary to recognize the importance of peer and sibling relationships, and one should perhaps call into question the "preponderant attention usually given to parents" (Sutton-Smith *et al.,* 1964).

Despite the general prevalence of peer-group ties in the United States, the most intensive peer-group relationships are to be found during adolescence. This is a time of transition for the adolescent between his family of orientation and his family of procreation; prior to adolescence he has a greater investment in relationships with his parents and siblings; subsequently, he develops an investment in relationships with his spouse and children. Perhaps the most noticeable illustration of strong peer-group ties during adolescence is found among delinquent gangs, where peers exert a tremendous degree of influence over each other's behavior. Of special interest is the tendency for a delinquent gang to break up once its members have passed out of the adolescent years, and for its once-delinquent members to become, on the whole, law-abiding adults (Miller, 1962).

It is David Riesman (*14*), above all, who has referred to the tremendous importance and influence of the peer group in the United States. Aided and abetted by parents, the other-directed child comes to look to his peers as the source of his tastes and standards, and the dominance of the peer group may stifle individual differences and creativity as it cuts everyone down to size.* Once again, it is a question of the value that is placed in American life upon independence from the parents, and of achieving this independence from the parents by relying upon the support of the peer group. The issue that Riesman raises, however, is whether

---

* Some of the issues involved in this area of parental versus peer-group control are also discussed in *12* and *22.*

the early parental pressure toward "good" peer-group relationships, and the consequent dependence of the child (and later, the adolescent and adult) upon the peer group, is necessarily the best thing for the mental health of Americans.

REFERENCES

ADELSON, JOSEPH. 1964. "The Mystique of Adolescence," *Psychiatry*, XXVII, 1–5.

AUSUBEL, DAVID P. 1958. *Theory and Problems of Child Development*, New York: Grune & Stratton.

BELL, ROBERT R., and JACK V. BUERKLE. 1962. "The Daughter's Role During the 'Launching Stage,'" *Marriage and Family Living*, XXIV, 384–388.

BOEHM, LEONORE. 1957. "The Development of Independence: A Comparative Study," *Child Development*, XXVIII, 85–92.

BOWERMAN, CHARLES E., and JOHN W. KINCH. 1959. "Changes in Family and Peer Orientation of Children Between the Fourth and Tenth Grades," *Social Forces*, XXXVII, 206–211.

BRITTAIN, CLAY V. 1963. "Adolescent Choices and Parent–Peer Cross–Pressures," *American Sociological Review*, XXVIII, 385–391.

CAMPBELL, JOHN D. 1964. "Peer Relations in Childhood," in Martin L. Hoffman, and Lois W. Hoffman, eds., *Review of Child Development Research*, Vol. I, New York: Russell Sage Foundation.

COHEN, YEHUDI A. 1964. *The Transition from Childhood to Adolescence*, Chicago: Aldine.

COLEMAN, JAMES S. 1961. (With John W. C. Johnstone and Kurt Jonassohn.) *The Adolescent Society*, New York: Free Press of Glencoe.

DAVIS, KINGSLEY. 1948. *Human Society*, New York: Macmillan.

DOUVAN, ELIZABETH, and MARTIN GOLD. 1966. "Modal Patterns in American Adolescence," in Lois W. Hoffman and Martin L. Hoffman, eds., *Review of Child Development Research*, Vol. II, New York: Russell Sage Foundation.

FORD, CLELLAN S., and FRANK A. BEACH. 1951. *Patterns of Sexual Behavior*, New York: Harper.

GANS, HERBERT J. 1962. *The Urban Villagers*, New York: Free Press of Glencoe.

GOTTLIEB, DAVID, and JON REEVES. 1963. *Adolescent Behavior in Urban Areas: A Bibliographic Review and Discussion of the Literature*, New York: Free Press of Glencoe.

GRINDER, ROBERT E., and CHARLES E. STRICKLAND. 1963. "G. Stanley Hall and the Social Significance of Adolescence," in Robert E. Grinder, ed., *Studies in Adolescence*, New York: Macmillan.

GUTHRIE, GEORGE M., and PEPITA JIMENEZ JACOBS. 1966. *Child Rearing and Personality Development in the Philippines*, Penn. State Univ. Press.

HALL, G. STANLEY. 1904. *Adolescence, Its Psychology and Its Relations to Physiology, Anthropology, Sociology, Sex, Crime, Religion, and Education*, 2 vols., New York: Appleton.

HARLOW, HARRY F. 1962. "The Heterosexual Affectional System in Monkeys," *American Psychologist*, XVII, 1–9.

HOLLINGSHEAD, AUGUST B. 1949. *Elmtown's Youth*, New York: Wiley.

IRISH, DONALD P. 1964. "Sibling Interaction: A Neglected Aspect in Family Life Research," *Social Forces*, XLII, 279–288.

JANOWITZ, MORRIS. 1959. *Sociology and the Military Establishment*, New York: Russell Sage Foundation.

KAMMEYER, KENNETH. 1965. Personal communication.

KIELL, NORMAN. 1964. *The Universal Experience of Adolescence*, New York: International Universities Press.

MEAD, MARGARET. 1928. *Coming of Age in Samoa*, New York: William Morrow.

MILLER, WALTER B. 1962. "The Impact of a 'Total–Community' Delinquency Control Project," *Social Problems*, X, 168–191.

NEIMAN, LIONEL J. 1954. "The Influence of Peer Groups upon Attitudes Toward the Feminine Role," *Social Problems*, II, 104–111.

OPIE, IONA, and PETER OPIE. 1959. *The Lore and Language of Schoolchildren*, New York: Oxford University Press.

PITTS, JESSE. 1960. "The Family and Peer Groups," in Norman W. Bell, and Ezra F. Vogel, eds., *A Modern Introduction to the Family*, Glencoe, Ill.: Free Press.

POLSKY, HOWARD W. 1959. "The Sociology of Adolescence," *Human Relations*, VII, 251–270.

REMMERS, H. H., and D. H. RADLER. 1957. *The American Teenager*, New York: Bobbs-Merrill.

RITCHIE, OSCAR W., and MARVIN R. KOLLER. 1964. *Sociology of Childhood*, New York: Appleton-Century-Crofts.

RODMAN, HYMAN. 1965. "The Textbook World of Family Sociology," *Social Problems*, XII, 445–457.

ROSEN, BERNARD C. 1955. "Conflicting Group Membership: A Study of Parent–Peer Group Cross Pressures," *American Sociological Review*, XX, 155–161.

SMITH, ERNEST A. 1962. *American Youth Culture*, New York: Free Press of Glencoe.

STONE, L. JOSEPH, and JOSEPH CHURCH. 1957. *Childhood and Adolescence*, New York: Random House.

A Study of Adolescent Boys. 1955. Ann Arbor: University of Michigan, Survey Research Center.

SUTTON-SMITH, BRIAN, JOHN M. ROBERTS, and B. G. ROSENBERG. 1964. "Sibling Associations and Role Involvement," *Merrill-Palmer Quarterly*, X, 25–38.

VOGEL, EZRA F., and SUZANNE H. VOGEL. 1961. "Family Security, Personal

Immaturity, and Emotional Health in a Japanese Sample," *Marriage and Family Living*, XXIII, 161–166.

WHYTE, WILLIAM F. 1955. *Street Corner Society*, enlarged ed., Chicago: University of Chicago Press.

————. 1964. "On 'Street Corner Society,'" in Ernest W. Burgess, and Donald J. Bogue, eds., *Contributions to Urban Sociology*, Chicago: University of Chicago Press, pp. 256–268.

WILSON, BRYAN R. 1961. *Sects and Society*, Berkeley: University of California Press.

⇜ 12 ⇝ Parent-Youth Conflict:
A Sociological Interpretation

by KINGSLEY DAVIS

It is in sociological terms that this paper attempts to frame and solve the sole question with which it deals, namely: Why does contemporary western civilization manifest an extraordinary amount of parent-adolescent conflict?* In other cultures, the outstanding fact is generally not the rebelliousness of youth, but its docility. There is practically no custom, no matter how tedious or painful, to which youth in primitive tribes or archaic civilizations will not willingly submit. What, then, are the peculiar features of our society which give us one of the extremest examples of filial friction in human history?

Our answer to this question makes use of certain constant and variable conditions, the constants being the universal factors in the parent-youth relation, the variables being the factors which differ from one society to another.

Adapted by the editor from Kingsley Davis, "The Sociology of Parent-Youth Conflict," *American Sociological Review*, V, Aug., 1940, 523–535; and Kingsley Davis, "Adolescence and the Social Structure," *The Annals of the American Academy of Political and Social Science*, CCXXXVI, Nov., 1944, 8–16. By permission of the author, the *American Sociological Review*, and *The Annals*.

* In the absence of statistical evidence, exaggeration of the conflict is easily possible. Yet sufficient non-quantitative evidence lies at hand in the form of personal experience, the outpour of literature on adolescent problems, and the historical and anthropological accounts of contrasting societies to justify the conclusion that in comparison with other cultures ours exhibits an exceptional amount of such conflict. If this paper seems to stress conflict, it is simply because we are concerned with this problem rather than with parent-youth harmony.

The Rate of Social Change

The first important variable is the rate of social change. Extremely rapid change in modern civilization, in contrast to most societies, tends to increase parent-youth conflict, for within a fast-changing social order the time-interval between generations, ordinarily but a mere moment in the life of a social system, becomes historically significant, thereby creating a gap between one generation and the next. Inevitably, under such a condition, youth is reared in a milieu different from that of the parents; hence the parents become old-fashioned, youth rebellious, and clashes occur which, in the closely confined circle of the immediate family, generate sharp emotion. If, for example, the conflict is sharper in the immigrant household, this can be due to one thing only, that the immigrant family generally undergoes the most rapid social change of any type of family in a given society.

Decelerating Socialization and Parent-Child Differences

Rapid social change would, however, have no power to produce conflict were it not for two universal factors: first, the decelerating rate of socialization in the development of personality; and second, the age differential between the generations.

The sequential development of personality involves a constantly decelerating rate of socialization, perhaps with the exception of the time of early infancy. This deceleration is due to the human being's organic development, from infant plasticity to senile rigidity, and to his cumulative cultural and social development. Its effect is to make the period of youth—the interval between a person's birth and the birth of his child—the time of major socialization.

The age difference between the generations therefore takes on special importance. This is because the cultural content which the parent acquired is a different content from that which the child is now acquiring. Since the parent is supposed to socialize the child, he tends to apply the former but now inappropriate content. He makes this mistake, and cannot remedy it, because his basic orientations were formed by the experiences of his own childhood. He cannot "modernize" his point of view, because *he* is the product of those experiences. He can change in superficial ways, such as learning a new tune, but it is much more difficult for him to change (or *want* to change) the initial modes of thinking upon which his subsequent social experience has been built. To change the basic conceptions by which he has learned to judge the rightness and reality of all specific situations might render subsequent experience meaningless, and might make an empty caricature of what has been his life.

Physiological Differences

Though the disparity in chronological age remains constant through life, the precise physiological differences between parent and offspring vary radically from one period to another. The organic contrasts between parent and infant, for example, are far different from those between parent and adolescent. Yet whatever the period, the organic differences produce contrasts in those desires which, at least in part, are organically determined. Thus, at the time of adolescence the contrast is between an organism which is just reaching its full powers and one which is just losing them.

The adolescent period seemingly has one outstanding characteristic—namely, it is a time when the individual is attaining physical and social maturity. In terms of growth, strength, fecundity, and mental capacity, full maturity tends to be attained only a short time after puberty; however, the adolescent's acquired knowledge, judgment, insight, and self-reliance are generally far from their peak. As a result of this disparity between physical maturity and social maturity, in the adolescent as well as in the parent, there is a potential for parent-youth conflict.

Most societies avoid the potential clash of old and young by using sociological position as a neutralizing agent. They assign definite and separate positions to persons of different ages, thereby eliminating competition between them for the same position and avoiding the competitive emotions of jealousy and envy. Also, since the expected behavior of old and young is thus made complementary, the performance of each age group can be suited to its physiological capacity. In our culture, however, where most positions are theoretically based on accomplishment rather than age, inter-age competition arises, superior organic propensities lead to a high evaluation of youth (the so-called "accent on youth"), a dispro-portionate lack of opportunity for youth manifests itself, and con-sequently, arrogance and frustration appear in the young, fear and envy in the old.

Sociological Differences: Parental Authority

Since social status and office are everywhere partly distributed on the basis of age, personality development is intimately linked with the network of social positions successively occupied during life. Western society, in spite of an unusual amount of interage competition, maintains differences of social position between par-ent and child, the developmental gap between them being too clearcut, the symbiotic needs too fundamental, to escape being made a basis of social organization. Hence, parent and child, in a variety of ways, find themselves enmeshed in different social con-texts and possessed of different outlooks. The much publicized critical attitude of youth toward established ways, for example, is partly a matter of being on the outside looking in. The "established ways" under criticism are usually institutions (such as property, marriage, profession) which the adolescent has not yet entered. He looks at them from the point of view of the outsider (especially since they affect him in a restrictive manner), either failing to imagine himself finding satisfaction in such patterns or else feeling resentful that the old have in them a vested interest from which he is excluded.

Because of his strategic position with reference to the new-born child, the parent is given considerable authority. It is important to note that this authority, in addition to its function in socialization, is a case of authority within a primary group. It has been pointed out that authority is bearable for the subordinate because it touches only one aspect of his life. Impersonal and objective, it permits all other aspects of his life to be free from its dominance. This escape, however, is lacking in parental authority, for since the family in-cludes most aspects of life, its authority is not limited, specific, or impersonal. What, then, can make this authority bearable? Three factors associated with the familial primary group help to give the answer: (1) the child is socialized within the family, and therefore knowing nothing else and being utterly dependent, the authority of the parent is internalized, accepted; (2) the family, like other primary groups, implies identification, its members being responsive to each other's sentiments, so that the harshness of authority is ameliorated; (3) in the intimate interaction of the family control can never be purely one-sided—there are too many ways in which the child can exert the pressure of his will. For these reasons, parental authority, however inclusive, is not felt as despotic.

Let us now take up, point by point, the manner in which western civilization has affected parental authority.

1. *Conflicting norms.*   To begin with, rapid change has, as we saw, given old and young a different social content, so that they possess conflicting norms. More than this, social complexity has confused the standards *within* the generations. Faced with conflicting goals, parents become inconsistent and confused in their own minds in rearing their children. The children, for example, acquire an argument against discipline by being able to point to some family wherein discipline is less severe, while the parent can retaliate by pointing to still other families wherein it is firmer. The acceptance of parental attitudes thus becomes less complete than formerly.

2. *Competing authorities.*   We took it for granted, when discussing rapid social change, that youth acquires new ideas, but we did not ask how. The truth is that, in a specialized and complex culture, they learn from competing authorities. Today, for example, education is largely in the hands of professional specialists, some of whom, as college professors, resemble the sophists of ancient Athens by virtue of their work of accumulating and purveying knowledge, and who consequently have ideas in advance of the populace at large. By giving the younger generation these advanced ideas, they (and many other extrafamilial agencies, including youth's contemporaries) widen the intellectual gap between parent and child.*

* The essential point is not that there are other authorities—in every society there are extrafamilial influences in socialization—but that, because of specialization and individualistic enterprise, they are *competing* authorities. Because they make a living by their work and are specialists in socialization, some authorities have a competitive advantage over parents who are amateurs or at best merely general practitioners.

3. *Little explicit institutionalization of steps in parental authority.* Our society provides little explicit institutionalization of the progressive readjustments of authority as between parent and child. The failure of our culture to institutionalize this readjustment by a series of well-defined, well-publicized steps is undoubtedly a cause of much parent-youth dissension. The exact time when authority is relinquished, the exact amount, and the proper ceremonial behavior are not clearly defined. Not only do different groups and families have conflicting patterns, and new situations arise to which old definitions will not apply, but the different spheres of life (legal, economic, religious, intellectual) do not synchronize, maturity in one sphere and immaturity in another often coexisting.

The adolescent's sociological exit from his family, via education, work, marriage, and change of residence, is fraught with potential conflicts of interest which only a definite system of institutional controls can neutralize. The parents have a vital stake in what their children will do. Because the acquisition of independence by the child will free the parents of many obligations, they are willing to relinquish their authority; yet, precisely because their own status is socially identified with that of their child, they wish to insure satisfactory conduct on the latter's part and are tempted to prolong their authority, by making the decisions themselves. In the absence of institutional prescriptions, the conflict of interest may lead to a struggle for power, the parents fighting to keep control in matters of importance to themselves, the son or daughter clinging to personally indispensable family services while seeking to evade the concomitant control.

4. *Concentration within the small family.* Our family system is peculiar in that it involves a very small kinship unit within which there is an intensity of family feeling. Since this strong family sentiment is directed toward a few individuals who are very important to one's emotional life, complexes easily develop. Emotional intensity and situational instability (for example, the breakup of the small family unit through death, desertion, or divorce) increase both the probability and severity of conflict.

In a familistic society, where there are several adult male and female relatives within the effective kinship group to whom the child turns for affection and aid, and many members of the younger generation in whom the parents have a paternal interest, there appears to be less intensity of emotion for any particular kinsman and consequently less chance for severe conflict. Also, if conflict between any two relatives does arise, it may be handled by shifting mutual rights and obligations to another relative.[1]

5. *Open competition for socioeconomic position.* In our society occupation is a matter of choice rather than ascription. This means that one's future occupation and destiny are determined more at adolescence than at birth, the adolescent himself (as well as the parents) having some part in the decision. Before him are many possible occupations and avenues of advancement, all of them fraught with the uncertainties of competitive vicissitude. The youth is ignorant of most of the facts. So is the parent, but less so. Both attempt to collaborate on the future, but because of previously mentioned sources of friction, the collaboration is frequently stormy. They evaluate future possibilities differently, and since the decision is uncertain yet important, a clash of wills results. The necessity of choice at adolescence extends beyond the occupational field to practically every phase of life, the parents having an interest in each decision. A culture in which more of the choices of life were settled beforehand by ascription, where the possibilities were fewer and the responsibilities of choice less urgent, would have much less parent-youth conflict.[2]

6. *Sex tension.* If until now we have ignored sex taboos, the omission has represented a deliberate attempt to place them in their proper context with other factors, rather than in the unduly prominent place usually given them. Undoubtedly, because of a constellation of cultural conditions, sex looms as an important bone of parent-youth contention. Our morality, for instance, demands both premarital chastity and postponement of marriage, thus creating a long period of desperate eagerness when young persons practically at the peak of their sexual capacity are forbidden to enjoy it. Naturally, tensions arise—tensions which adolescents try to relieve, and adults hope they will relieve, in some socially acceptable form. Such tensions not only make the adolescent intractable and capricious, but create a genuine conflict of interest between the two generations. The parent, with respect to the child's behavior, represents morality, while the adolescent reflects morality

plus his organic cravings. The stage is thereby set for conflict, evasion, and deceit. For the mass of adolescents, sublimation is never sufficient. Given our system of morality, conflict seems inevitable.

Among most peoples of the world, at least until recently, the sexual problem of adolescence was resolved in one of a number of ways. Either marriage occurred shortly after puberty or premarital intercourse prevailed. The choice of a marital partner was generally in the hands of parents or kinsmen. Wedlock did not usually imply a separate household, and did not convey full emancipation from the parents. Although there were countless variations on this generalized pattern, the underlying theme was extremely widespread. Its main characteristic was that it gave a sexual and reproductive function to the adolescent but carefully controlled the exercise of this function.

By way of contrast, American society is unusual, though not entirely unique, in the following ways: It maintains the ideal of premarital chastity in the face of a long period of postponement of marriage after puberty. In connection with this, it upholds the freedom of marital choice and fosters a competitive attitude in courtship. Finally, it emphasizes the independence and separateness of the wedded couple. As a consequence, the adolescent period becomes one of considerable strain. The young person is permitted to associate closely with the opposite sex but is put on his honor to remain virtuous; he is supposed to choose his own mate independently but is in many ways still under the authority of the parents; and he is forced to compete for love in a rating and dating system that may interfere with his educational or occupational goals.

The extraordinary preoccupation of modern parents with the sex life of their adolescent offspring is easily understandable. First, our morality is sex-centered. The strength of the impulse which it seeks to control, the consequent stringency of its rules, and the importance of reproductive institutions for society, make sex so morally important that being moral and being sexually discreet are synonymous. Small wonder, then, that parents, charged with responsibility for their children and fearful of their own status in the eyes of the moral community, are preoccupied with what their offspring will do in this matter. Moreover, sex is intrinsically involved in the family structure and is therefore of unusual significance to familial relationships. Offspring and parent are not simply two persons who happen to live together; they are two persons who happen to live together because of past sex relations between the parents. Also, between parent and child there stand strong incest taboos, and doubtless the unvoiced possibility of violating these unconsciously intensifies the interest of each in the other's sexual conduct. In addition, since sexual behavior is connected with the offspring's formation of a new family of his own, it is naturally of concern to the parent. Finally, these factors taken in combination with the delicacy of the authoritarian relation, the emotional intensity within the small family, and the confusion of sex standards, make it easy to explain the parental interest in adolescent sexuality. Yet because sex is a tabooed topic between parent and child,[3] parental control must be indirect and devious, which creates additional possibilities of conflict.

Summary and Conclusion

Parent-youth conflict thus results from the interaction of certain universals of the parent-child relation and certain variables the values of which are peculiar to modern culture. The universals are (1) the basic age differential between parent and child, (2) the decelerating rate of socialization with advancing age, and (3) the resulting intrinsic differences between old and young on the physiological and sociological planes.

Though these universal factors *tend* to produce conflict between parent and child, whether or not they do so depends upon at least the following variables: (1) the rate of social change; (2) the extent of complexity in the social structure; (3) the degree of integration in the culture; and (4) the frequency of social (vertical) mobility, involving cultural change as one moves from one social class to another.

In contemporary western society rapid social change has crowded historical meaning into the family time-span, has thereby given the offspring a different social content from that which the parent acquired, and consequently has added to the universal features of parent-youth relations a set of variable features which double the chance of alienation. Moreover, our great societal complexity, our evident cultural conflict, and our emphasis upon open competition for socioeconomic status have all added to this initial effect. We have seen, for instance, that they have unsettled parental authority by confusing the goals of child control, by setting up competing authorities, by creating a small family system, and by making necessary certain significant choices at the time of adolescence. The parent-youth conflict that results from this, moreover, has not been mitigated by the development of institutional mechanisms to symbolize and enforce the progressively changing stages of parental power.

NOTES

1. MARGARET MEAD, *Coming of Age in Samoa,* New York: William Morrow, 1928.
2. *Ibid.*
3. "Even among the essentially 'unrepressed' Trobrianders the parent is never the confidant in matters of sex." Bronislaw Malinowski, *Sex and Reproduction in Savage Society,* London, 1927, p. 36n.

᷅ 13 ᷥ᷾ Family Structure and Sex Role
Learning by Children

by O R V I L L E G . B R I M , J R .

The structure of a social group, delineated by variables such as size, age, sex, power, and prestige differences, is held to be a primary influence upon the patterns of interaction within the group, determining in major part the degree to which any two group members interact. It is held, second, that social roles are learned through interaction with others, such interaction providing one with the opportunity to practice his own role as well as to take the role of the other. On this basis one may hypothesize that group structure, by influencing the degree of interaction between group members, would be related to the types of roles learned in the group: one would learn most completely those roles which he himself plays, as well as the roles of the others with whom he most frequently interacts. This argument is applied in this paper specifically to the relation between family structure, described in terms of age, sex, and ordinality of children, and the sex role learning by the children.

The process of role learning through interaction, which has been described by Mead (see Strauss, 1956), Cottrell (1942), and others, can be sketched as follows. One learns the behavior appropriate to his position in a group through interaction with others who hold normative beliefs about what his role should be and who are able to reward and punish him for correct and incorrect actions. As part of the same learning process, one acquires expectations of how

Adapted by the editor from Orville G. Brim, Jr., "Family Structure and Sex Role Learning by Children: A Further Analysis of Helen Koch's Data," *Sociometry*, XXI, Mar., 1958, 1–16; used with permission of the author and *Sociometry*.

others in the group will behave. The latter knowledge is indispensable to the actor, in that he must be able to predict what others expect of him, and how they will react to him, in order to guide his own role performance successfully. Accurate or erroneous understanding and prediction are respectively rewarding and punishing to the actor, and learning proceeds systematically through the elimination of incorrect responses and the strengthening of correct ones.

It has been the distinctive contribution of sociology to demonstrate that learning the role of others occurs through the actor's taking the role of the other, i.e., trying to act as the other would act. While this role-taking of the other can be overt, as with children who actively and dramatically play the role of the parent, it is commonly covert in adults, as with the husband who anticipates what his wife will say when he returns home late, or the employee who tries to foresee his employer's reaction when he asks for a raise.

It follows that, whether taking the role of others is overt or covert, certain responses (belonging to the role of the other) are in fact made, run through, completed, and rewarded if successful, i.e., accurate, and that this process adds to the repertoire of possible actions of a person those actions taken by others in their own roles. Such actions, as part of one's repertoire or pool of learned responses, are available for performance by an actor, not now simply in taking the role of the other, but as resources which he can use as part of his *own* role performances.

The critical fact is that the actor not only can, but *does,* make use of responses learned in role-taking in his own role performances. There are two senses in which this happens. The first, which does not concern us in this paper, involves the direct transfer of the role of the other to a new and parallel status of one's own, where there is a straightforward adoption of the other's role. Such transfer may be appropriate and rewarded, as where the oldest child performs the role of the parent to his sibs, or simply interesting and tolerated, as where the new assistant professor plays the department chairman to the graduate students.

The second sense, which is our major concern here, involves a more complex process of convergence between one's own role and that of the other which he takes, where there is a spill-over of elements belonging to another's role into one's own performance when it is not necessarily appropriate. Our basic hypothesis, set forth by Cottrell (1942) and others, is that interaction between two persons leads to assimilation of roles, to the incorporation of elements of the role of the other into the actor's role. Thus, one says, husbands and wives grow more alike through time, and long-time collaborators in research begin to think alike.

While not pretending to a full analysis of the process underlying assimilation, several causes can be described. First, the actor may note that the other is successful to a high degree in some of his behavior and consciously transfer to his own role such behavioral elements for trial. To the extent that they prove successful for him, in his performance, and are not eliminated through punishment from others for being inappropriate, he will adopt them. Second, faced with novel situations where his "own" behavior fails, the elements of others' roles are already learned and available for trial and hence would tend to be tried prior to the development of totally new responses; again, if successful, they tend to be assimilated to the role. Third, the actions learned by taking the role of others are ordinarily performed implicitly and under limited conditions, e.g., in interaction with the other. However, the cues which guide and elicit one's own role performance may be difficult to differentiate from cues eliciting taking the role of the other. It would appear that for the young child this is especially difficult, and data indeed show that the child has difficulty discriminating between reality and fantasy, between what his role is or even what his self is, and what belongs in the category of the "other." In this way, behavior learned through role-taking and appropriate to the other is confused with and undifferentiated from behavior learned as part of one's own role. The latter becomes tinged or diluted with characteristics belonging to someone else's role.

Among the hypotheses which are derivative of the general hypothesis of assimilation through interaction, two are pertinent here. First, the process of discrimination between what belongs to oneself and what belongs to the other is aided by the guidance of other persons. Thus, the parent helps the son differentiate between what belongs to him and what belongs to his sister; the fledgling nurse is assisted in a proper demeanor and in separating her duties from those of the physician. Rewards and punishments administered by others govern the discrimination process. Where the process of assimilation comes primarily from inability to discriminate between roles, it follows that where greater attention is paid to helping the learner discriminate, the process of assimilation is to a greater degree arrested.

Second, given two other persons with whom one interacts and who differ in power over the actor, i.e., differ in the degree to which they control rewards and punishments for the actor, one would predict that the actor would adopt more of the characteristics of the powerful, as contrasted to the less powerful, other person. This follows from the fact that it is more important to the actor to predict the behavior of the powerful figure, that he is motivated more strongly to take his role, that the rewards and punishments are more impressive and the learning consequently better. Interaction between two figures of unequal power should give a parallel result, namely, there would be a greater assimilation of the role of the other into the actor's role for the less powerful figure, for the same reasons as above. Thus the employee gravitates toward the boss more than the reverse, and the child becomes more like the parent than the other way round. However, this is not to imply that the more powerful figure need not take the role of the other, nor that he does not assimilate (to a lesser degree) elements from the other's role. The weaker figure always has some control over rewards and punishments, requiring therefore that his reaction be considered. The displeased employee can wound his boss through expressions of dislike, and the angry child can hurt his parents in a variety of ways, from refusing to eat to threatening to leave home.

Turning now to a consideration of sex-role learning specifically, pertinent reviews (Brim, 1957; Terman and Tyler, 1954) of the data show that sex-role prescriptions and actual performance begin early. The accepted position is that children in a family learn their appropriate sex roles primarily from their parents. There is remarkably little data, other than clinical materials, on this topic, perhaps because of its obviousness. What systematic data there is, is not inconsistent with the role-learning propositions set forth above. Sears, Pintler, and Sears (1946) have shown that in families where the father is absent the male child is slower to develop male sex-role traits than in families where the father is present, a finding predictable from the fact that there is no father whose role the child needs to take. Both Sears (1953) and Payne and Mussen (1956) have shown that father role-playing, identification with the father, and masculinity of attitudes are positively related to the father's being warm, affectionate, and rewarding. This strikes one as the same type of finding as the first, but at the other end of the interaction range; insofar as warm, affectionate, and rewarding fathers interact more with their sons, or are perceived as such because they interact more, it follows that the sons have more experience in taking their role.

In regard to the effects of sibling characteristics upon sex-role learning, there is again almost no information. Fauls and Smith (1956) report that only children choose sex-appropriate activities more often than do children with older same-sex siblings, a finding which seems to fit none of our role-learning propositions. While one might hold that the only child has more interaction, because of sibling absence, with his same-sex parent, hence learns his sex role better, one might equally say, especially for the young boys, that it is the cross-sex parent with whom the child interacts and hence the only child should not learn his sex role well. In any case, the finding serves to stress one important limitation of the data we are to report, namely, that they pertain to variations within two-child families, and that generalization to families of varying sizes is unwarranted.

Even with respect to theory concerning the effects of siblings on sex-role learning, we have not noted any systematic predictions in the literature. It is against this background of comparative absence of research and theory on the effects of siblings on sex-role learning that our own report must be viewed. The very valuable data on personality traits of children presented in recent publications by Helen Koch (1954, 1955a, 1955b, 1956a, 1956b, 1956c, 1956d) provide the opportunity to apply several of the general hypotheses set forth above to the substantive area of sibling effects on sex-role learning. The specific application of these hypotheses can be summarized as follows:

First, one would predict that cross-sex, as compared with same-sex, siblings would possess more traits appropriate to the cross-sex role. When taking the role of the other in interaction, cross-sex siblings must take the role of the opposite sex, and the assimilation of roles as delineated above should take place.

Second, one would predict that this effect would be more noticeable for the younger, as compared with the older, sibling in that the latter is more powerful and is more able to differentiate his own from his sibling's role.

Procedures

Our description of procedures must of necessity be broken into two parts. The first consists of a brief description of the procedures in Helen Koch's original study; complete details are available in the publications cited previously. The second consists of our mode of further analysis of the reported data.

In her series of papers Koch has reported results from a major research project concerned with the relation between structural characteristics of the family (sex of child, sex of sibling, ordinal position of child) and the child's ratings on more than fifty personality traits. In her study, all 384 subjects were obtained from the Chicago public schools and one large private school. The characteristics of the children used as subjects can be summarized as follows. All children were from unbroken, native-born, white, urban, two-child families. The children were five- and six-year-olds, free of any gross physical or mental defect. In most cases only one sibling in a family was a subject in the study.

Teachers' ratings were made for each child on 58 traits. The relation between personality trait ratings and the structure of the family from which the children came was assessed by Koch for each of the 58 traits. It is this data on which we made our further study.

The procedures for the further analysis involved several steps. First, each of the 58 traits was judged in terms of its pertinence to either a masculine or feminine role. Our conception of the characteristics of the two sex roles was based on recent empirical studies describing sex-role differences in small problem-solving groups (Strodtbeck and Mann, 1956) and in the nuclear family (Zelditch, 1955), and on the major theoretical treatment of such differences by Talcott Parsons (1955). In these studies the now-familiar distinction between the instrumental or task role and the expressive or socio-emotional role in a social group is shown to be related to sex-role differentiation, particularly in the family, with the male customarily taking the instrumental role and the female the expressive role. Hence in the judging process our decision as to whether a trait was masculine or feminine was essentially dependent on whether we believed the trait to belong to the instrumental or expressive role respectively.

Substantial descriptive data are available on sex-role differences in children for some of the traits which we judged. These findings, summarized by Terman and Tyler (1954), were consulted after the judging was completed and strongly corroborate our assignment of traits: e.g., male children are judged higher on traits we believed instrumental, such as dominance and aggression, and lower on traits we judged to pertain to the expressive role, such as affection and absence of negativism.

In judging the traits it was recognized that many of them would be part of the role requirements for both roles. It was, however, possible to assign 31 of the 58 traits to either the instrumental or expressive role. Some examples of expressive traits are: affectionateness, obedience, sympathy, cheerfulness, kindness, and friendliness. Some examples of instrumental traits are: tenacity, aggressiveness, ambition, originality, competitiveness, and self-confidence.

Results and Discussion. The data presented in Table 1 can be brought to bear upon our hypotheses by considering the distribution by subgroups of the masculinity and femininity scores. With respect to our first hypothesis, that through interaction and taking the role of the other the cross-sex sibs would have more traits of the opposite sex than would same-sex sibs, an examination of the distribution in Table 1 shows that this is clearly the case. The older girl with a younger brother has a higher masculinity score than does her counterpart, the older girl with a younger sister. This is even more pronounced for the girls in the second ordinal position, the younger girl with older brother being substantially higher on masculinity than her counterpart with an older sister. One will note that the acquisition of male traits does not reduce the femininity scores of the girls with brothers. As a matter of fact, a higher masculinity score seems to be associated with a higher femininity score. It therefore appears that certain feminine traits may be accentuated in order to compensate for the heightening of the masculine traits.

TABLE 1

Masculinity and Femininity Scores*
of Five- and Six-Year-Old Children

	Masculinity Score	Femininity Score
GIRLS		
With younger sister	11	58
With younger brother	38	67
With older sister	10	63
With older brother	41	89
BOYS		
With younger brother	58	0
With younger sister	53	11
With older brother	60	18
With older sister	42	49

* [Scores are derived from the original data by subtracting the number of low masculine traits from the number of high masculine traits for the preliminary masculinity score. A similar procedure was followed with the feminine traits to obtain the preliminary femininity score. Forty-one was then added to each score in order to eliminate negative numbers, and 20 was subtracted from the girls' masculinity scores while 20 was added to the boys' masculinity scores in order to compensate for certain biases noted by Brim in the teachers' ratings. This considerably simplifies the presentation of the data, but the original article should be consulted by anyone who wants additional details.—ED.]

Examination of Table 1 shows that the first hypothesis holds for boys also. While not pronounced for boys in the eldest child position, the boy with the sister is feminine to a greater degree than the boy with the brother. For the boys who are second-born, the difference is clear: the boy with the older sister is substantially more feminine than his counterpart with an older brother. For the boy with the older sister the acquisition of feminine traits would seem to have displaced his masculinity and he thus contrasts with the girls for whom this did not occur. We can offer no explanation for this, but it may provide a lead for further study in this area.

In connection with this result, the role of the parent requires attention. While all would agree that parents actively assist cross-sex sibs in separating their sex roles, the data show they are unsuccessful in completely arresting the process of assimilation. Perhaps in earlier times, when children's sex roles were stressed more strongly, and perhaps today for some parents making an extreme effort, the effects of interaction would be reduced. However, it certainly appears that the average parent today cannot completely avoid the effects of such sib interaction. Even were more attention given by parents to cross-sex as opposed to same-sex sibs in this matter, we believe that the tremendously greater cross-sex interaction of the former would leave its mark.

With respect to our second hypothesis, that because of differences in control of rewards and punishments and in ability to discriminate between self and other roles the effects of role-taking would be more pronounced for the younger child, an examination of Table 1 again seems to support the hypothesis. While the younger, as contrasted with the older, girl with a brother manifests only a slightly greater degree of masculinity, this difference for boys is quite striking: the younger, as contrasted with the older, boy with a sister is substantially more feminine.

To conclude, our analysis of Koch's data indicates that cross-sex siblings tend to assimilate traits of the opposite sex, and that this effect is most pronounced in the younger of the two siblings. These findings support the role-learning theory presented here, and also stand as a substantive contribution to the area of sex-role learning.

We wish now to stress two points mentioned earlier. First, these findings must be subject to strict limitations to two-child families. Not only does the Fauls and Smith study demonstrate this limitation with regard to only-child families, but observation suggests that in larger families other variables come into play; e.g., in the four-child family with a three and one sex split, parents may actively help the solitary child in differentiating sex roles; or in the four-child family with a two and two split, siblings may pair off by sex and the cross-sex role-taking effect is minimized.

Second, with respect to the substantive value of these results, we would point out that even though parents must remain as the major source of sex-role learning, almost every child has a mother and father to learn from. Hence the *variations* in type and amount of sex-role learning occur on top of this base, so to speak, and in this variability the effect of a same or a cross-sex sib may play as large or larger a role than variations in parental behavior, mixed versus single-sexed schooling, sex of neighborhood playmates, and the like. Speculations on the durable and considerable effects of sex of sib on sex-role learning thus seem warranted and lead one to consider problems such as the effect of sex of sibling on one's later role in the marital relation, on career choices, and on other correlates of the adult sex role.

Summary

This paper reports some relations between ordinal position, sex of sibling, and sex-role learning by children in two-child families. The findings are based on a further analysis of Koch's data. In the present analysis the personality traits were classified as pertaining either to the instrumental (masculine) role or the expressive (feminine) role. The distribution of such traits in children as a correlate of family structure was then assessed.

General propositions describing role learning in terms of interaction with others, including taking the role of the other, leads to hypotheses that cross-sex siblings will have more traits of the opposite sex than will same-sex siblings, and that this effect will be greater for the younger, as contrasted with the older, sibling. Both hypotheses are confirmed by the data presented.

REFERENCES

BRIM, O. G., JR., "The Parent-Child Relation as a Social System: I. Parent and Child Roles," *Child Development*, 1957, 28, 344–364.

COTTRELL, L. S., JR., "The Analysis of Situational Fields in Social Psychology," *American Sociological Review*, 1942, 7, 370–382.

FAULS, L. B., and W. D. SMITH, "Sex Role Learning of Five-Year-Olds," *Journal of Genetic Psychology*, 1956, 89, 105–117.

KOCH, H. L., "The Relation of 'Primary Mental Abilities' in Five- and Six-Year-Olds to Sex of Child and Characteristics of His Sibling," *Child Development*, 1954, 25, 209–223.

KOCH, H. L., "Some Personality Correlates of Sex, Sibling Position, and Sex of Sibling Among Five- and Six-Year-Old Children," *Genetic Psychology Monographs*, 1955, 52, 3–50.

KOCH, H. L., "The Relation of Certain Family Constellation Characteristics and the Attitudes of Children Toward Adults," *Child Development,* 1955, 26, 13–40.

KOCH, H. L., "Attitudes of Children Toward Their Peers as Related to Certain Characteristics of Their Sibling," *Psychological Monographs,* 1956, 70, No. 19 (whole No. 426).

KOCH, H. L., "Children's Work Attitudes and Sibling Characteristics," *Child Development,* 1956, 27, 289–310.

KOCH, H. L., "Sibling Influence on Children's Speech," *Journal of Speech and Hearing Disorders,* 1956, 21, 322–328.

KOCH, H. L., "Sissiness and Tomboyishness in Relation to Sibling Characteristics," *Journal of Genetic Psychology,* 1956, 88, 231–244.

PARSONS, T., "Family Structure and the Socialization of the Child," in T. Parsons and R. F. Bales, *Family, Socialization and Interaction Process,* Glencoe, Illinois: Free Press, 1955.

PAYNE, D. E., and P. H. MUSSEN, "Parent-Child Relations and Father Identification Among Adolescent Boys," *Journal of Abnormal and Social Psychology,* 1956, 52, 358–362.

SEARS, P. S., "Child-Rearing Factors Related to Playing of Sex-Typed Roles," *American Psychologist,* 1953, 8, 431 (abstract).

SEARS, R. R., M. H. PINTLER, and P. S. SEARS, "Effect of Father Separation on Preschool Children's Doll Play Aggression," *Child Development,* 1946, 17, 219–243.

STRAUSS, A., *The Social Psychology of George Herbert Mead,* Chicago: Phoenix Books, University of Chicago Press, 1956.

STRODTBECK, F. L., and R. D. MANN, "Sex Role Differentiation in Jury Deliberations," *Sociometry,* 1956, 19, 3–11.

TERMAN, L. M., and L. E. TYLER, "Psychological Sex Differences," in L. Carmichael (ed.), *Manual of Child Psychology* (2d ed.), New York: Wiley, 1954.

ZELDITCH, M., JR., "Role Differentiation in the Nuclear Family: A Comparative Study," in T. Parsons and R. F. Bales, *Family, Socialization and Interaction Process,* Glencoe, Illinois: Free Press, 1955.

by D A V I D   R I E S M A N , *with* N A T H A N
G L A Z E R *and* R E U E L   D E N N E Y

1. The Peer-Group in the Stage of Inner-Direction

With the decline of the extended kinship family (the type of tradition-directed family that may include uncles, aunts, cousins, and other relatives), the child is often confronted in the inner-directed home with the close oppressiveness of idealized parents. He may compete with his brothers and sisters for the parents' favors, or to ward off their disapprobation. In theory the children in a family can unite against tyrannical parents, but, judging from the novels, it is more likely that parents divide and rule. Children in a family cannot react as a peer-group because of the age differentials among them. Consequently any given child at any single moment faces obviously unique problems and is alone with them—barring the luck of a sympathetic maid or aunt.

The fate of many inner-directed children is therefore loneliness in and outside the home. Home, school, and way-stations between may be places for hazing, persecution, misunderstanding. No adult intervenes on behalf of the lonely or hazed child to proffer sympathy, ask questions, or give advice. Adults do not think children's play is very important anyway; they will criticize children who seem too much concerned with play and too little with work. No sociometrically inclined teacher will try to break up friendship cliques in school to see that no one is left out. How savagely snobbish boys and girls can be is typified by the story, in the Lynd's *Middletown,* of the daughter who quit high school because her mother could not

Reprinted from David Riesman, with Nathan Glazer and Reuel Denney, *The Lonely Crowd,* New Haven: Yale University Press, abridged ed., 1961, pp. 66, 69–76. With permission of the publisher.

of three- and four-year-olds, just as, in earlier eras, the adults managed marriages. Hence, while "self-demand" feeding schedules are gaining ground for infants, self-demand is not observed when it comes to socialization outside the home. The daily schedule is an effort, with mother as chauffeur and booking agent, to cultivate all the currently essential talents, especially the gregarious ones. It is inconceivable to some supervising adults that a child might prefer his own company or that of just one other child.

The child is thus confronted by what we have termed his socio-metric peers and is not surrounded by those who are his peers in less visible matters, such as temperament and taste. Yet since there are no *visible* differences he finds it difficult to justify, even to be aware of, these *invisible* differences. On the overt level the situation is highly standardized: any given child faces the culture of the fives or the sixes at a particular moment of the fashion cycle in child-training and child-amusement practices. Indeed it is this very standardization which, as we saw, weakens the power of the parents, whose deviation from the standards is felt by them and by the child to demonstrate their inexperience and inadequacy. In this setting the adults are anxious that the child succeed in the peer-group and therefore are concerned with his "adjustment." They, too, tend to ignore and even suppress invisible differences between their child and the children of others. Such differences might cast doubt on their own adjustment, their own correct tuning to the signals concerning child rearing.

The majority of children learn very fast under these conditions; the same adult authorities who patronize children's intellects (and therefore slow them down) are perhaps not sufficiently impressed with how poised in many social situations modern other-directed children are. These children are not shy, either with adults or with the opposite sex whom they have accompanied to proms and parties and seen daily in and out of school. This adaptability, more-over, prepares the child for a type of social mobility somewhat different from the social-climbing experiences of the parvenu in an inner-directed environment. The latter only rarely acquired the intellectual and social graces of his new associates—or he ridicu-lously accentuated them. He either kept his rough and lowly man-ners or painfully tried to learn new ones as he moved up; in either case the standard, limited code of conduct expected of him was

afford to give her silk stockings. Often the children, unawai
they have rights to friendship, understanding, or agreeable p
unaware, indeed, that the adults could be greatly interested in
matters—suffer in silence and submit to the intolerable.

Only with the perspective of today can we see the advantag
these disadvantages. We can see that in a society which values in
direction, loneliness and even persecution are not thought of as
worst of fates. Parents, sometimes even teachers, may have crush
moral authority, but the peer-group has less moral weight, glam
ous or menacing though it may be. While adults seldom interv
to guide and help the child, neither do they tell him that he sho
be part of a crowd and *must* have fun.

II. *The Peer Group in the Stage of Other-Direction*

The parents in the era dominated by other-direction lose thei
once undisputed role; the old man is no longer "the governor"—an
the installer of governors. Other adult authorities such as th
governess and grandmother either almost disappear or, like the
teacher, take on the new role of peer-group facilitator and mediator
—a role not too different from that of many clergymen who, in the
adult congregation, move from morality to morale.

As already indicated, moreover, the city in which the other-
directed child grows up is large enough, and stratified enough—
taking into account its ring of suburbs—to create an age- and class-
graded group for him. It will be possible to put him into school and
playground, and camp in the summer, with other children of
virtually the same age and social position. If the adults are the
judge, these peers are the jury. And, as in America the judge is
hemmed in by rules which give the jury a power it has in no other
common-law land, so the American peer-group, too, cannot be
matched for power throughout the middle-class world.

The Trial. While the inner-directed parent frequently forced the
pace of the child in its home "duties," as, for example, in cleanliness and toilet-training habits, the other-directed parent, more apt
to be permissive in such matters, forces the pace, with like im-
patience, in the child's social life, though often hardly aware of
doing so. Parents today are the stage managers for the meetings

unequivocal. In contrast with this the other-directed child is able to move among new associates with an almost automatic adjustment to the subtlest insignia of status.

Bearing in mind these positive achievements of other-directed sociability, let us turn our attention from what the peer-group teaches and evokes to what it represses. Today six-year-olds and up have a phrase—"he [or she] thinks he's *big*" (or "he thinks he's *something*")—which symbolizes the role of the peer-group in the creation of other-directed types. The effort is to cut everyone down to size who stands up or stands out in any direction. Beginning with the very young and going on from there, overt vanity is treated as one of the worst offenses, as perhaps dishonesty would have been in an earlier day. Being high-hat is forbidden.

Temper, manifest jealousy, moodiness—these, too, are offenses in the code of the peer-group. All knobby or idiosyncratic qualities and vices are more or less eliminated or repressed. And judgments of others by peer-group members are so clearly matters of taste that their expression has to resort to the vaguest phrases, constantly changed: cute, lousy, square, darling, good guy, honey, swell, bitch (without precise meaning), etc. Sociometry reflects this situation when it asks children about such things as whom they like to sit next to or not to sit next to, to have for a friend, a leader, and so on. The judgments can be meaningfully scaled because, and only because, they are all based on uncomplicated continua of taste, on which the children are constantly ranking each other.

But to say that judgments of peer-groupers are matters of taste, not of morality or even opportunism, is not to say that any particular child can afford to ignore these judgments. On the contrary he is, as never before, at their mercy. If the peer-group were—and we continue to deal here with the urban middle classes only—a wild, torturing, obviously vicious group, the individual child might still feel moral indignation as a defense against its commands. But like adult authorities in the other-directed socialization process, the peer-group is friendly and tolerant. It stresses fair play. Its conditions for entry seem reasonable and well meaning. But even where this is not so, moral indignation is out of fashion. The child is therefore exposed to trial by jury without any defenses either from the side of its own morality or from the adults. All the morality is the group's. Indeed, even the fact that it is a morality is concealed by the confusing notion that the function of the group is to have fun, to play; the deadly seriousness of the business, which might justify the child in making an issue of it, is therefore hidden.

"The Talk of the Town": The Socialization of Preferences. In the eyes of the jury of peers one may be a good guy one day, a stinker the next. Toleration, let alone leadership, depends on having a highly sensitive response to swings of fashion. This ability is sought in several ways. One way is to surrender any claim to independence of judgment and taste—a kind of plea of *nolo contendere*. Another is to build a plea for special consideration by acquiring unusual facility in one's duties as a consumer—in performance, that is, of the leisurely arts. With good luck one may even become a taste and opinion leader, with great influence over the jury.

Each particular peer-group has its fandoms and lingoes. Safety consists not in mastering a difficult craft but in mastering a battery of consumer preferences and the mode of their expression. The preferences are for articles or "heroes" of consumption and for members of the group itself. The proper mode of expression requires feeling out with skill and sensitivity the probable tastes of the others and then swapping mutual likes and dislikes to maneuver intimacy.

Now some of this is familiar even in the period depending on inner-direction; it is important, therefore, to realize the degree to which training in consumer taste has replaced training in etiquette. Formal etiquette may be thought of as a means of handling relations with people with whom one does not seek intimacy. It is particularly useful when adults and young, men and women, upper classes and lower classes, are sharply separated and when a code is necessary to mediate exchanges across these lines. Thus etiquette can be at the same time a means of approaching people and of staying clear of them. For some, etiquette may be a matter of little emotional weight—an easy behavioral cloak; for others the ordering of human relations through etiquette can become highly charged emotionally—an evidence of characterological compulsiveness. But in either case etiquette is concerned not with encounters between individuals as such but with encounters between them as representatives of their carefully graded social roles.

In comparison with this, training in consumer taste, which tends to replace etiquette among the other-directed, is useful not so much across age and social class lines as within the jury room of one's age and class peers. As in some groups—children as well as adults —discussion turns to the marginal differentiation between Cadillacs and Lincolns, so in other groups discussion centers on Fords and Chevrolets. What matters in either case is an ability at continual sniffing out of others' tastes, often a far more intrusive process than the exchange of courtesies and pleasantries required by etiquette. Not, of course, that the child always gets close to the others with whom he is exchanging and ratifying preferences—these exchanges are often mere gossip about goods. Yet a certain emotional energy, even excitement, permeates the transaction. For one thing, the other-directed person acquires an intense interest in the ephemeral tastes of the "others"—an interest inconceivable to the tradition-directed or inner-directed child whose tastes have undergone a less differentiated socialization. For another thing, the other-directed child is concerned with learning from these interchanges whether his radar equipment is in proper order.

It has alway been true in social classes dominated by fashion that to escape being left behind by a swing of fashion requires the ability to adopt new fashions rapidly; to escape the danger of a conviction for being different from the "others" requires that one can be different—in look and talk and manner—from *oneself* as one was yesterday. Here, also, it is necessary to see precisely what has changed. In general the processes of fashion are expanded in class terms and speeded in time terms. In the leisure economy of incipient population decline the distributive machinery of society improves, in terms of both distribution of income and of commodities. It becomes possible to accelerate swings of fashion as well as to differentiate goods by very minute gradients. For, in its late stages, mass production and mass distribution permit and require a vast increase not only in quantity but in qualitative differences among products—not only as a consequence of monopolistic efforts at marginal differentiation but also because the machinery and organization are present for rapidly designing, producing, and distributing a wide variety of goods.

This means that the consumer trainee has a lot more to learn than in the early days of industrialization. To take one example, the foreigner who visits America is likely to think that salesgirls, society ladies, and movie actresses all dress alike, as compared with the clear status differences of Europe. But the American knows—has to know if he is to get along in life and love—that this is simply an error: that one must look for small qualitative differences that signify style and status, to observe for instance the strained casualness sometimes found in upper-class dress as against the strained formality of working-class dress. In the days of etiquette the differences were far more sharp.

One must listen to quite young children discussing television models, automobile styling, or the merits of various streamliners to see how gifted they are as consumers long before they have a decisive say themselves—though their influence in family councils must not be underestimated. Children join in this exchange of verdicts even if their parents cannot afford the gadgets under discussion; indeed, the economy would slow down if only those were trained as consumers who at any given moment had the wherewithal.

The wider ambit of socialization of taste today is shown in still another decisive change from the era depending on inner-direction. Then, by the rules of etiquette and class, certain spheres of life were regarded as private: it was a breach of etiquette to intrude or permit intrusion on them. Today, however, one must be prepared to open up on cross-examination almost any sphere in which the peer-group may become interested. It may become fashionable, as some articles in the "Profile of Youth" series in the *Ladies' Home Journal* have shown, for young girls to discuss their rivals' necking techniques with their particular partner.* While the game of post office is old, the breakdown of privacy for reasonably serious love-making is new. Dating at twelve and thirteen, the child is early made aware of the fact that his taste in emotions as well as in consumer goods must be socialized and available for small talk. Whereas etiquette built barriers between people, socialized exchange of consumer taste requires that privacy either be given up, or be kept, like a liberal theologian's God, in some interstices of one's nature. Before the peer-group jury there is no privilege against self-incrimination.

* A student has written me: "In male bull sessions one can no longer play the gentleman and keep quiet about sexual adventures. He has to furnish names, dates, and all the exact details of the conquest. Where fellows get into trouble is when they have a sincere feeling for a girl and yet are forced to tell. The measure of the peer-group's strength and their other-directedness is that they *can* be forced to tell."

Six

EXTENDED KINSHIP RELATIONSHIPS

✺ INTRODUCTION ✺

There are many different role relationships within family and kinship groups. The socialization of children, economic cooperation, and the sexual and reproductive functions are carried out within these groups. At times, the nuclear family of husband, wife, and children is the major repository of these functions; at other times extended kinship groups share some of these functions. In addition, members of the extended family may have an influence upon the members of a nuclear family. As a consequence, a study of the family should pay attention (in addition to marital, sibling, and parent-child relationships) to relations between extended kinsmen: uncle and nephew, for example, or grandmother and grandson, or various in-law relationships.

Kinship Responsibilities

With so many kinship relationships, each individual is liable to face a situation of kinship role conflict. If called upon by various kinsmen for financial support that he cannot provide out of his limited resources he may have to decide where the priorities lie; or he may be called upon for emotional support from two conflicting kinsmen. How is he to choose between two kinsmen under such circumstances? (Or how is he to choose between a kinsman and a close friend?) This kinship role conflict problem is especially in evidence with respect to the possible claims of a person's nuclear family of orientation and his nuclear family of procreation. Conflicting claims upon a person's loyalty can be particularly disturbing here because of the strong ties that are usually established within both these nuclear families. A solution to such potential role conflict is ordinarily worked out culturally—for example, a man's major loyalty in traditional Chinese society was to his parents, while a man's major loyalty in the United States is to his spouse. Since the solution is culturally patterned, a person does not have to face up to conflicting claims upon his loyalty without any guidelines as to what he should do. There is a ready-made solution available.

Cultural guidelines, however, are not always very clear. In addition, they do not always apply unambiguously to the specific circumstances a person may face. Moreover, different groups within the same society may hold very different cultural expectations. For example, what are the responsibilities of adult children to their aged parents in Western societies? The aged cannot command respect by virtue of their position, in the way that this is often possible in other societies (Simmons, 1952). Nevertheless, adult children usually do show considerable responsibility in their relationships with their parents, albeit with much ethnic, regional, and individual variation (Dinkel, 1944; Brown, 1952; Garigue, 1956; Cullingworth, 1960; Young and Geertz, 1961; *15; 18*).

The following generalizations about the relationships between parents and their married children appear to be well established: (1) There is a great deal of social contact and mutual aid between parents and the families of their married children. (2) The flow of financial aid goes mainly from parents to the families of their married children, especially during the early years of marriage. (3) The norm, however, is strongly in the direction of financial and residential independence for married children as well as for their parents (Sussman and Burchinal, 1962a, 1962b). A residence is therefore ordinarily shared only under special circumstances; and financial aid is often given in disguised form: for example, as expensive gifts for special occasions.

There are times, however, when the law is not in accord with the normative patterns that have developed regarding parent-child relations, or other aspects of family life. This is true, at least in some measure, with regard to such matters as sexual relations, birth control, abortion, and divorce (St. John-Stevas, 1960; Harper and Skolnick, 1962; Ploscowe and Freed, 1963; Pilpel and Zavin, 1964), and Kinsey *et al.* (1953), for example, were very much concerned about the backwardness of many laws. An example of such a law is provided by Schorr (*15*). He asks about the impact of the legal requirement that adult children support their parents, despite the norm of financial independence. In view of the evidence, it is clear that a good deal of help is voluntarily provided by children to elderly parents in need—under such circumstances the norm of financial independence is probably reversed, and calls for aid from the children. But aid is not always provided voluntarily, and the legal requirement to support parents is therefore usually enforced upon those who can least afford it. This has the effect of maintaining poverty from one generation to another by taking funds away from those who desperately need the funds if they are ever to escape from poverty. Schorr's article is therefore an interesting sidelight not only on parental relations with adult children, but also on one aspect of the system of social stratification and of the current American "war" against poverty. It shows that the poor are hampered by legal considerations in addition to the social, economic, and political deprivations they face.

Kinship Terms

The kinship terms that are used by kinsmen may be indicative of the nature of their relationship (in the same way that the terms of address used between a student and instructor may be indicative of the nature of that relationship; cf. Frumkin, 1964). We would expect differences in the relationship if a child addresses his father by his first name, by the term "Dad," or the term "Sir." Knowledge of the terms of address used, however, usually cannot tell us a great deal about a relationship because there are only a small number of terms to characterize a limitless variety of relationships. It is therefore helpful to know not only what terms are used but also *why* certain terms are or are not used in particular situations.

In Western societies there is a good deal of selectivity among one's kinsmen. A person may have many different kin with whom he can maintain relationships, but he typically maintains a strong relationship with only a certain number of these kin. Mogey (1956) points out that "acceptance or rejection of kinship ties is permissive in England" and that "kinship is regarded as a purely personal affair." Similarly, in the United States, a strong personal element enters into the choice of the kinsmen with whom one associates (*17; 18*), and such a choice is often made on the basis of shared interests and values (Zimmerman and Cervantes, 1960). Michel (1959), Mogey (1962), Pitts (1964), and others have pointed out the way in which the relationship to extended kinsmen takes on a friend-like aspect, while relationships to friends take an a kin-like aspect, so that one may find it difficult, simply by looking at the interaction that takes place, to distinguish between close friends and close relatives.

The selection by Schneider and Homans (*17*) gives evidence of the personal element that enters into the relationship with uncles and aunts. This is shown through a consideration of the different terms of address that are used for uncles and aunts. For example, where the relationship is highly charged positively or negatively, the first name alone may be used as a term of address—in the first instance to indicate especially friendly feelings, and in the second to indicate a lack of respect. This is a particularly good example of the limited extent to which we can rely upon a kinship term alone for our information about a relationship, because the same term (the use of the first name) is used in diametrically opposite types of relationships.

Shlien (*16*) also deals with an extended kinship relationship through considering the terms of address that may be used. He points out that there are no standardized terms to draw upon in addressing a mother-in-law. As a result there is much confusion and misunderstanding, and frequently no term at all is used, unless one wants to characterize "Uh" as an all-purpose term of address! (In the same way a student may not use any term of address toward certain of his instructors, because he feels that the first name is too familiar and that "Mr." or "Professor" is too formal.) The general implication is that it is usually much easier for members of a society to be able to draw upon culturally acceptable solutions to perennial kinship problems. For example, a couple is not usually faced with a difficult decision about where to live upon marriage (patrilocally, matrilocally, or neolocally) because there is a cultural rule that they follow in this connection. In the United States they are expected to live neolocally—away from both sets of parents. Does this mean that having a standardized term of address for mothers-in-law would ease this in-law relationship? Since the term of address used is only one aspect of the relationship it does not follow that agreement upon a term would lead to a satisfactory relationship. Shlien, however, does give an interesting example of how compelling a problem over the term of address can be, and of how drastically a relationship can change once this problem is solved. Goody (1962) cites R. W. Chapman regarding a solution to the problem of what to call the mother-in-law that is very similar to the solution illustrated by Shlien: "If I am obliged to name my mother-in-law direct, I call her, by invitation, *'Granny'*; a solution not wholly satisfactory, but made possible by a nursery atmosphere."

Extended Kin Relations: Revival or Rediscovery?

There has been a great deal of recent research into the nature of extended kinship relationships in urban industrial society. As a consequence, it has been well established that such relationships are very common, and that we must pay attention to them as well as to the relationships within the nuclear family. Have extensive relationships with members of the extended family been in existence all along, and is it that researchers have just rediscovered them? Or is it that there has been a revival of such relationships? We simply do not know. Most researchers imply that it is a rediscovery rather than a revival. Reiss (*18*), however, in summarizing much of the data about extended family relationships in the United States, takes a different position. He acknowledges that his position is debatable, but he does point to a number of factors that indicate an intensified degree of extended family relationships in the United States. His article, in addition, tells us about the nature of extended kinship relationships in the United States, and about certain factors, such as distance, degree of relationship, and personal interests, that account for some of the variation in these relationships (cf. Bott, 1957).

Reiss draws an interesting parallel between his commentary on nuclear and extended families and the "three-generation hypothesis" of Hansen (1952) and Herberg (1955) in the religious area. According to Hansen and Herberg, first-generation immigrants were still attached to the religion and values of the old country and were looked down upon by "native" Americans; second-generation immigrants were aware of the social handicaps of immigrant status, and therefore shed many of the old-country values, including their strong religious affiliations; third-generation immigrants, being more securely placed as Americans and seeking cultural roots in an industrialized society, began to return to the cultural heritage of their grandparents, and developed closer ties with their church than their parents had. Lazerwitz and Rowitz (1964) have presented some data that partially support the Hansen-Herberg hypothesis, particularly for the religious affiliations of Catholic men. (This is an indication, of course, that when we test an idea with empirical data we may not get "clean" results, and differences may be found as between men and women, different religious groups, etc.) The novel idea put forward by Reiss is that the nuclear family in the United States once was more isolated from kin than at present. On first coming to the United States, ties to members of one's extended family were usually very close. But social and geographic mobility made it desirable to develop a greater degree of independence for the nuclear family. The independence of the nuclear family, however, was not yet normatively established. As a result, it became necessary to make a thorough break with one's family in order to maintain one's independence. However, as the norm of nuclear family independence became established, it was no longer necessary to make such a break, and it was possible to maintain strong ties with members of one's extended family without threatening the independence of the nuclear family (cf. 22, pp. 275-276).

REFERENCES

BOTT, ELIZABETH. 1957. *Family and Social Network,* London: Tavistock Publications.

BROWN, JAMES S. 1952. "The Conjugal Family and the Extended Family Group," *American Sociological Review,* XVII, 297-306.

CULLINGWORTH, J. B. 1960. "Social Implications of Overspill: The Worsley Social Survey," *Sociological Review,* VIII, 77-96.

DINKEL, ROBERT M. 1944. "Attitudes of Children Toward Supporting Aged Parents," *American Sociological Review,* IX, 370-379.

FRUMKIN, ROBERT M. 1964. "Titles and the Professor," *Improving College and University Teaching*, XII, 203–205.

GARIGUE, P. 1956. "French Canadian Kinship and Urban Life," *American Anthropologist*, LVIII, 1090–1101.

GOODY, JACK. 1962. "On Nannas and Nannies," *Man*, LXII, 179–184.

HANSEN, MARCUS L. 1952. "The Third Generation in America," *Commentary*, XIV, 492–500.

HARPER, FOWLER V., and JEROME H. SKOLNICK, eds. 1962. *Problems of the Family*, rev. ed., Indianapolis: Bobbs-Merrill.

HERBERG, WILL. 1955. *Protestant–Catholic–Jew*, Garden City, N.Y.: Doubleday.

KINSEY, ALFRED C., *et al.* 1953. *Sexual Behavior in the Human Female*, Philadelphia: Saunders.

LAZERWITZ, BERNARD, and LOUIS ROWITZ. 1964. "The Three-Generations Hypothesis," *American Journal of Sociology*, LXIX, 529–538.

MICHEL, ANDRÉE. 1959. *Famille, Industrialisation, Logement*, Paris: CNRS.

MOGEY, JOHN M. 1956. *Family and Neighbourhood: Two Studies in Oxford*, London: Oxford University Press.

———. 1962. "Introduction," *International Social Science Journal*, XIV, 411–424.

PILPEL, HARRIET F., and THEODORA ZAVIN. 1964. *Your Marriage and the Law*, New York: Collier Books.

PITTS, JESSE R. 1964. "The Structural–Functional Approach to the Family," in Harold T. Christensen, ed., *Handbook on Marriage and the Family*, Chicago: Rand McNally.

PLOSCOWE, MORRIS, and DORIS J. FREED. 1963. *Family Law: Cases and Materials*, Boston: Little, Brown.

ST. JOHN-STEVAS, NORMAN. 1960. *Birth Control and Public Policy*, Santa Barbara, Calif.: Center for the Study of Democratic Institutions.

SIMMONS, LEO W. 1952. "Social Participation of the Aged in Different Cultures," *The Annals of the American Academy of Political and Social Science*, CCLXXIX, 43–51.

SUSSMAN, MARVIN B., and LEE BURCHINAL. 1962a. "Kin Family Network: Unheralded Structure in Current Conceptualizations of Family Functioning," *Marriage and Family Living*, XXIV, 231–240.

———. 1962b. "Parental Aid to Married Children: Implications for Family Functioning," *Marriage and Family Living*, XXIV, 320–332.

YOUNG, MICHAEL, and HILDRED GEERTZ. 1961. "Old Age in London and San Francisco: Some Families Compared," *British Journal of Sociology*, XII, 124–141.

ZIMMERMAN, CARLE C., and LUCIUS F. CERVANTES, S. J. 1960. *Successful American Families*, New York: Pageant Press.

‒§ 15 §‒ Filial Responsibility and the Aging

by A L V I N   L .   S C H O R R

Attitudes about the responsibility of adult children for their aging parents are rooted in personal ideas about family relationships and social goals. This broad frame of reference is seldom clarified, however, in discussions of filial responsibility. It is possible, even likely, that differences of opinion about the administrative difficulties in enforcing children's responsibility, for example, arise from deeper differences. Let us, therefore, examine this frame of reference with some care.

Image of the Family

There are two kinds of things to say about the frame of reference into which we fit filial responsibility. The first has to do with our image of the American family. The term "image" is used with premeditation to suggest a perception that may or may not be accurate, that is manipulable, and that is used by a profession or a business to advance its own interests. We have possibly become too charmed with images. The great danger is in dealing with them as if their tie to facts is not consequential; what matters is whether an image serves our purposes or someone else's. The image of the American family that is commonly held is an example of this separation of image from fact. Though fantasy can be pleasant, in this case it may be a major single factor in perpetuating relatives' responsibility laws.

Adapted from *Journal of Home Economics,* LIV, April, 1962, 271–276; and *Social Security Bulletin,* XXV, May, 1962, 4–9. With permission of the author and the American Home Economics Association. The article was originally written for public welfare workers.

What shape does this image take? The American family is deteriorating! In what was once a family-centered society, industrialization and urbanization have separated our old people from their children and everyone from his home. Margaret Mead announces the end of the war of the sexes—women have attained emancipation and need not struggle further. Suffragists may applaud, but equality leaves men and women uncertain about sex roles. The age of permissiveness was ushered in by Freud. We pay for its glories with character disorders in adults and—who knows—delinquency in children. Our civilization has become so complex that all of us feel adrift, uncertain of our purposes, unable even to achieve genuine intimacy. The man who survives the driving thirties, the dangerous forties, and the frantic fifties may live to be 65—and aged! What awaits him? His children—anxious, ambitious, and hedonistic—have neither time nor material support to offer.

This description is a bit of a caricature, but with small changes it would make a sober, persuasive, and typical description of the American family. Though each of the parts of this description contains an insight that is valid, much as the whale contained Jonah, in sum it is chiefly interesting for clinical purposes—as a symptom of the anxiety with which we view ourselves and of the ease and inaccuracy with which we generalize. The flat statement that the American family is deteriorating cannot be supported. The family *is changing.* Some of the changes may be bad, and others are all to the good. As far as the relations of older men and women and their children are concerned, to say that the net effect is on the debit side is a distortion.

The Changing Family. A review of some of the changes in the American family should be helpful. The greatest change of all, of course, is that so many persons live to be old. It would be a rash man who would suggest that this is a change for the worse. At the same time, it must be apparent that the doubling or tripling of the aged population creates a problem of income maintenance, even if nothing else in family relationships changes.

This growth in the number of the aged has been going on for the past century or longer. So, too, there has been a steady, long-run shift from a property-centered to a wage-centered economy.

When a parent owned his handicraft tools or farm he had an income, whoever did the work, but gradually his income has become dependent on selling a marketable skill that can evaporate. Here is a change that has produced a new problem of support and that one may evaluate as unfortunate. (A rural, handicraft society would be a lot further from reaching the moon, to be sure.) On the other hand, it may not be said that the adult child once supported his father because he cared for him and that today he does not. It is more exact to say that it was, many years ago, in the nature of the situation of many aged people that they commanded support. Today this is less often the case. If feelings or morality have much to do with the change, the evidence has yet to be presented.

A third change, considerably related to the shift to wages, is the ascendancy of the nuclear family. The nuclear family—a man, his wife, and their young children—is becoming as well-known as nuclear fallout and, to judge from the tone in which it is discussed, as unpopular. It is sometimes said that the larger families, including several generations and several degrees of relationship, became obsolete in response to the requirements of industrialization. One must be wary of reading this kind of direct purpose into our preference for nuclear families, but it is clear that small, mobile families work well in an industrial society.

The Real Family.   Now, the argument goes, since grandpa and grandma are no longer part of their children's family, they are forgotten, frequently lonesome, and in any case not supported. The main thing wrong with this argument is that it is not in accord with the facts. Part of it does appear to be true; adult children in the United States do not habitually make cash contributions to their parents. Perhaps 5 percent—certainly not more than 10 percent— of the aged get cash contributions in a given year from children with whom they do not live.[1]

Money is more likely to flow in the opposite direction.[2] Sussman and Burchinal, in reviewing available studies recently, concluded that "financial assistance appears generally to flow from parents to children."[3] It seems likely that it is chiefly the middle-aged parents who are giving to their children, but the reason that they give continues into their old age. In other words, an American parent is ambitious for his children and grandchildren, as they are for themselves. He is reluctant to take money from them if he believes that it interferes with their meeting their own needs. (And where is the family that feels it has enough money to meet its own needs?) Even when the parent is less ambitious for his children, he may prefer to do without such contributions and make some sacrifice in his standard of living so that he may keep his feeling of independence.

The older and younger generations are usually in agreement that, if a choice is to be made, the cash must be spent on the children. The aged do not, however, go without help. For obvious reasons, those who are most in need of help usually turn to adult children who have comparatively little to spare. The preferred method of helping that these families use is to share living quarters. For one thing, it leads to the most efficient use of money. For another, living together may provide the older person with natural ways of reciprocating—babysitting, help with housework, and so on. Often, the old people are also in need of nursing care or of benevolent supervision. Indeed, living together is more common with the parent's advancing age and ill health.

If the giving of cash is not a common pattern, living together is. Of the old people who have children, more than a third live with one child or another.[4] (It should be noted that helping the old person is only one reason for a family to live together; sometimes help goes the other way.) Others live together simply because they always have. There are as many old people living with their children today as the total number of old people who were alive as recently as 1920. This is something of a blow to the theory that nuclear families spin off their aging parents, careless of love and heedless of responsibility.

The intangibles that are exchanged between parents and their children—the feeling, the visiting, the marketing—are as important as the material exchanges. It is a common concept that the old are lonely, uncared for, and in fact, alone. Public welfare workers may have some excuse for thinking this, since the lonely and deserted loom larger in their caseloads than elsewhere.

Nevertheless, there is a growing body of solid evidence that this view is wide of the mark. As Ethel Shanas has observed, only 15 percent of all aged parents live more than a short ride from some child. About half live within walking distance or a short ride, and about a third live with a child. These figures are especially impressive if one considers the rate at which Americans move about and the fact that young families move most rapidly of all. Physical proximity aside, an exchange of services between the parents and their children—an exchange that is typically spontaneous and reciprocal—is noted in a number of studies. More than 2 out of 3 aged parents see their children at least weekly. When there are no visits, they keep in touch—perhaps daily—by telephone.[5] What of the help that children and parents give each other in emergencies? Quarantelli writes that disaster studies lend little support to the notion that the extended family is now of little importance. This group, he says, "is the preferred, sought, and major source of short and long term help in time of crises."[6]

One must conclude that the view that the American family is deteriorating is oversimplified and in error, at least so far as it concerns parents and their adult children. Obviously, this is not to say that there are no needy or lonely old people. The case for filial responsibility laws rests most firmly on a powerful feeling that frequently goes unstated. It is the feeling that families are falling apart and that somehow limits must be established. It is the feeling that morals and responsibility are dissolving everywhere and that somehow a halt must be called. It is the feeling that the government is being expected to do everything and that it cannot. The image of the American family described earlier, unreal though it is, aggravates these feelings. As long as this inaccurate, popular image of the family and this general, semiconscious feeling of deterioration support each other, no change is likely to occur.

Concept of Poverty

Filial responsibility has been discussed so far in the frame of reference of the American family. Let us shift now to consider filial responsibility in the context of poverty. There was a time not so long ago when poverty might have been defined as the absence of money. This definition is influenced perhaps by the Horatio Alger notion that, if money is lacking, with work and determination one provides it. Another definition of poverty may be more useful; a point about Horatio Alger will serve to introduce the definition.

The Alger Heroes. The Alger heroes had a lack of money that impresses one from the first pages of their story. Luke Larkin swept out his school twice a week to earn money to attend it. Ragged Dick shined a gentleman's shoes but couldn't make change for a quarter. It would be hard to be worse off than these street boys, but one should pause to count their blessings. They were white, these heroes of Horatio Alger. They came from homes with a proper, legal view of what a family is. Sometimes, if their fathers had died, they were left with anonymous but well-heeled guardians, who came through at crucial points. Because of their early training and associations, our heroes were polite and well-mannered. Only Phil the Fiddler was an Italian immigrant and could not even manage English. (By then some social workers had been talking to Horatio Alger and spoiled the purity of his story line, but only for one book.)

Horatio Alger's heroes had a solid early education. They had a degree of ambition that suggests they had seen the last pages of the book. As if this cornucopia of blessings were not enough, in the last act fortune favored them with a rich little girl to rescue from runaway horses or a river in flood. Take nothing away from Horatio Alger—he figures in our country's adolescence and gave us what we needed, or wanted—but these street boys did not know poverty. They knew an episode when money was less plentiful, so they could enjoy it when it became more plentiful. That is not poverty in our country today.

Today's Definition. A definition of poverty more appropriate to the present day would go like this. Poverty is a complex set of circumstances, each caused by and in turn reinforcing the others, that combine to keep a person without money despite such energy or hope as he is able to muster. It may be exact to say that in our country today those people are poor who can least afford it.

If a person is poor, there is a fair chance—1 chance in 5—that he is Negro, or Puerto Rican, or Mexican, or Indian.[7] There is a better chance—1 in 4—that he is in a home where there is no father. (The average income in such cases is one-third the average for intact families.)[8] If he is poor, he is relatively uneducated (2 chances out of 3). You may think that therefore he needs better schools, but on the whole the schools he attends are poor. As Dr. Conant has said: "The contrast in the money available to the schools in a wealthy suburb and to the schools in a large city jolts one's notion of the meaning of equality of opportunity."[9]

Where does he live, this non-Alger hero? In Chicago today, half the poorer, broken families that include children live in housing that is seriously crowded, dilapidated, or lacks central heat, electricity, or plumbing.[10] The aged do not fare so badly in terms of housing. If they live with relatives, they share their fortunes so far as housing is concerned. Of those living alone or with nonrelatives, from a fourth to a third are in substandard housing.

These figures on housing underline a point that is insufficiently appreciated in this somewhat psychiatric age: Substandard housing affects personal behavior and family patterns. It means, for example, that there is not adequate opportunity for study or even for parental control. Questioning once, at Hull House, a program that kept 13-year-olds out 5 nights a week until 10 o'clock curfew brought the following reply: It is hopeless to attempt keeping children inside the apartments in which these youngsters live. After they have had supper, sitting on beds and stools around a table, they wander outside. One draws them to a settlement house or leaves them in the streets. Hylan Lewis has observed that poor children are not given their freedom at an early age. They seize it.[11]

How would parents keep control in the kind of housing that drives children outside? Crowded housing means early, and not especially pleasant, acquaintance with sexual facts. It means tension; it means weariness. A study of working-class Negroes in Chicago during World War II revealed that most of them had less than 5 hours' sleep per night. They slept from three to five to a bed, and the beds were filled day and night.[12] Matters have undoubtedly improved since the war. Nevertheless, one reads public assistance case records with a somewhat different attitude if these facts are borne in mind.

Poverty means other things. For many, it means living in a state of despair or bitterness that, if it represents a realistic and even necessary reaction to their experiences, in itself becomes a barrier to improving their circumstances. Poverty means that a man's family is not likely to be able to help him get ahead. Not only are they not able to help, but they may turn to him when they are in such desperate need that he must share with them anything extra that he has managed to scrape together.

What Filial Responsibility Means. The point of this catalogue of the elements of poverty has now been reached. Filial responsibility legislation is not examined realistically when it is examined in isolation. Taken as an abstraction, the requirement to provide support may be a small, not to say reasonable, requirement to make of a person. Its appearance may be different if it is seen as one element in a network of circumstances that combine to handicap a person at every turn.

It would be another matter if people of average means or better were being considered. The fact is that those with good income tend to have parents with adequate income. The fact is that persons with good income do not need to be required by law to help their parents when they are in need; they tend to do it voluntarily. The fact is, finally and ironically, that those with good income know best how to evade the law if this is what they want. In Pennsylvania, for example, a study of shared households found that half the support contributions to clients came from adult children whose family income was less than $2,400 a year. In no case was there a contribution from a son or a daughter whose family income was over $5,400 a year.[13]

One might grant the thesis that many factors in a poor person's situation interact to keep him poor and yet doubt whether support requirements are in themselves a significant handicap. As far as is known, the matter has never been studied in just these terms. Yet, one must take note of the extent to which the self-improvement of adults is subsidized by their parents today. Sussman and Burchinal observe, for example, that we are well on our way to a new norm, that parents should, if at all possible, provide a college education for their children. College education is not the only subsidy; middle-class parents make substantial contributions at marriage, in connection with grandchildren, and so on. The adult children being considered here not only fail to get this assistance; they are required to give the assistance.

Visualize a child on the aid to dependent children rolls reaching the landmark of his eighteenth birthday. Obviously, his family is not going to be able to help him towards the goal of self-improvement—financially, at least. Much less than that, the child is now a legally responsible relative. The Pennsylvania study mentioned earlier counted 5,180 children over age 18 who were living in homes receiving aid to dependent children and were regarded as legally responsible relatives. North Carolina assumes a contribution from an employed child over age 18—50 percent of his net income or $75 a month, whichever is smaller. Utah assumes a contribution from any child earning more than $75 a month—50 percent of the amount over $75.

Not all of these children, or even most of them, will achieve earnings that bring these requirements to bear on them. Nor are all of those who do achieve such earnings striving for self-improvement. What of those who are? Shall we debate how to provide specialized services to encourage self-improvement while we require them to give up the means for it?

Filial responsibility and poverty can be viewed in two ways. One can put the emphasis on support and consider questions of justice and reasonableness. Using this approach, it is possible to establish a definition of moderate income and to require that all or part of any sums above that amount be contributed to the needy parent. Some states set this level low indeed. In addition, one's concept of justice must somehow encompass the fact that most Americans, of any income level, do not make cash contributions.

At least implicitly, a second approach is being proposed here. This approach puts the emphasis on poverty and asks at how many points and how substantially it is possible, within the framework of the public assistance programs, to interrupt the cycle that keeps people poor. Interfering with poverty is, it must be apparent, far from a simple thing to do. It requires change on a variety of fronts—education, race relations, employment, family relationships, and so on—many of them outside the reach of our everyday work. One small area can lie within our reach: if we deal with an old man, we may include his children in our stated goal of fostering independence.

Indivisibility of Family Welfare

With respect to the points made so far in this article, a few qualifications are necessary. Why, for example, so much talk about children when the subject is filial responsibility and the aged? The reason has already been stated in another connection: The welfare of the aged and their children and their grandchildren is indivisible. It is not possible to have old people comfortable at the expense of their children. No one wants it that way, but in any case it could not be achieved.

Second, it is not intended to give the impression that parents and adult children are necessarily distinct groups of people. A great many people are parent and child at once. It has been noted, for example, that support requirements may be a handicap to the child after he is dropped from the rolls of aid to dependent children because of his age. Similarly, a youth may be handicapped because support for an older relative is required from his 40-year-old father. Further, increasing numbers of aged Americans are finding that they have even older relatives who might be considered to be dependent on them. The proportion of those just over age 60 to the really old—over age 80—is now about 3 to 1; in a generation or so, the proportion should be 3 to 2.[14] Thus, contributions to the aged might have to be enforced from the aged.

There is a third qualification: In speaking about poverty, human spirit and drive have been referred to only negatively—that is, in terms of despair and bitterness. This is not to say that the human spirit will not assert itself despite all obstacles. The human drive towards self-respect may surmount decades of repression and indignity. It does seem clear, however, that poverty will be left behind only bit by bit, here and there, unless we create the conditions for leaving it behind.

Finally, it may seem that it is being suggested here that children should not help their parents but should think only of themselves. Far from it. Evidence that children freely and spontaneously help their parents has been noted. It is the effect of the legal requirement that has been discussed specifically, in particular its effect

on adult children who are being denied the right to the smallest
surplus income that may be applied to self-advancement. These
are not the people on whom one should choose, as in effect the law
chooses, to enforce support.

Conclusions

To sum up: Filial responsibility laws cannot be considered alone,
for they should have some rational relationship to the way families
live. These laws do not represent the normal pattern of American
family life, nor are they likely to be enforced except on public
assistance families. In fact, a case for the repeal of these laws can
be based solely on their effects on family relationships. (This was
probably the primary motivation of the recommendations against
support requirements made by the 1961 White House Conference
on Aging.) Support laws appear to be intimately related to vague,
though powerful, fears about the deterioration of families. The
anxiety may be real, but it is not tied to objective trends in family
life.

Filial responsibility laws must also be considered in relation to
poverty. The requirement to support is one of the network of handicaps that surrounds a poor family; it may, on occasion, be the
crucial handicap that persuades a person that improvement is not
in the cards for him. Earlier in this article images and their dangers
were discussed. Visions merit rather more respect. We have had
the vision from time to time of so organizing public welfare, and
our society, that we shall wipe out poverty as we know it today.
Eliminating support requirements in public assistance is only one
element in this program, but it is an element.

NOTES

1. ALVIN L. SCHORR, *Filial Responsibility in the Modern American Family*
   (Social Security Administration, Division of Program Research), 1961,
   p. 6.
2. There was speculation about this as long ago as 1940. Barkev S.
   Sanders wrote then that "As a group, the aged may spend as much

from their own resources for the support of younger persons as is spent, in the aggregate, by younger persons toward the support of the aged." He proposed a statistical method of testing this speculation but did not, so far as is known, carry it out ("Economic Status of the Aged in Urban Households," *Social Security Bulletin,* October 1940).

3. MARVIN B. SUSSMAN and LEE BURCHINAL, *Parental Aid: Prospects and Implications for Family Theory,* September 1961. Processed. [See p. 210, below, footnotes 10 and 17, for references to publications.—Ed.]

4. ETHEL SHANAS, "Living Arrangements of Older People in the United States," *The Gerontologist,* March 1961, pp. 27–29.

5. ALVIN L. SCHORR, *op. cit.,* pp. 15–17.

6. ENRICO L. QUARANTELLI, "A Note on the Protective Function of the Family in Disasters," *Marriage and Family Living,* August 1960, p. 264.

7. These odds and those that follow are inferred from Robert J. Lampman, *The Low Income Population and Economic Growth,* Study Paper No. 12, prepared for the Joint Economic Committee, U.S. Congress, December 16, 1959.

8. LENORE A. EPSTEIN, "Some Effects of Low Income on Children and Their Families," *Social Security Bulletin,* February 1961, pp. 12–17.

9. JAMES BRYANT CONANT, *Slums and Suburbs,* McGraw-Hill Book Co., Inc., 1961.

10. BEVERLY DUNCAN and PHILIP M. HAUSER, *Housing a Metropolis— Chicago,* The Free Press, 1960, p. 137.

11. HYLAN LEWIS, *Child Rearing Practices Among Low Income Families,* National Conference on Social Welfare, May 16, 1961. [Cf. Lewis's article in Louis A. Ferman, Joyce L. Kornbluh, and Alan Haber, eds., *Poverty in America: A Book of Readings,* Ann Arbor: University of Michigan Press, 1965.—ED.]

12. ALLISON DAVIS, "The Motivation of the Under-Privileged Worker," in *Industry and Society,* edited by William Foote Whyte, McGraw-Hill Book Co., Inc., 1946, p. 94.

13. Pennsylvania Department of Public Welfare, *Composition of Shelter Groups, Latter Half of January 1958, Special Analysis,* June 9, 1958.

14. Senate Subcommittee on Problems of the Aged and Aging, Report to the Senate Committee on Labor and Public Welfare, *The Aged and the Aging in the United States—A National Problem,* January 29, 1960.

✌ 16 ❧   Mother-in-Law: A Problem

in Kinship Terminology

by J O H N   M.   S H L I E N

In our own society, I have tried to inquire into terms of address used in connection with a single relationship status—the mother-in-law. It seems a privileged case for study. It is active and prevalent. It contains a broad range of social distances and psychological attributes. It is unstable, changing over time, both in individual cases and in the culture at large. It takes place *de novo* in the rather sudden meetings of two adults who have, usually, no experience of growing together, or no attraction for each other. They are thrust together, almost as side effects, as it were, with *nothing given in the way of a relationship or term of address,* and they may have to invent one from scratch. Finally, the relationship is a crucial one, with much intensity of emotion attached. That seems always and everywhere to be so. Much of this emotion is negative. Clear evidence lies in the degree to which avoidance, deliberate and often ritually prescribed, is the practice between parents and children-in-law.

In more than three-fifths of the world's societies, severe penalties follow upon the meeting of a man and his mother-in-law, and they shun each other accordingly. In northern Australia, a man who speaks to his mother-in-law must be put to death. In parts of the South Pacific, both parties would commit suicide. In Yucatan, men believe that to meet one's mother-in-law face to face would render a man sterile for life, so he may travel miles out of his way over

Adapted by the editor from *ETC.,* XIX, July, 1962, 161–171. Copyright 1962 by the International Society for General Semantics. By permission of the author and the publisher.

dangerous territory to avoid being near her. Navaho men believe that they will go blind if they should see their mothers-in-law, so she is not even allowed to attend the wedding.* This strenuous avoidance of son and mother-in-law has been analyzed from the point of view of the sexual potential and shame in the relationship by Freud, Margaret Mead, and many others. There is the possibility of socially disruptive pseudo-incest between parents and children-in-law, and there may also be various feelings of jealousy or outrage against the intruder who "steals" a mother's coveted son, or "defiles" the precious daughter.

In our own culture, the range of attitudes towards the mother-in-law is wide. Many people, especially women (who may be mothers-in-law themselves some day), like their mothers-in-law. Nevertheless, the mother-in-law is overwhelmingly named on all surveys as the most difficult of all relatives. Extreme avoidance is not customary, but an alternative technique, the mother-in-law joke, is very common. Professor Fred Eggan hypothesizes that the more inevitable the conflict, the greater the social necessity to avoid it, thus the stronger the "obligatory joking relationship." (This is an anthropological phrase for a relationship in which quarrelsomeness is prohibited by convention, and only a jolly, somewhat oblique communication is the mode.) We Americans do not have the technical form of the joking relationship—only the joke itself. It is never directed at the son or daughter-in-law, only at the mother-in-law, and it is based on hostility and rejection. It often suggests the death of the mother-in-law. An example from a burlesque show: "Definition of conflict—your mother-in-law driving over a cliff in your new Cadillac." Sometimes the "joke" is built into more subtle and enduring forms, such as the popular name of the houseplant with sharp-pointed and spiny-edged leaves (San-sevieria), which is usually called "Mother-in-Law's Tongue." In the lower classes, the jokes abound, and often take the form of a curse. To illustrate from the lower depths, consider the man called "Blind Pig" in Nelson Algren's *Man With the Golden Arm*. Blind Pig was so vile that he was repulsive even in his own society, and just his foul breath made the tavern owner "shudder and wish he

---

* Navaho men also believe that blindness follows the viewing of a naked woman. One is authentically reported to have entered a circus side-show with one eye covered by his hand. Of such curiosity and daring experimentation, social change is born.

had finished high school." In all his hatred and self-loathing, the nastiest thing Blind Pig could say was, "Aw, yer mother-in-law," which means, "May you not be able to avoid her, sexually."

What do Americans call their parents-in-law, particularly the female parent-in-law? Approximately half of my informants *say* they use Mother, or Mother X. Other terms of address, used less frequently, are: Given name (Mary, or Elmer); Mrs. X (first initial, or surname); Nickname; Ma'am or Sir; Local conventions, such as Mammy or Big Daddy in southern small town cliques.

These are the terms informants give if they are simply *asked*. But one may sit through whole evenings with in-law pairs who never use the terms they say they use. For instance, a man had just told me that he called his mother-in-law "Mother" or some-times "Mother Smith." The telephone rang. It was a call for his mother-in-law, who was at the moment visiting there. He walked over to her, in another room, and said directly to her, "Uh, it's for you." He had, in fact, *no* term of address. To get such facts one must directly observe, or at least ask searching questions. The in-formant who says he uses "Mother" will often be observed, in situations such as the above, to call out to his wife and say some-thing like, "Honey, it's for your mother." Or he may call out in an announcer's voice, "Call for Mrs. Surname."

In the absence of settled behavior patterns or names, the situa-tion can become distressing for the whole family. Consider the case of Mrs. Gravely. Her only daughter was newly married to a man who was not good enough for her. Mrs. Gravely was a power-ful matriarch, used to authority, money, respect, and from her daughter, rebellion. To the son-in-law, no term of address seemed to fit. "Mother" was too intimate and affectionate for this for-bidding woman. "Mrs. Gravely" offended her. "Mrs. G." seemed too distant; her first name too forward. Not only for the son-in-law but for his entire family, this was a terrible problem. His sisters, brothers, nieces, nephews, were all at a loss.

The problem of what to call Mrs. Gravely was eventually re-solved when her first grandchild began to call her "Yamah." Every-one seized upon it with enthusiasm and relief. They address her as "Yamah." They also refer to her as "Yamah." She even calls her-self "Yamah," so signs her letters, and receives them. By means of this bridge, she is written to and called upon freely by members of the in-law family who had avoided her before, and everyone is genuinely cordial, although no basic personality change is observable.

This is more than an academic problem to be debated as one of the questions raised by differences in kinship terminology. The mother-in-law is a special case. In it we can see an unusual amount of tension between principals *for whom there is no term of address*. Lack of such terms does not create the problem, but surely contributes to it, leaving an uneasy situation to be solved only by individuals who develop an unusual degree of personal maturity in their relationship. For the rest, the strain continues, perhaps ameliorated over time by yielding accommodations and weariness.

⋘ 17 ⋙   Uncle and Aunt: A Problem in Kinship Terminology

by D A V I D   M.   S C H N E I D E R   *and*

G E O R G E   C.   H O M A N S

An interesting finding emerged from a study of terms for aunts and uncles. Although the combination of aunt- or uncle-plus-first-name is the most frequently employed term, many informants reported the use of first name alone. In working over particular genealogies with informants we encountered a sizable group which did not apply any particular term consistently for all aunts or for

Adapted by the editor from "Kinship Terminology and the American Kinship System," *American Anthropologist*, LVII, Dec., 1955, 1199–1202. With permission of the publisher and authors.

all uncles. That is, one informant called his mother's elder brother "Uncle Jim" and his mother's younger brother "Bill." Another reported that he called his mother's sister "Aunt Jane" and his mother's sister's husband "John."

We spent some time trying to determine when the aunt or uncle term plus-first-name would be used as against the use of the first name alone, and a few interesting facts emerged.

First, there was a tendency for more first-name-alone designations to be applied to aunts and uncles on the mother's side than on the father's. About as many uncles as aunts were called by first names, and about as many affinal (marriage-related) uncles and aunts as consanguineal (blood-related) ones. The only apparently significant difference was the side of the family they happened to be on. Does this represent a tendency, in a society with a patrilateral bias (e.g. being named after the father, place of residence being selected with reference to father's place of work), for ego's close and warm ties to be with his mother's kin?

Second, there was a slight tendency for male speakers to use the first name alone more often than female speakers. This may mean that women are more concerned with and perceptive of kinship obligations and relations than men, or that women still think of themselves as being of somewhat lower status than men and so are less willing to assert the equality implied by the use of the first name, or, finally, that women are less inclined to allow themselves the display of affect that is also, as we shall see, implied by the first name alone.

Third, some informants reported that they dropped aunt and uncle terms and used first names alone after they started going to college. Here, far more surely, the use of the first name implies a role of equality with uncle and aunt. The formal term is dropped when children view themselves, and are viewed, as being grown-up and so almost on the same plane as uncle and aunt.

Fourth, we ran across a number of situations of the following sort. An informant with three uncles would call one "John," one "Uncle Bill," and the other "Jim." When pressed to explain why he called the first uncle just plain "John," he would reply by saying that the person was a dirty so-and-so and that he would not dignify the man by calling him uncle. (This, by the way, was never said of mother or father.) The next question would be, "Well, how about your other uncle, Jim? Why don't you call him Uncle Jim?" And the explanation would be, "Jim is a wonderful guy! He and I have always been the closest friends. When I was a kid we would . . ." and out would come a picture of an idyllic relationship. The final question, of course, would be, "What about Uncle Bill?" And Uncle Bill would usually prove to be liked—a nice guy— "He's o.k.," or some such mildly positive or mildly negative sentiment.

The pattern seemed to be that wherever there was strong affect, either positive *or* negative, the "uncle" form would be dropped and the first name alone used. Alternatively, if we think of these terms as status designators, the first name may imply either the equality of the speaker with the person referred to *or* the inferiority of the latter. Where the affect was mild, one way or the other, and the relative statuses were simply those expected in the kinship norms, the uncle term was used.

It is, of course, a statement of some significance about the nature of the American kinship system that there can be three broad possibilities in the relationship between ego and uncles or aunts; the relationship may be intensely close, warm and intimate with egalitarian overtones; or it may be intensely hostile with or without the prominent display of this affect; or it can be mildly positive, mildly negative, or, to put it in another way, the affect can be subordinate to other, primarily kinship, considerations. Not all bilateral systems permit ego to say quite bluntly: "I wouldn't dignify that S.O.B. by the use of a kinship term"; or even, conversely, "We are the closest of friends and always have been."

It is worth noting the obvious point that in uncle and aunt designations the dominant tendency is toward a combination of first name and kinship term. In a very important sense the American system classes all uncles together and then differentiates individuals within each class. This is clearly in line with the tendency to treat kinsmen as particular people with particular and unique qualities of a personal nature. Uncles, for instance, might be distinguished as elder, second, third, or younger and yield the same differentiation. But there the stress would be on the ranking among uncles and not, as in the American system, the stress on the person as such within the kinship setting.

In our study of the use of personal names for kin, especially for uncles and aunts, we recur again to our fundamental point—that the nature of the relationship between the speaker and the person referred to is an important determinant of the term used. But in the uncle-aunt case, there are really only two available terms— "Jim" or "Uncle Jim"—yet the elements that enter the relationship are many: status similarities or differences, affect or lack of it, kinship or personal interest. The disproportion between the number of terms and the number of elements in the relationship means that, though the terms do reflect the relationship, they often do so crudely and sometimes ambiguously.

⤳§ 18 §⤶ Extended Kinship Relationships in American Society

by P A U L J . R E I S S

While discussion of the family in American society ordinarily centers on the nuclear family consisting of a husband and wife and their unmarried children, an individual also usually has social relationships with a wider number of kin. In some societies a number of related nuclear families live and work together as a larger extended family. The most salient characteristic of kinship systems in America, however, is undoubtedly the fact that the nuclear family is the only important kinship unit socially, economically, and residentially and is relatively independent of other kin. Not only has the establishment of independent nuclear family units been the cultural ideal in the United States but it has also generally been realized in practice. In 1960, 97.8 per cent of all

Written especially for this reader.

married couples maintained their own households.[1] The Biblical injunction that a man should leave his father and mother and cleave to his wife is well followed in the United States where the marital relationship, which is the basis of independent nuclear families, clearly takes precedence over other relationships.

The independence of the nuclear family has been related to the differentiation of social structures and the specialization of functions in modern industrial society. The consequences of such specialization and differentiation are revealed in the American kinship system. Economic, political, educative, and other functions formerly handled by kinship groups have been taken over by other units such as governments, schools, and business firms. This loss of functions by kinship systems has been accompanied by the development of the independent, specialized, nuclear family and the decline in importance of wider kinship units.[2]

American society has also been characterized as an achievement-oriented society in which it is the individual's personal achievements, particularly in his occupation, rather than inherited status, which primarily determine his position in society. Such a society is characterized by geographic mobility and by social mobility based upon individual achievement. An individual nuclear family may therefore be residentially separated from related nuclear family units and these nuclear families may be at varying social status levels. Extended family units can hardly be maintained in the face of such extensive social and geographic mobility. A lack of good information, however, obscures the historical development of the present nuclear family. At what time in the history of Western society extended family units were common, or whether they followed or preceded industrialization, is not known.[3]

While it is recognized that the independence of the nuclear family is institutionalized in American society and that there is normally no solidary extended family operating as a unit, there has been controversy over the nature of the relationship of individuals to their kin beyond the nuclear family. For some time it was assumed that the nuclear family was isolated from kin and that relationships to relatives were generally unimportant. As a result there was little research on the question of extended kin and little mention of them in texts on the family except for occasional references to the "in-law problem."

Recent studies have shown, however, that individuals do maintain relationships with their relatives. In Detroit it was discovered that about one-half of the population see their relatives at least once a week.[4] Another sample in Los Angeles[5] and one in San Francisco[6] revealed very similar patterns. In each case there was more social participation with relatives than with co-workers, neighbors, or friends. Several studies have also shown that there is a great deal of aid exchanged among extended kin, particularly between parents and married children. In Detroit about 70 per cent of the wives in a sample indicated that they exchanged aid of some type with relatives.[7] In a study of middle-class parents in New Haven, Connecticut, it was discovered that 79 per cent had established a pattern of providing aid for their married children.[8] Another study in Cleveland indicated that about one-half of the respondents received help of some sort from parents and from siblings while 93 per cent provided some aid to parents and about 80 per cent to siblings.[9] This aid may include financial assistance, help during illness or in emergencies, taking care of children, or just giving advice. Relatives are the first ones most people turn to for aid in emergencies.[10] Schorr (15) discusses the nature of this aid between adult children and their aged parents, showing that financial aid flows to the children from the parents, but that married children more often provide living quarters and other types of personal service for their aged parents.

It is apparent from these studies that functioning extended kin relationships do exist for most people in urban American society.[11] Nevertheless, as the figures indicate, there is a great deal of variation from family to family in the amount of contact or aid exchanged with kin. When it is stated that one-half of the respondents visited relatives at least once a week, it also means that the other half did not. Likewise 30 per cent of the wives in Detroit did not exchange any type of aid with any relatives. People also see some relatives frequently but others very seldom; they give or receive aid from some but not others.

Two of the most important factors accounting for these variations are: how closely related are the kinsmen? and how close together do they live? One study found that in a middle-class sample most of the difference in the amount of contact respondents had with various relatives was explained by these two factors: 98

per cent of the respondents who had parents or children in the same town visited them at least monthly, but this was true of only 42 per cent of the cousin relationships in which the cousin lived in the same town, and in only 10 per cent of the parent–married child relationships in which the kinsmen lived in a different region of the country.[12]

In addition to degree of relationship, another study found that the role of the woman in maintaining kin ties was an important variable in explaining the degree of closeness to various kin.[13] Other factors such as the presence of common interests, compatible personalities, and similarity of family situations also explained differences in the amount of contact and feelings of closeness between individuals and their various relatives. While at least some contact among kin is expected, individuals in general exercise a great deal of choice in selecting those kinsmen with whom they will maintain especially close relationships. Similar factors account for the development of close friendship relationships among non-kin and among kin. The studies of Schneider and Homans (*17*) and of Shlien (*16*) show how some of this variation in the quality of kin relationships is revealed by kinship terminology.

It appears, then, that certain types of extended family relationships can exist in an achievement-oriented, industrial society. An extended family, however, in which the members live and work together, is not found. The kin relationships which have been noted in urban America are relationships between independent nuclear families which do not hinder geographic mobility.[14] If a family desires to move away from kin, it is free to do so although the distance will ultimately affect kinship relationships. These kinship relationships also do not hinder social mobility; the resources of kin may even be used to further social mobility.[15] Kinship relationships of this type are thus compatible with an industrial, achievement-oriented society.

The specialization which has occurred in industrial society has meant, as we have mentioned, that kinship units no longer have the economic, political, and educative functions they once possessed. However, the fact that extended kin relationships continue to be maintained indicates that they could not be entirely functionless. The functions of these extended kin relationships appear to be basically those performed by primary friendship relationships; personality satisfactions including a sense of belonging, companionship, and security. While impersonal bureaucratic organizations pursue common societal goals, close personal relationships are still required to satisfy the needs of the individual personality. The nuclear family does provide personality satisfactions but these are based on a very small number of individuals. Extended kin relationships provide additional personnel and material resources, and therefore function as a second-line support system for the nuclear family in the performance of vital functions for the individual personality.

Extended kin relationships of the type noted in the studies mentioned above may or may not always have existed in urban, industrial America. It is possible that they always did exist but were overlooked by sociologists concentrating on the study of the nuclear family. It may also be that a revival of extended kinship relationships has taken place in recent decades. The question as to whether or not the nuclear family was ever more completely isolated from kin cannot now be resolved. There are several factors, however, which help to explain the revival of extended kin relationships in recent decades, if indeed such a revival has taken place. In the first place, with about 20 years added to life expectancy during this century, there are more apt to be three generations of kin living at the same time. Some kin, such as grandparents, if they are living, may serve as a focus of kin interest and contact among a wide group of their descendants.

In the second place, the additional years now required to complete an education and the younger age at marriage may make more young couples dependent upon their parents. Greater prosperity may make it possible for the parents to assist their married children and thus establish a kin relationship which may endure after the aid is no longer required.

Thirdly, with the independence of the nuclear family established, even in the minds of the older generation, nuclear families can now afford to maintain close relationships with extended kin without threat to their independence or to their social or geographic mobility. It may even be that this freedom to engage in closer extended kin relationships is analogous to the situation described by Herberg and others wherein the grandchildren of immigrants, once they are firmly established in American society, return to the religion and traditions of the grandparents.[16] Further research is needed, however, to discover how close a relationship can be developed with kin or how much aid exchanged before the independence of the nuclear family is seriously compromised.

A fourth reason for the re-establishment of extended kin ties may stem from the closer, more personal relationships that have developed in the nuclear family in recent decades. The core of extended kin relationships for an individual are the members of his nuclear family of orientation. Close personal relationships within the nuclear family in one generation may be continued as close relationships between extended kin in the next generation.

In general, the work of sociologists during the past decade has opened up the subject of extended kinship relationships in modern society as an important area of family study.[17] Much more research is needed in order to clarify the nature of these relationships and the manner in which they function in an urban, industrial society.

NOTES

1. U.S. Bureau of the Census. *U.S. Census of Population: 1960*, Vol. I, *Characteristics of the Population*, Part I, United States Summary, Table 79.

2. TALCOTT PARSONS and ROBERT F. BALES (1955) *Family, Socialization and Interaction Process*, Glencoe, Ill.: Free Press, Chap. 1. [Also see below, pp. 264 ff.—ED.]

3. WILLIAM J. GOODE (1963) *World Revolution and Family Patterns*, New York: Free Press of Glencoe, pp. 6–7.

4. MORRIS AXELROD (1956) "Urban Structure and Social Participation," *American Sociological Review*, 21: 13–19.

5. SCOTT GREER (1956) "Urbanism Reconsidered: A Comparative Study of Local Areas in a Metropolis," *American Sociological Review*, 21: 19–25.

6. WENDELL BELL and N. D. BOAT (1957) "Urban Neighborhoods and Informal Social Relations," *American Journal of Sociology*, 43: 381–398.

7. HARRY SHARP and MORRIS AXELROD (1956) "Mutual Aid Among Relatives in an Urban Population," in Ronald Freedman *et al.*, *Principles of Sociology*, New York: Holt.

8. MARVIN B. SUSSMAN (1953) "The Help Pattern in the Middle Class Family," *American Sociological Review*, 18: 22–28.

9. MARVIN B. SUSSMAN (1959) "The Isolated Nuclear Family: Fact or Fiction," *Social Problems*, 6: 333–340.

10. For a review of research on aid among kin see Marvin B. Sussman and Lee Burchinal (1962) "Parental Aid to Married Children: Implications for Family Functioning," *Marriage and Family Living*, 24: 320–332.

11. Similar results were obtained in studies of working-class families in London, England. See Michael Young and Peter Willmott (1957) *Family and Kinship in East London*, Glencoe. Ill.: Free Press; and Raymond Firth (1956) ed., *Two Studies of Kinship in London*, London: University of London, Athlone Press.

12. PAUL J. REISS (1962) "The Extended Kinship System: Correlates of and Attitudes on Frequency of Interaction," *Marriage and Family Living*, 24: 333–339.

13. LEE ROBINS and MIRODA TOMANEC (1962) "Closeness to Blood Relatives Outside the Immediate Family," *Marriage and Family Living*, 24: 340–346.

14. EUGENE LITWAK (1960) "Geographic Mobility and Extended Family Cohesion," *American Sociological Review*, 25: 385–394.

15. EUGENE LITWAK (1960) "Occupational Mobility and Extended Family Cohesion," *American Sociological Review*, 25: 9–21.

16. WILL HERBERG (1955) *Protestant-Catholic-Jew*, Garden City, N.Y.: Doubleday.

17. For a review of much of this recent research see Marvin B. Sussman and Lee Burchinal (1962) "Kin Family Network: Unheralded Structure in Current Conceptualizations of Family Functioning," *Marriage and Family Living*, 24: 231–240.

Seven

SOCIAL CLASS AND FAMILY RELATIONS

◦§ INTRODUCTION* §◦

A person's social class background has a pervasive influence upon his life. The lower the class background of people the likelier they are to have tuberculosis, to die early, to receive poor physical care, to get poor justice in the courts, to bear illegitimate children, to have unstable marital relationships, and to have "less" motivation and "lower" aspirations. An exceedingly wide variety of injustices and deprivations can be documented for members of the lower classes of society—physical, social, occupational, legal, economic, and political. Even in an affluent society like the United States, the poor are plentiful, and the injustices and deprivations they face are facts of life. The moves in the direction of providing adequate counsel to all citizens in criminal cases, and of providing adequate medical care to all people, help to eliminate some of these deprivations. So are all the efforts of the current civil rights movement and the "war on poverty" in the United States. The focus in this section, however, will be less upon the political activist orientation toward the problems of the poor,† and more upon the sociological orientation—what are the consequences of poverty, or more generally, what are the consequences of membership in any social class.

* The emphasis in this section is upon the lower class. For additional details see Rainwater, Coleman, and Handel (1959); Rainwater and Weinstein (1960); Bell (1963); Cavan (1963); Komarovsky (1964); McKinley (1964); Shostak and Gomberg (1964); and Rodman (in preparation).
    † For a variety of writings that begin to deal with some of the political and practical issues see Galbraith (1958); Miller and Riessman (1961); Harrington (1962); Theobald (1961, 1963); Keyserling (1963, 1964); Silberman (1964); and Burns (1965).

Understanding Lower-Class Behavior

In many respects it is lower-class behavior that is most different from the behavior of other classes, and the most difficult to understand. While it is often easy for us to recognize differences in another cultural group—Samoans or Trobrianders, for example—it is more difficult to understand social class differences within one's own society. We too readily assume that all Americans should act alike, and our reactions to differences often are ethnocentric and uncharitable. As a result, there are many middle-class misunderstandings of lower-class behavior and values. Rodman (*19*) deals with these misunderstandings: for example, illegitimacy, desertion, and unmarried motherhood are often seen as lower-class *problems,* from a middle-class viewpoint; Rodman suggests that one can see these as *solutions* rather than problems. They are solutions to other, more basic, problems that are faced by members of the lower class. These problems reside in the social, economic, and political deprivations of the lower class. In coping with these problems lower-class people tend to develop family patterns that involve flexibility (or instability)—this flexibility helps them to deal with such problems as unemployment and low-pay employment. As a result one finds a greater degree of marital instability within the lower class, a greater degree of casualness in the relations between the sexes, a greater willingness to enter a sexual relationship even where there is not much ego involvement, and a greater degree of illegitimacy (Rodman, (*19*); Hollingshead, 1950; Vincent,* 1954,

* Vincent has ably pointed to the stereotypes in our society regarding the supposedly lower-class status of unwed mothers. He indicates that higher-status unwed mothers use private physicians and that most studies of unwed mothers ignore these cases. He therefore exposes this bias by including the patients of private physicians in his study. Not only does he indicate that there are a substantial number of middle-class unwed mothers, but he goes on to suggest that there are no class differences in the distribution of illegitimacy. This is highly questionable, however; although there are many middle-class unwed mothers, it is likely that proportionately more lower-class mothers are unwed. Even Vincent agrees that his own data bear this out if we consider the probable social class distribution of the cases for which he was unable to obtain information. But he cautions that "the data available concerning this point may be misleading because of the unknown but presumably high number of unwed mothers from the middle and upper socioeconomic groups who migrate to one of the 15 states where illegitimacy is not recorded" (personal communication).

1959, 1961; Goode, 1962). The important thing to recognize is that these differences are best seen in terms of the conditions of life in the different social classes, and not in judgmental terms of right or wrong.

Differences in behavior between the social classes are often related to value differences, and it is therefore desirable to know what the values are in the different social classes. For example, within the lower class, it is often assumed that there is a lower level of aspiration, or, as it is sometimes expressed, less motivation. This is not the whole story, however. It has been suggested (Rodman, 1963) that within the lower class it is more accurate to speak of a wider range of values with a lesser degree of commitment to each level of the range, rather than a lower level of aspiration. This is consistent with the life conditions of members of the lower class. In other words, members of the lower class aspire to the same things that middle-class people aspire to, but they are also aware of their lesser chance of attaining these things. As a result, they are not as committed to these aspirations, and they have stretched their aspirations in such a way that they have also become more satisfied with a lesser degree of attainment. It is therefore possible to speak of a wider range of aspirations, or of a lower-class value stretch.

Parent-Child Relationships

It has already been pointed out that social class differences have an impact upon husband-wife relationships and family relationships in general. For example, infant care practices vary by social class (pp. 106 ff.), and parental discipline techniques vary by social class. In the selection by Kohn (20) we can see the way in which certain value differences are translated into behavioral differences —in this instance into differences in the disciplinary techniques used by parents. Working-class parents are more concerned with the immediate consequences of their children's behavior, while middle-class parents are more concerned with the child's intent. In other words, working-class parents are likelier to punish rowdy behavior that disturbs them or that results in broken objects; they are less likely to punish rowdy behavior that does not have such consequences. Middle-class parents, on the other hand, are likelier to punish rowdy behavior that they perceive as a loss of self-control; they are less likely to punish such behavior if they see it as merely an emotional release.

We must be careful, however, not to translate research differences that are reported between the social classes into descriptive statements of class characteristics. Johnsen and Leslie (1965) make this clear by referring to a study in which 20 per cent of middle-class mothers stress obedience on the part of their children, while 33 per cent of lower-class mothers stress obedience. This turns out to be a significant difference between the two classes; but it does not mean that we can then say, without qualification, that the lower class is characterized by a stress upon obedience, because a majority of the lower-class mothers did not stress it. Although this is a rather simple point, it is also fundamental, and Johnsen and Leslie indicate that it is often ignored in textbooks and other secondary accounts of the original research data.

Kohn looks upon the values of the middle class and working class as mediating between the conditions of class life and the ensuing behavior. In this sense there is a good deal of similarity in the selections by Kohn and by Rodman. (It must be remembered. however, that Rodman is contrasting the lower class with the middle class, while Kohn is contrasting the working class with the middle class.) The conditions of social class life give rise to different values; the value differences give rise to differences in behavior. Kohn suggests that occupational differences call forth different requirements in the middle class and the working class. Within the former there is a greater need for self-direction; within the latter there is a greater need for following rules. As a result it may be more advantageous for the working-class child to be trained to follow externally imposed rules. The causal sequence that can be inferred here—from the conditions of life to values, and from values to behavior—is conjectural. Nevertheless, it offers us a more insightful way of looking at social class differences in behavior.

We can therefore see that differences in class behavior are related to differences in class values, and that differences in class values are related to the conditions of class life. In this way we avoid the narrow judgmental approach to social class differences, which views such differences in moral terms—as better or worse, right or wrong. And the step from moral judgments about human behavior to scientific understanding of such behavior is a giant stride that too few people are prepared to take.

REFERENCES

BELL, ROBERT R. 1963. *Marriage and Family Interaction,* Homewood, Ill.: Dorsey.

BURNS, EVELINE M. 1965. "Social Security in Evolution: Toward What?" *Social Service Review,* XXXIX, 129–140.

CAVAN, RUTH S. 1963. *The American Family,* 3d ed., New York: Crowell.

GALBRAITH, JOHN KENNETH. 1958. *The Affluent Society,* Boston: Houghton Mifflin.

GOODE, WILLIAM J. 1962. "Marital Satisfaction and Instability: A Cross-Cultural Class Analysis of Divorce Rates," *International Social Science Journal,* XIV, 507–526.

HARRINGTON, MICHAEL. 1962. *The Other America: Poverty in the United States,* New York: Macmillan.

HOLLINGSHEAD, AUGUST B. 1950. "Class Differences in Family Stability," *The Annals of the American Academy of Political and Social Science,* CCLXXII, 39–46.

JOHNSEN, KATHRYN P., and GERALD R. LESLIE. 1965. "Methodological Notes on Research in Childrearing and Social Class," *Merrill–Palmer Quarterly,* XI, 345–358.

KEYSERLING, LEON H. 1963. "What Can We Do Now," *New University Thought,* III, 14–26.

———. 1964. *Progress or Poverty: The U.S. at the Crossroads,* Washington, D.C.: Conference on Economic Progress.

KOMAROVSKY, MIRRA. 1964. *Blue-Collar Marriage,* New York: Random House.

McKINLEY, DONALD G. 1964. *Social Class and Family Life,* New York: Free Press of Glencoe.

MILLER, S. M., and FRANK RIESSMAN. 1961. "The Working Class Subculture: A New View," *Social Problems,* IX, 86–97.

RAINWATER, LEE, RICHARD P. COLEMAN, and GERALD HANDEL. 1959. *Workingman's Wife,* New York: Oceana.

RAINWATER, LEE and KAROL K. WEINSTEIN. 1960. *And the Poor Get Children,* Chicago: Quadrangle.

RODMAN, HYMAN. 1963. "The Lower-Class Value Stretch," *Social Forces,* XLII, 205–215.

———. In preparation. *Lower-Class Families.*

SHOSTAK, ARTHUR B., and WILLIAM GOMBERG, eds. 1964. *Blue-Collar World,* Englewood Cliffs, N.J.: Prentice-Hall.

SILBERMAN, CHARLES E. 1964. *Crisis in Black and White*, New York: Random House.

THEOBALD, ROBERT. 1961. *The Challenge of Abundance*, New York: Clarkson N. Potter.

——. 1963. "Needed: A New Definition of Work," *New University Thought*, III, 9–14.

VINCENT, CLARK E. 1954. "The Unwed Mother and Sampling Bias," *American Sociological Review*, XIX, 562–567.

——. 1959. "Ego Involvement in Sexual Relations: Implications for Research on Illegitimacy," *American Journal of Sociology*, LXV, 287–295.

——. 1961. *Unmarried Mothers*, New York: Free Press of Glencoe.

৭৪ 19 ৪৯ Middle-Class Misconceptions About Lower-Class Families

by HYMAN RODMAN

How well can middle-class persons understand lower-class life? To what extent do their middle-class values lead them to misinterpret lower-class behavior? It is worthwhile asking these questions about middle-class persons—including social scientists and professional practitioners—who have ideas about members of the lower class. Whyte asked these questions a long time ago when he studied the structure of a lower-class Italian community in Boston,[1] and they have been asked many times since by students of the lower class. But these questions have not usually been asked directly, nor have they been explored in much detail. For the most part, as in Whyte, they underlie the discussions about lower-class life. I therefore propose to focus upon these questions and to discuss their general implications. Although the discussion will be, for the most part, a general one, special attention will be paid to commonly held views about lower-class family life.

Lower-Class and Negro Stereotypes

If we consider the general attitudes of middle-class people toward the lower class, it is clear that there is a great deal of misunder-

Adapted from Hyman Rodman, "Middle-Class Misconceptions About Lower-Class Families," in Arthur B. Shostak and William Gomberg, eds., *Blue-Collar World: Studies of the American Worker.* © 1964. Adapted by permission of Prentice-Hall, Inc., Englewood Cliffs, N.J. This article is based upon two prior publications: "On Understanding Lower-Class Behaviour," *Social and Economic Studies,* Vol. VIII, Dec., 1959; and "Marital Relationships in a Trinidad Village," *Marriage and Family Living,* Vol. XXIII, May, 1961.

standing. Members of the lower class often are thought to be "immoral," "uncivilized," "promiscuous," "lazy," "obscene," "dirty," and "loud." Many writers make it clear that this is the way the lower class is frequently viewed within the United States[2] as well as within many other countries.[3] The dominant characterization of the lower class is perhaps in terms of its "immorality," and this reflects the tendency on the part of the middle-class person to judge the lower-class person in terms of his own middle-class values.

Such social class biases are extremely widespread and they appear to be found in most stratified communities. For example, the same biases are found within Negro as well as white communities; thus Davis and Dollard state that "upper-class and middle-class Negroes often criticize lower-class Negroes for being loud, ignorant, black, or dirty persons."[4]

One result of the existence of these biases has been their extension to other than a narrowly defined lower-class group. For example, whites often characterize Negroes by the same stereotypes that middle-class people use in characterizing the lower class—obscene, dirty, loud, lazy, promiscuous, irresponsible, happy. Inkeles[5] and Copeland,[6] among others, have commented on the parallel stereotypes applied to the poor and to Negroes. Part of the explanation for the extension of lower-class stereotypes to Negroes as a group is the larger proportion of Negroes who are in the lower class, and the development of a racially competitive tradition in which Negroes are a physically distinguishable, and therefore vulnerable, minority group.[7]

Simpson and Yinger point out that it is not racial difference which leads to these prejudiced stereotypes—indeed, how can it be when similar stereotypes are used toward white Protestant immigrants (from Arkansas and Oklahoma) to California? toward Polish workers in Germany in the late 1800's? and toward minority groups, racial groups, and lower-class groups generally?[8]

The Social Scientist's Biases

It is also worth asking to what extent the social scientist who studies the lower class, and who is himself a member of the middle class, is influenced by his middle-class values.

The question on the bias of the social scientist is much more difficult to answer. Social scientists do not, for example, use labels such as "immoral" or "uncivilized" in writing about the lower class. They do, however, speak of the lower class as being less well socialized, "unintegrated," "immature," "pathological," and more frequently as being "disorganized."[9] In many cases social scientists who use these terms actually have a fairly good understanding of the effect of life's deprivations upon the lower class, but in applying such terms to the lower-class person or to the lower-class family they are temporarily implying middle-class judgments. Why not speak of the total society as being pathological—if it is necessary to use this word—since this is what contributes to the lower-class behavior that we are concerned about? Many years ago Davis and Dollard made a similar point about the bias of social scientists by noting "that it is common practice, even of sociologists, to speak of the lower class as 'unsocialized,' from their middle-class point of view."[10] C. Wright Mills documented this tendency, and pointed to the use of terms like "unadjusted," "demoralized," and "disorganized."[11] These practices have not disappeared.

Another technique that social scientists sometimes use is to describe the lower class by indirection. This is done by giving an account of lower-class behavior as it has been presented by middle-class informants. It is certainly significant that so many middle-class stories and quotations are used to characterize the lower class, and that very few lower-class statements are used to characterize the middle class.

The Professional Practitioner's Biases

It is also of interest to ask to what extent social workers (and professional practitioners generally) are handicapped by their middle-class values in working with and understanding lower-class clients. This is a point that a number of social scientists have raised. For the most part, they have held that social workers do a poor job in contacting or in meeting the needs of lower-class people; for example, this position has been stated by Koos, Whyte, and Spinley,[12] three social scientists who have themselves worked with the lower class. Historically, social workers started out with a moralistic approach to lower-class behavior, and it is only recently that they have become more psychiatric in their approach. This, of course, has paralleled the fact that more and more social workers are being professionally trained, especially within the United States. One of the most significant and promising approaches toward dealing with the lower class has been made by social workers within the past decade, and this is an approach that is beginning to spread to other practicing professions. The approach is best symbolized in the social work literature by such phrases as "hard-to-reach," "hard core," and "multi-problem" families (or individuals or gangs). This approach recognizes the fact that many lower-class clients are difficult to work with, and it emphasizes the need to understand and accept lower-class families or delinquent gangs before making any attempts to reform them.

Social workers have not been alone in having difficulties with lower-class clients. Davis, Hollingshead, Sexton, and Riessman have referred to the cultural differences that underlie the problems that may be faced by teachers and their lower-class pupils;[13] and Hollingshead, Redlich, Overall, and Aronson have made the same point with respect to psychiatrists and their lower-class patients.[14] They have indicated, for example, that lower-class patients frequently expect the psychiatrist to play an authoritarian role, and that this runs counter to the psychiatrist's therapeutic principles. Without really understanding the lower-class patient, the psychiatrist may then label the lower-class patient as being "unable to profit from therapy" or simply as "untreatable."

A fact of great significance, as I have already suggested, is that there has been a trend away from thinking of certain patients or clients as being "untreatable" toward thinking of them as being "resistive" and "hard to reach." This trend reflects the greater realization on the part of professionals that there is a two-way relationship between the professional person and his client, and that the professional shares in the responsibility of establishing a relationship that will be of help to his client. The change from the notion of "untreatable" clients to "resistive" or "hard-to-reach" ones implies that the resistance can be overcome and that the client can be reached. A common saying, in reaction to the strong psychiatric orientation of social work, refers to the need to put the "social" back into social work. The current trend toward seriously trying to reach certain "hard-to-reach" clients may be referred to as putting the "work" back into social work.

Lower-Class Family Behavior

It is lower-class family behavior that presents the greatest challenge to the person who tries to understand lower-class life. The following have all been considered as characteristic of the lower class: "promiscuous" sexual relationships; "illegitimate" children; "deserting" husbands and fathers; and "unmarried" mothers. These characteristics are frequently viewed in a gross manner as, simply, *problems* of the lower class. It makes better sense, however, to think of them as *solutions* of lower-class persons to problems that they face in the social, economic, and perhaps legal and political spheres of life.

How is it that lower-class behavior can so easily be misunderstood? That a middle-class view of lower-class behavior can lead to misunderstanding has already been pointed out. And one of the major ways in which alien values become incorporated into one's view of the lower class is through the use of middle-class terms to describe lower-class behavior. It is little wonder that if we describe the lower-class family in terms of "promiscuous" sexual relationships, "illegitimate" children, "deserting" men, and "unmarried" mothers, we are going to see the situation as disorganized and chock-full of problems. It should be stressed that words like "promiscuity," "illegitimacy," and "desertion" are not part of the lower-class vocabulary, and that it is misleading to describe lower-class behavior in this way. These words have middle-class meanings and imply middle-class judgments, and it is precisely because of this that we ought not to use them to describe lower-class behavior— unless, perhaps, our intention is to judge this behavior in a middle-class manner in order to bolster a sagging middle-class ego.

No claim is being made here, of course, that demographers or social scientists should not discuss rates of desertion or rates of illegitimacy. In a scientific sense these rates have a clear enough meaning and they provide very important pieces of information for certain kinds of analyses. But these terms can also be used in a judgmental sense, and it is this judgmental use that I am cautioning against. I am also cautioning against the rather easy way in which a scientific stance on these matters can buckle under the weight of a middle-class morality. Consider the following example, in which the author rushes headlong into a *non sequitur:*

> In my opinion, it is indefensible to write off as "culturally ac-
> ceptable" to a certain group poverty and its terrible hardships,
> personality disturbances and their painful results, or the pervasive
> effect of impaired relationships. How often we have heard that in
> a particular cultural group it's acceptable for a teen-age girl to
> have a baby out of wedlock. Whether or not this is a valid
> generalization is for the sociologist to study. The social worker,
> on the other hand, must be concerned about the loneliness a teen-
> age girl feels when she has no husband with whom to share her
> parenthood, when she cannot return to school, when her friends
> go out on dates while she stays at home to care for the baby, or
> when her friends get their first jobs and she must apply for public
> assistance.[15]

The social scientist who studies lower-class families should pay more attention to the language of the lower class itself. In a practical vein this means that lower-class family patterns are usually best described in lower-class terms:

> The language problem is . . . involved in the terms used for
> the different forms of marital or quasi-marital relationships in
> the different parts of the West Indies. R. T. Smith has discussed
> some of the difficulties that develop when the observer sets up his
> own classification scheme for dealing with lower-class marital
> unions. In addition, the great variety of terms used by different
> observers for a marital union that is socially but not legally sanc-
> tioned, and the reasons they give for a particular usage, also sug-
> gest that the observer's terms may not be the most satisfactory
> ones. Henriques and R. T. Smith use common-law marriage;
> Clarke rejects the term "common law" because it suggests legal
> recognition, and uses concubinage; Stycos rejects "concubinage"
> and uses consensual union; Matthews, more simply and perhaps
> more sensibly, uses non-legal union. Although all of these writers
> recognize the distinctions between the legal and social aspects of
> the union, it seems to me that in using their own particular terms
> for the union, they may be causing unnecessary confusion. Would
> it not make better sense to use the terms that are used by the lower
> class itself to refer to these unions?[16]

Accordingly, in my own study of lower-class families in Coconut Village, Trinidad, I discuss three different kinds of marital or quasi-marital relationships—"friending," "living," and married. Through a consideration of some of the findings of this study we can come to a better understanding of what I regard as a major middle-class misconception of lower-class families—viewing certain patterns as *problems* when, in reality, they can as easily be viewed as *solutions*.

Although the details that follow refer to lower-class marital relationships in Coconut Village, I believe that the description, in a broad sense, applies to lower-class families in many societies.[17] The "friending" relationship is one in which a man visits a woman at intervals for sexual intercourse, and in which he has certain limited obligations to the woman and to any children of his that she may bear. Although this relationship is not fully acceptable, it is the most frequent type of relationship, and it usually precedes one of the other relationships. The "living" relationship is one in which the man and woman live together under one roof, but in which they are not legally married. It is an acceptable marital relationship and it occurs more frequently than marriage. A married relationship is similar to a "living" relationship, but it involves a church marriage and a legal bond between the man and woman. It occurs least frequently within the lower class. From one point of view, these patterns reflect a reluctance to take on responsibility, since a greater degree of marital responsibility is involved in the "living" than in the "friending," and in the married than in the "living" relationship.

One man put it this way when I asked him why the people were reluctant to marry: "Matrimony is a money that you can't spend." He explained this to mean that it was something you could not easily get rid of. Another man answered the same question this way: "You can buy a penny milk, so what you want with a cow, na?" Such comments are by no means unique to Coconut Villagers, but they do point out for us the reluctance of the villager to enter a strong marital alliance.

What are the reasons for this reluctance, especially on the man's part, to take on responsibilities within the marital relationship? Also, why is there a good deal of "marital shifting" within Coconut Village, such that most villagers in their lifetime will have gone through several "friending" and "living" relationships? Part of the answer to these questions must be sought in the relation of family life to the structure of the society as a whole, particularly to its economy.

Almost all Coconut Villagers are members of the lower class of Trinidad society and face serious economic deprivations. Although someone in approximately half the households of Coconut Village owns some land, not one household is able to earn its living from the land alone. The land is poor and the hoe and cutlass are the only tools used. Transportation is a severe problem because the lands are practically all at a considerable distance from the main road, so that the meager crops are difficult to market. Wage labor must therefore be relied upon by all households within Coconut Village, and here they share, with other members of the lower class, a situation in which wages are low, unemployment and underemployment are high, and geographical mobility is at times necessary in order simply to find a job.[18]

It is the man who is responsible for the financial support of his wife and children. However, since the economic circumstances faced by the lower-class man often make it difficult or impossible for him to meet these responsibilities, it becomes clear as to why there is a reluctance to accept such responsibilities in the first place. We can therefore understand why "friending" occurs more frequently than "living," and "living" more frequently than marriage within lower-class communities. We can also understand why a marital relationship such as "living" becomes such an acceptable lower-class pattern, for it provides the lower-class person with a fluid marital bond.

In addition to the greater number of acceptable marital relationships the lower-class person can choose from, there is also a ready acceptance of a separation when economic circumstances make it necessary for the man to move in order to find employment.* In this way the man can later set up another marital relationship, when he is in a position to do so, while the woman may be able to set up a new marital relationship with a man who can support her.

Fluidity is therefore strategic in marital life. On the one hand there is fluidity with respect to the type of relationship a person enters into, and on the other hand there is fluidity with respect to the permanence of the marital bond such that it is possible to shift from one marital partner to another. Therefore these marital relationships are functional in that they provide the lower-class

* Since a separation is easy under such conditions, it often takes place for personal as well as for economic reasons.

person with acceptable alternatives which permit him to live with both his conscience and his economic uncertainties.

This fluidity of the marital bond is, I believe, characteristic of lower-class families generally. Within the United States the higher rates of divorce and desertion within the lower class, as well as of "common-law" unions and illegitimacy, are indicative of such fluidity. If, as I am suggesting, these lower-class patterns are responses to the deprivations of lower-class life, and if they are functional for lower-class individuals, then we can see the sense in which many of the lower-class family patterns that are often regarded as problems are actually solutions to other, more pressing, problems.

Concluding Remarks

We have seen that middle-class folk frequently are biased about the lower-class, and that they tend to hold many misconceptions about lower-class family life. Social scientists and professional practitioners may share these biases in some measure. Illustrating this danger is a story told about a social work convention:

> A social worker was presenting a paper that included case material about a lower-class client. She reported that her client's husband entered the room during one of her home visits and described him as a burly and taciturn man. One of her colleagues rose to object: "I beg your pardon. That's my husband you're talking about. He's not burly and taciturn. He's strong and silent!"

This recalls Merton's "engagingly simple formula of moral alchemy":

> The proficient alchemist will at once know that the word "firm" is properly declined as follows:
>
> > I am firm,
> > Thou art obstinate,
> > He is pigheaded.
>
> There are some, unversed in the skills of this science, who will tell you that one and the same term should be applied to all three instances of identical behavior. Such unalchemical nonsense should simply be ignored.[19]

The moral of these stories is obvious. If middle-class persons regard immorality as the special province of the lower classes, then they are not going to be successful in their relations with lower-class people—whether as researchers, practitioners, or in everyday discourse.

There are still many questions in the area of lower-class family relationships and values to which we do not have the answers. With additional research we may eventually begin to get some answers to the many different questions that are being asked about lower-class families. In the meantime, additional research should at least help us to eliminate some of our biases about lower-class families. As Barbara Wootton has said: "The first result of a demand for evidence which will stand up to rigorous scientific examination is the destruction of myths, and such destructive activity is likely for sometime to come to be the main preoccupation of the social sciences."[20]

NOTES

1. It is of interest that in his enlarged edition of *Street Corner Society,* published in 1955 by the University of Chicago Press, Whyte has added a section which deals with the difficulties he had in moving from a middle-class to a lower-class milieu.

2. HERMAN R. LANTZ, *People of Coal Town,* New York: Columbia University Press, 1958, pp. 227–228; Richard Centers, *The Psychology of Social Classes,* Princeton, N.J.: Princeton University Press, 1949, pp. 95–96; W. Lloyd Warner *et al., Democracy in Jonesville,* New York: Harper, 1949, pp. 249–250; August B. Hollingshead, *Elmtown's Youth,* New York: Wiley, 1949, pp. 110–111; St. Clair Drake and Horace R. Cayton, *Black Metropolis,* New York: Harcourt, 1945, pp. 559–563; James West, *Plainsville, U.S.A.,* New York: Columbia University Press, 1945, p. 125; Allison Davis, Burleigh B. Gardner, and Mary R. Gardner, *Deep South,* Chicago: University of Chicago Press, 1941, p. 230.

3. For such views in the West Indies, for example, see F. M. Henriques, *Family and Colour in Jamaica,* London: Eyre and Spottiswoode, 1953, p. 145; Lloyd Braithwaite, "Social Stratification in Trinidad," *Social and Economic Studies,* Vol. II, Nos. 2 and 3, p. 126.

4. ALLISON DAVIS and JOHN DOLLARD, *Children of Bondage,* Washington, D.C.: American Council on Education, 1940, p. 44.

5. ALEX INKELES, "Industrial Man: The Relations of Status to Experience, Perception, and Value," *American Journal of Sociology,* Vol. LXVI, July, 1960, p. 14.

6. LEWIS C. COPELAND, "The Negro as a Contrast Conception," in Edgar T. Thompson, ed., *Race Relations and the Race Problem,* Durham, N.C.: Duke University Press, 1939, p. 157.

7. It must also be remembered that the development of prejudiced stereo-
   types of Negroes, and the often accompanying discrimination, is largely
   responsible for the greater proportion of Negroes in the lower class.
   For a more detailed statement of the origin of prejudices toward
   Negroes see George E. Simpson and J. Milton Yinger, *Racial and
   Cultural Minorities,* rev. ed., New York: Harper, 1958, pp. 153–154
   et passim; Gordon W. Allport, *The Nature of Prejudice,* Garden City,
   N.Y.: Doubleday, 1958.

8. SIMPSON and YINGER, *op. cit.,* pp. 124, 167–168, *et passim.*

9. DAVIS and DOLLARD, *op. cit.,* p. 267; Madeline Kerr, *Personality and
   Conflict in Jamaica,* Liverpool: Liverpool University Press, 1952,
   p. 193; Madeline Kerr, *The People of Ship Street,* London: Routledge
   & Kegan Paul, 1958, p. 156 *et passim;* Dom Basil Matthews, *Crisis of
   the West Indian Family,* Trinidad: University of the West Indies, Extra
   Mural Department, 1952, pp. xiii, 19, 125.

10. DAVIS and DOLLARD, *op. cit.,* pp. 264–265.

11. C. WRIGHT MILLS, "The Professional Ideology of Social Pathologists,"
    American Journal of Sociology, Vol. XLIX, Sept., 1942, p. 179.

12. EARL LOMON KOOS, *Families in Trouble,* New York: King's Crown
    Press, 1946, pp. 84–86; William F. Whyte, *Street Corner Society,* Chi-
    cago: University of Chicago Press, 1943, pp. 98–104; B. M. Spinley,
    The Deprived and the Privileged, London: Routledge & Kegan Paul,
    1953.

13. ALLISON DAVIS, *Social Class Influences upon Learning,* Cambridge:
    Harvard University Press, 1952; August B. Hollingshead, *op. cit.;*
    Patricia Cayo Sexton, *Education and Income,* New York: Viking, 1961;
    Frank Riessman, *The Culturally Deprived Child,* New York: Harper,
    1962.

14. AUGUST B. HOLLINGSHEAD and FREDERICK C. REDLICH, *Social Class and
    Mental Illness,* New York: Wiley, 1958; Betty Overall and H. Aronson,
    "Expectations of Psychotherapy in Patients of Lower Socioeconomic
    Class," *American Journal of Orthopsychiatry,* Vol. XXXIII, April, 1963,
    421–430.

15. CAROL H. MEYER, "Individualizing the Multiproblem Family," *Social
    Casework,* Vol. XLIV, May, 1963, p. 269.

16. HYMAN RODMAN, "On Understanding Lower-Class Behaviour," *Social
    and Economic Studies,* Vol. VIII, Dec., 1959, p. 445. See original article
    for footnotes.

17. HYMAN RODMAN, *Lower-Class Families,* in preparation. Cf. Lee
    Rainwater, Richard P. Coleman, and Gerald Handel, *Workingman's
    Wife,* New York: Oceana Publications, 1959; Lee Rainwater, *And the
    Poor Get Children,* Chicago: Quadrangle Books, 1960; Oscar Lewis,
    Five Families, New York: Basic Books, 1959; E. Franklin Frazier, *The
    Negro Family in the United States,* New York: Citadel Press, rev. and
    abridged ed., 1948; Albert K. Cohen and Harold M. Hodges, "Char-

acteristics of the Lower-Blue-Collar Class," *Social Problems,* Vol. X, Spring, 1963.

18. Geographic mobility is therefore not a good index of status mobility. For a brief discussion related to this point see Hyman Rodman, "The 'Achievement Syndrome' and Negro Americans," and Bernard C. Rosen, "Reply to Rodman," *American Sociological Review,* Vol. XXIV, Oct., 1959, pp. 691–692.

19. ROBERT K. MERTON, *Social Theory and Social Structure,* rev. and enlarged ed., New York: Free Press of Glencoe, 1957, p. 428.

20. BARBARA WOOTTON, *Social Science and Social Pathology,* London: Allen and Unwin, 1959, p. 328.

⇜§ 20 §⇝   Social Class and Parent-Child Relationships: An Interpretation

by MELVIN L. KOHN

This essay is an attempt to interpret, from a sociological perspective, the effects of social class upon parent-child relationships. Many past discussions of the problem seem somehow to lack this perspective, even though the problem is one of profound importance for sociology. Because most investigators have approached the problem from an interest in psychodynamics, rather than social structure, they have largely limited their attention to a few specific techniques used by mothers in the rearing of infants and very young children. They have discovered, *inter alia,* that social class has a decided bearing on which techniques parents use. But, since they have come at the problem from this perspective, their interest in social class has not gone beyond its effects for this very limited aspect of parent-child relationships.

Reprinted from *American Journal of Sociology,* Vol. LXVIII, Jan., 1963, 471–480. With permission of the author and The University of Chicago Press. Copyright 1963 by The University of Chicago.

The present analysis conceives the problem of social class and parent-child relationships as an instance of the more general problem of the effects of social structure upon behavior. It starts with the assumption that social class has proved to be so useful a concept because it refers to more than simply educational level, or occupation, or any of the large number of correlated variables. It is so useful because it captures the reality that the intricate interplay of all these variables creates different basic conditions of life at different levels of the social order. Members of different social classes, by virtue of enjoying (or suffering) different conditions of life, come to see the world differently—to develop different conceptions of social reality, different aspirations and hopes and fears, different conceptions of the desirable.

The last is particularly important for present purposes, for from people's conceptions of the desirable—and particularly from their conceptions of what characteristics are desirable in children—one can discern their objectives in child-rearing. Thus, conceptions of the desirable—that is, values[1]—become the key concept for this analysis, the bridge between position in the larger social structure and the behavior of the individual. The intent of the analysis is to trace the effects of social class position on parental values and the effects of values on behavior.

Since this approach differs from analyses focused on social class differences in the use of particular child-rearing techniques, it will be necessary to re-examine earlier formulations from the present perspective. Then three questions will be discussed, bringing into consideration the limited available data that are relevant: What differences are there in the values held by parents of different social classes? What is there about the conditions of life distinctive of these classes that might explain the differences in their values? What consequences do these differences in values have for parents' relationships with their children?

Social Class

Social classes will be defined as aggregates of individuals who occupy broadly similar positions in the scale of prestige.[2] In dealing with the research literature, we shall treat occupational posi-

tion (or occupational position as weighted somewhat by education) as a serviceable index of social class for urban American
society. And we shall adopt the model of social stratification implicit in most research, that of four relatively discrete classes: a
"lower class" of unskilled manual workers, a "working class" of
manual workers in semiskilled and skilled occupations, a "middle
class" of white-collar workers and professionals, and an "elite,"
differentiated from the middle class not so much in terms of occupation as of wealth and lineage.

Almost all the empirical evidence, including that from our own
research, stems from broad comparisons of the middle and working class. Thus we shall have little to say about the extremes of
the class distribution. Furthermore, we shall have to act as if
the middle and working classes were each homogeneous. They
are not, even in terms of status considerations alone. There is
evidence, for example, that within each broad social class, variations in parents' values quite regularly parallel gradations of social
status. Moreover, the classes are heterogeneous with respect to
other factors that affect parents' values, such as religion and
ethnicity. But even when all such considerations are taken into
account, the empirical evidence clearly shows that being on one
side or the other of the line that divides manual from non-manual
workers has profound consequences for how one rears one's children.[3]

Stability and Change

Any analysis of the effects of social class upon parent-child
relationships should start with Urie Bronfenbrenner's analytic
review of the studies that had been conducted in this country
during the twenty-five years up to 1958.[4] From the seemingly
contradictory findings of a number of studies, Bronfenbrenner
discerned not chaos but orderly change: there have been changes
in the child-training techniques employed by middle-class parents in
the past quarter-century; similar changes have been taking place
in the working class, but working-class parents have consistently
lagged behind by a few years; thus, while middle-class parents
of twenty-five years ago were more "restrictive" than were working-

class parents, today the middle-class parents are more "permissive"; and the gap between the classes seems to be narrowing.

It must be noted that these conclusions are limited by the questions Bronfenbrenner's predecessors asked in their research. The studies deal largely with a few particular techniques of child-rearing, especially those involved in caring for infants and very young children, and say very little about parents' over-all relationships with their children, particularly as the children grow older. There is clear evidence that the past quarter-century has seen change, even faddism, with respect to the use of breast-feeding or bottle-feeding, scheduling or not scheduling, spanking or isolating. But when we generalize from these specifics to talk of a change from "restrictive" to "permissive" practices—or, worse yet, of a change from "restrictive" to "permissive" parent-child relationships—we impute to them a far greater importance than they probably have, either to parents or to children.[5]

There is no evidence that recent faddism in child-training techniques is symptomatic of profound changes in the relations of parents to children in either social class. In fact, as Bronfenbrenner notes, what little evidence we do have points in the opposite direction: the over-all quality of parent-child relationships does not seem to have changed substantially in either class.[6] In all probability, parents have changed techniques in service of much the same values, and the changes have been quite specific. These changes must be explained, but the enduring characteristics are probably even more important.

Why the changes? Bronfenbrenner's interpretation is ingeniously simple. He notes that the changes in techniques employed by middle-class parents have closely paralleled those advocated by presumed experts, and he concludes that middle-class parents have changed their practices *because* they are responsive to changes in what the experts tell them is right and proper. Working-class parents, being less educated and thus less directly responsive to the media of communication, followed behind only later.[7]

Bronfenbrenner is almost undoubtedly right in asserting that middle-class parents have followed the drift of presumably expert opinion. But why have they done so? It is not sufficient to assume that the explanation lies in their greater degree of education. This might explain why middle-class parents are substantially more likely than are working-class parents to *read* books and articles on child-rearing, as we know they do.[8] But they need not *follow* the experts' advice. We know from various studies of the mass media that people generally search for confirmation of their existing beliefs and practices and tend to ignore what contradicts them.

From all the evidence at our disposal, it looks as if middle-class parents not only read what the experts have to say but also search out a wide variety of other sources of information and advice: they are far more likely than are working-class parents to discuss child-rearing with friends and neighbors, to consult physicians on these matters, to attend Parent-Teacher Association meetings, to discuss the child's behavior with his teacher. Middle-class parents seem to regard child-rearing as more problematic than do working-class parents. This can hardly be a matter of education alone. It must be rooted more deeply in the conditions of life of the two social classes.

Everything about working-class parents' lives—their comparative lack of education, the nature of their jobs, their greater attachment to the extended family—conduces to their retaining familiar methods.* Furthermore, even should they be receptive to change, they are less likely than are middle-class parents to find the experts' writings appropriate to their wants, for the experts predicate their advice on middle-class values. Everything about middle-class parents' lives, on the other hand, conduces to their looking for new methods to achieve their goals. They look to the experts, to other sources of relevant information, and to each other not for new values but for more serviceable techniques.† And within the limits of our present scanty knowledge about means-ends relationships in child-rearing, the experts have provided practical and useful advice. It is not that educated parents slavishly

---

* The differences between middle and working-class conditions of life will be discussed more fully below.

† Certainly middle-class parents do not get their values from the experts. In our research, we compared the values of parents who say they read Spock, Gesell, or other books on child-rearing, to those who read only magazine and newspaper articles, and those who say they read nothing at all on the subject. In the middle class, these three groups have substantially the same values. In the working-class, the story is different. Few working-class parents claim to read books or even articles on child-rearing. Those few who do have values much more akin to those of the middle class. But these are atypical working-class parents who are very anxious to attain middle-class status. One suspects that for them the experts provide a sort of handbook to the middle class; even for them, it is unlikely that the values come out of Spock and Gesell.

follow the experts but that the experts have provided what the parents have sought.

To look at the question this way is to put it in a quite different perspective: the focus becomes not specific techniques nor changes in the use of specific techniques but parental values.

Values of Middle- and Working-Class Parents

Of the entire range of values one might examine, it seems particularly strategic to focus on parents' conceptions of what characteristics would be most desirable for boys or girls the age of their own children. From this one can hope to discern the parents' goals in rearing their children. It must be assumed, however, that a parent will choose one characteristic as more desirable than another only if he considers it to be both important, in the sense that failure to develop this characteristic would affect the child adversely, and problematic, in the sense that it is neither to be taken for granted that the child will develop that characteristic nor impossible for him to do so. In interpreting parents' value choices, we must keep in mind that their choices reflect not simply their goals but the goals whose achievement they regard as problematic.

Few studies, even in recent years, have directly investigated the relationship of social class to parental values. Fortunately, however, the results of these few are in essential agreement. The earliest study was Evelyn Millis Duvall's pioneering inquiry of 1946.[9] Duvall characterized working-class (and lower middle-class) parental values as "traditional"—they want their children to be neat and clean, to obey and respect adults, to please adults. In contrast to this emphasis on how the child comports himself, middle-class parental values are more "developmental"—they want their children to be eager to learn, to love and confide in the parents, to be happy, to share and co-operate, to be healthy and well.

Duvall's traditional-developmental dichotomy does not describe the difference between middle- and working-class parental values quite exactly, but it does point to the essence of the difference: working-class parents want the child to conform to externally

imposed standards, while middle-class parents are far more atten-
tive to his internal dynamics.

The few relevant findings of subsequent studies are entirely
consistent with this basic point, especially in the repeated indica-
tions that working-class parents put far greater stress on obedience
to parental commands than do middle-class parents.[10] Our own
research, conducted in 1956–57, provides the evidence most directly comparable to Duvall's.[11] We, too, found that working-class
parents value obedience, neatness, and cleanliness more highly
than do middle-class parents, and that middle-class parents in turn
value curiosity, happiness, consideration, and—most importantly
—self-control more highly than do working-class parents. We further found that there are characteristic clusters of value choice in
the two social classes: working-class parental values center on
conformity to external proscriptions, middle-class parental values
on *self*-direction. To working-class parents, it is the overt act that
matters: the child should not transgress externally imposed rules;
to middle-class parents, it is the child's motives and feelings that
matter: the child should govern himself.

In fairness, it should be noted that middle- and working-class
parents share many core values. Both, for example, value honesty
very highly—although, characteristically, "honesty" has rather
different connotations in the two social classes, implying "trust-
worthiness" for the working-class and "truthfulness" for the middle-
class. The common theme, of course, is that parents of both social
classes value a decent respect for the rights of others; middle- and
working-class values are but variations on this common theme.
The reason for emphasizing the variations rather than the common
theme is that they seem to have far-ranging consequences for
parents' relationships with their children and thus ought to be
taken seriously.

It would be good if there were more evidence about parental
values—data from other studies, in other locales, and especially,
data derived from more than one mode of inquiry. But, what
evidence we do have is consistent, so that there is at least some
basis for believing it is reliable. Furthermore, there is evidence
that the value choices made by parents in these inquiries are not
simply a reflection of their assessments of their own children's
deficiencies or excellences. Thus, we may take the findings of

these studies as providing a limited, but probably valid, picture of the parents' generalized conceptions of what behavior would be desirable in their preadolescent children.

Explaining Class Differences in Parental Values

That middle-class parents are more likely to espouse some values, and working-class parents other values, must be a function of differences in their conditions of life. In the present state of our knowledge, it is difficult to disentangle the interacting variables with a sufficient degree of exactness to ascertain which conditions of life are crucial to the differences in values. Nevertheless, it is necessary to examine the principal components of class differences in life conditions to see what each may contribute.

The logical place to begin is with occupational differences, for these are certainly pre-eminently important, not only in defining social classes in urban, industrialized society, but also in determining much else about people's life conditions.[12] There are at least three respects in which middle-class occupations typically differ from working-class occupations, above and beyond their obvious status-linked differences in security, stability of income, and general social prestige. One is that middle-class occupations deal more with the manipulation of interpersonal relations, ideas, and symbols, while working-class occupations deal more with the manipulation of things. The second is that middle-class occupations are more subject to self-direction, while working-class occupations are more subject to standardization and direct supervision. The third is that getting ahead in middle-class occupations is more dependent upon one's own actions, while in working-class occupations it is more dependent upon collective action, particularly in unionized industries. From these differences, one can sketch differences in the characteristics that make for getting along, and getting ahead, in middle- and working-class occupations. Middle-class occupations require a greater degree of self-direction; working-class occupations, in larger measure, require that one follow explicit rules set down by someone in authority.

Obviously, these differences parallel the differences we have found between the two social classes in the characteristics valued by parents for children. At minimum, one can conclude that there is a congruence between occupational requirements and parental values. It is, moreover, a reasonable supposition, although not a necessary conclusion, that middle- and working-class parents value different characteristics in children *because* of these differences in their occupational circumstances. This supposition does not necessarily assume that parents consciously train their children to meet future occupational requirements; it may simply be that their own occupational experiences have significantly affected parents' conceptions of what is desirable behavior, on or off the job, for adults or for children.*

These differences in occupational circumstances are probably basic to the differences we have found between middle- and working-class parental values, but taken alone they do not sufficiently explain them. Parents need not accord pre-eminent importance to occupational requirements in their judgments of what is most desirable. For a sufficient explanation of class differences in values, it is necessary to recognize that other differences in middle- and working-class conditions of life reinforce the differences in occupational circumstances at every turn.

Educational differences, for example, above and beyond their importance as determinants of occupation, probably contribute independently to the differences in middle- and working-class parental values. At minimum, middle-class parents' greater attention to the child's internal dynamics is facilitated by their learned ability to deal with the subjective and the ideational. Further-

---

* Two objections might be raised here. (1) Occupational experiences may not be important for a mother's values, however crucial they are for her husband's, if she has had little or no work experience. But even those mothers who have had little or no occupational experience know something of occupational life from their husbands and others, and live in a culture in which occupation and career permeate all of life. (2) Parental values may be built not so much out of their own experiences as out of their expectations of the child's future experiences. This might seem particularly plausible in explaining working-class values, for their high valuation of such stereotypically *middle-class* characteristics as obedience, neatness, and cleanliness might imply that they are training their children for a middle-class life they expect the children to achieve. Few working-class parents, however, do expect (or even want) their children to go on to college and the middle-class jobs for which a college education is required. (This is shown in Herbert H. Hyman, "The Value Systems of Different Classes: A Social Psychological Contribution to the Analysis of Stratification," in Reinhard Bendix and Seymour Martin Lipset [eds.], *Class, Status and Power: A Reader in Social Stratification* [Glencoe, Ill.: Free Press, 1953], and confirmed in unpublished data from our own research.)

more, differences in levels and stability of income undoubtedly contribute to class differences in parental values. That middle-class parents still have somewhat higher levels of income, and much greater stability of income, makes them able to take for granted the respectability that is still problematic for working-class parents. They can afford to concentrate, instead, on motives and feelings —which, in the circumstances of their lives, are more important.

These considerations suggest that the differences between middle- and working-class parental values are probably a function of the entire complex of differences in life conditions characteristic of the two social classes. Consider, for example, the working-class situation. With the end of mass immigration, there has emerged a stable working class, largely derived from the manpower of rural areas, uninterested in mobility in the middle class, but very much interested in security, respectability, and the enjoyment of a decent standard of living.[13] This working class has come to enjoy a standard of living formerly reserved for the middle class, but has not chosen a middle-class style of life. In effect, the working class has striven for, and partially achieved, an American dream distinctly different from the dream of success and achievement. In an affluent society, it is possible for the worker to be the traditionalist—politically, economically, and, most relevant here, in his values for his children.[14] Working-class parents want their children to conform to external authority because the parents themselves are willing to accord respect to authority, in return for security and respectability. Their conservatism in child-rearing is part of a more general conservatism and traditionalism.

Middle-class parental values are a product of a quite different set of conditions. Much of what the working class values, they can take for granted. Instead, they can—and must—instil in their children a degree of self-direction that would be less appropriate to the conditions of life of the working class.* Certainly, there is

* It has been argued that as larger and larger proportions of the middle class have become imbedded in a bureaucratic way of life—in distinction to the entrepreneurial way of life of a bygone day—it has become more appropriate to raise children to be accommodative than to be self-reliant. But this point of view is a misreading of the conditions of life faced by the middle-class inhabitants of the bureaucratic world. Their jobs require at least as great a degree of self-reliance as do entrepreneurial enterprises. We tend to forget, nowadays, just how little the small- or medium-sized entrepreneur controlled the conditions of his own existence and just how much he was subjected to the petty authority of those on whose pleasure depended the sur-

substantial truth in the characterization of the middle-class way of life as one of great conformity. What must be noted here, however, is that *relative to* the working class, middle-class conditions of life require a more substantial degree of independence of action. Furthermore, the higher levels of education enjoyed by the middle class make possible a degree of internal scrutiny difficult to achieve without the skills in dealing with the abstract that college training sometimes provides. Finally, the economic security of most middle-class occupations, the level of income they provide, the status they confer, allow one to focus his attention on the subjective and the ideational. Middle-class conditions of life both allow and demand a greater degree of self-direction than do those of the working class.

Consequences of Class Differences in Parents' Values

What consequences do the differences between middle- and working-class parents' values have for the ways they raise their children?

Much of the research on techniques of infant- and child-training is of little relevance here. For example, with regard to parents' preferred techniques for disciplining children, a question of major interest to many investigators, Bronfenbrenner summarizes past studies as follows: "In matters of discipline, working-class parents are consistently more likely to employ physical punishment, while middle-class families rely more on reasoning, isolation, appeals to guilt, and other methods involving the threat of loss of love."[15] This, if still true,* is consistent with middle-class parents' greater attentiveness to the child's internal dynamics, working-class parents' greater concern about the overt act. For present purposes, however, the crucial question is not *which* disciplinary method

---

vival of his enterprise. And we fail to recognize the degree to which monolithic-seeming bureaucracies allow free play for—in fact, require—individual enterprise of new sorts: in the creation of ideas, the building of empires, the competition for advancement.

At any rate, our data show no substantial differences between the values of parents from bureaucratic and entrepreneurial occupational worlds, in either social class. But see Daniel R. Miller and Guy E. Swanson, *The Changing American Parent: A Study in the Detroit Area* (New York: John Wiley & Sons, 1958).

* Later studies, including our own, do not show this difference.

parents prefer, but when and why they use one or another method of discipline.

The most directly relevant available data are on the conditions under which middle- and working-class parents use physical punishment. Working-class parents are apt to resort to physical punishment when the direct and immediate consequences of their children's disobedient acts are most extreme, and to refrain from punishing when this might provoke an even greater disturbance.[16] Thus, they will punish a child for wild play when the furniture is damaged or the noise level becomes intolerable, but ignore the same actions when the direct and immediate consequences are not so extreme. Middle-class parents, on the other hand, seem to punish or refrain from punishing on the basis of their interpretation of the child's intent in acting as he does. Thus, they will punish a furious outburst when the context is such that they interpret it to be a loss of self-control, but will ignore an equally extreme outburst when the context is such that they interpret it to be merely an emotional release.

It is understandable that working-class parents react to the consequences rather than to the intent of their children's actions: the important thing is that the child not transgress externally imposed rules. Correspondingly, if middle-class parents are instead concerned about the child's motives and feelings, they can and must look beyond the overt act to why the child acts as he does. It would seem that middle- and working-class values direct parents to see their children's misbehavior in quite different ways, so that misbehavior which prompts middle-class parents to action does not seem as important to working-class parents, and vice versa.* Obviously, parents' values are not the only things that enter into their use of physical punishment. But unless one assumes a complete lack of goal-directedness in parental behavior, he would have to grant that parents' values direct their attention to some facets of their own and their children's behavior, and divert it from other facets.

The consequences of class differences in parental values extend far beyond differences in disciplinary practices. From a knowledge of their values for their children, one would expect middle-class parents to feel a greater obligation to be *supportive* of the children,

---

* This is not to say that the methods used by parents of either social class are necessarily the most efficacious for achievement of their goals.

if only because of their sensitivity to the children's internal dynamics. Working-class values, with their emphasis upon conformity
to external rules, should lead to greater emphasis upon the parents'
obligation to impose constraints.[17] And this, according to Bronfenbrenner, is precisely what has been shown in those few studies that
have concerned themselves with the over-all relationship of parents
to child: "Over the entire twenty-five-year period studied, parent-
child relationships in the middle-class are consistently reported as
more acceptant and equalitarian, while those in the working-class
are oriented toward maintaining order and obedience."[18]

   This conclusion is based primarily on studies of *mother*-child relationships in middle- and working-class families. Class differences
in parental values have further ramifications for the father's role.[19]
Mothers in each class would have their husbands play a role facili-
tative of the child's development of the characteristics valued in
that class: Middle-class mothers want their husbands to be supportive of the children (especially of sons), with their responsibility
for imposing constraints being of decidedly secondary importance;
working-class mothers look to their husbands to be considerably
more directive—support is accorded far less importance and constraint far more. Most middle-class fathers agree with their wives
and play a role close to what their wives would have them play.
Many working-class fathers, on the other hand, do not. It is not
that they see the constraining role as less important than do their
wives, but that many of them see no reason why they should have
to shoulder the responsibility. From their point of view, the important thing is that the child be taught what limits he must not
transgress. It does not much matter who does the teaching, and
since mother has primary responsibility for child care, the job
should be hers.

   The net consequence is a quite different division of parental responsibilities in the two social classes. In middle-class families,
mother's and father's roles usually are not sharply differentiated.
What differentiation exists is largely a matter of each parent taking
special responsibility for being supportive of children of the parent's
own sex. In working-class families, mother's and father's roles are
more sharply differentiated, with mother almost always being the
more supportive parent. In some working-class families, mother
specializes in support, father in constraint; in others, perhaps in

most, mother raises the children, father provides the wherewithal.*

Thus, the differences in middle- and working-class parents' values have wide ramifications for their relationships with their children and with each other. Of course, many class differences in parent-child relationships are not directly attributable to differences in values; undoubtedly the very differences in their conditions of life that make for differences in parental values reinforce, at every juncture, parents' characteristic ways of relating to their children. But one could not account for these consistent differences in parent-child relationships in the two social classes without reference to the differences in parents' avowed values.

Conclusion

This paper serves to show how complex and demanding are the problems of interpreting the effects of social structure on behavior. Our inquiries habitually stop at the point of demonstrating that social position correlates with something, when we should want to pursue the question, "Why?" What are the processes by which position in social structure molds behavior? The present analysis has dealt with this question in one specific form: Why does social class matter for parents' relationships with their children? There is every reason to believe that the problems encountered in trying to deal with that question would recur in any analysis of the effects of social structure on behavior.

In this analysis, the concept of "values" has been used as the principal bridge from social position to behavior. The analysis has endeavored to show that middle-class parental values differ from those of working-class parents; that these differences are rooted in basic differences between middle- and working-class conditions of life; and that the differences between middle- and working-class parental values have important consequences for their relationships

* Fragmentary data suggest sharp class differences in the husband-wife relationship that complement the differences in the division of parental responsibilities discussed above. For example, virtually no working-class wife reports that she and her husband ever go out on an evening or weekend without the children. And few working-class fathers do much to relieve their wives of the burden of caring for the children all the time. By and large, working-class fathers seem to lead a largely separate social life from that of their wives; the wife has full-time responsibility for the children, while the husband is free to go his own way.

with their children. The interpretive model, in essence, is: social class—conditions of life—values—behavior.

The specifics of the present characterization of parental values may prove to be inexact; the discussion of the ways in which social class position affects values is undoubtedly partial; and the tracing of the consequences of differences in values for differences in parent-child relationships is certainly tentative and incomplete. I trust, however, that the perspective will prove to be valid and that this formulation will stimulate other investigators to deal more directly with the processes whereby social structure affects behavior.

NOTES

1. "A value is a conception, explicit or implicit, distinctive of an individual or characteristic of a group, of the desirable which influences the selection from available modes, means, and ends of action" (Clyde Kluckhohn, "Values and Value Orientations," in Talcott Parsons and Edward A. Shils (eds.), *Toward A General Theory of Action* [Cambridge, Mass.: Harvard University Press, 1951], p. 395). See also the discussion of values in Robin M. Williams, Jr., *American Society: A Sociological Interpretation* (New York: Alfred A. Knopf, Inc., 1951), chap. xi, and his discussion of social class and culture on p. 101.

2. WILLIAMS, *op. cit.,* p. 89.

3. These, and other assertions of fact not referred to published sources, are based on research my colleagues and I have conducted. For the design of this research and the principal substantive findings see my "Social Class and Parental Values," *American Journal of Sociology,* LXIV (January, 1959), 337–51; my "Social Class and the Exercise of Parental Authority," *American Sociological Review,* XXIV (June, 1959), 352–66; and with Eleanor E. Carroll, "Social Class and the Allocation of Parental Responsibilities," *Sociometry,* XXIII (December, 1960), 372–92. I should like to express my appreciation to my principal collaborators in this research, John A. Clausen and Eleanor E. Carroll.

4. URIE BRONFENBRENNER, "Socialization and Social Class through Time and Space," in Eleanor E. Maccoby, Theodore M. Newcomb, and Eugene L. Hartley (eds.), *Readings in Social Psychology,* 3rd ed. (New York: Henry Holt & Co., 1958).

5. Furthermore, these concepts employ a priori judgments about which the various investigators have disagreed radically. See, e.g., Robert R. Sears, Eleanor E. Maccoby, and Harry Levin, *Patterns of Child Rearing*

(Evanston, Ill.: Row, Peterson & Co., 1957), pp. 444–47, and Richard A. Littman, Robert C. A. Moore, and John Pierce-Jones, "Social Class Differences in Child Rearing: A Third Community for Comparison with Chicago and Newton," *American Sociological Review,* XXII (December, 1957), 694–704, esp. p. 703.

6. BRONFENBRENNER, *op. cit.,* pp. 420–22 and 425.

7. Bronfenbrenner gives clearest expression to this interpretation, but it has been adopted by others, too. See, e.g., Martha Sturm White, "Social Class, Child-Rearing Practices, and Child Behavior," *American Sociological Review,* XXII (December, 1957), 704–12.

8. This was noted by John E. Anderson in the first major study of social class and family relationships ever conducted, and has repeatedly been confirmed (*The Young Child in the Home: A Survey of Three Thousand American Families* [New York: Appleton-Century, 1936]).

9. EVELYN M. DUVALL, "Conceptions of Parenthood," *American Journal of Sociology,* LII (November, 1946), 193–203.

10. ALEX INKELES has shown that this is true not only for the United States but for a number of other industrialized societies as well ("Industrial Man: The Relation of Status to Experience, Perception, and Value," *American Journal of Sociology,* LXVI (July, 1960), 20–21 and Table 9).

11. "Social Class and Parental Values," *op. cit.*

12. For a thoughtful discussion of the influence of occupational role on parental values see David F. Aberle and Kaspar D. Naegele, "Middle Class Fathers' Occupational Role and Attitudes Toward Children," *American Journal of Orthopsychiatry,* XXII (April, 1952), 366–78.

13. See, e.g., S. M. Miller and Frank Riessman, "The Working Class Subculture: A New View," *Social Problems,* IX (Summer, 1961), 86–97.

14. Relevant here is Seymour Martin Lipset's somewhat disillusioned "Democracy and Working-Class Authoritarianism," *American Sociological Review,* XXIV (August, 1959), 482–501.

15. BRONFENBRENNER, *op. cit.,* p. 424.

16. "Social Class and the Exercise of Parental Authority," *op. cit.*

17. The justification for treating support and constraint as the two major dimensions of parent-child relationships lies in the theoretical argument of Talcott Parsons and Robert F. Bales, *Family, Socialization and Interaction Process* (Glencoe, Ill.: Free Press, 1955), esp. p. 45, and the empirical argument of Earl S. Schaefer, "A Circumplex Model for Maternal Behavior," *Journal of Abnormal and Social Psychology,* LIX (September, 1959), 226–34.

18. BRONFENBRENNER, *op. cit.,* p. 425.

19. From the very limited evidence available at the time of his review, Bronfenbrenner tentatively concluded: "though the middle-class father typically has a warmer relationship with the child, he is also likely to have more authority and status in family affairs" (*ibid.,* p. 422). The discussion here is based largely on subsequent research, esp. "Social Class and the Allocation of Parental Responsibilities," *op. cit.*

Eight

THE
CHANGING
AMERICAN
FAMILY

⊰§ INTRODUCTION §⊱

A major change through which the American family has passed has been its transition from a domestic work group to a domestic group in which the individual members of the family are dispersed at work and at school. The farm family and the family that runs a small business firm are now unusual; the children go to school for a longer period of time; and the adult members of the family, often including the wife, leave the home to go to work. Although these changes have taken place gradually, they have had a dramatic impact upon American family life in the past one hundred years (Ogburn, 1938; *21; 22*).

From Institution to Companionship

The changes in economic organization in the United States have been accompanied by changes in family organization. A well-known statement of this change has been made by Burgess and Locke, who refer to a transition "from institution to companionship." As it is expressed in the latest edition of the book by Burgess, Locke, and Thomes (1963):

> the family has been in transition from an institution, with family behavior controlled by the mores, public opinion, and law, to a companionship, with behavior arising from the mutual affection, equality, and consensus of its members. The companionship form of the family is not to be conceived as having been realized but as emerging. . . . The most extreme conceptual formulation of the institutional family would be one in which its unity would be determined entirely by the traditional rules and regulations, specified duties and obligations, and other social pressures impinging on family members. The ideal construct of the family as a companionship would focus on the unity which develops out of mutual affection and intimate association of husband and wife and parents and children (p. 3).

A more comprehensive statement of the kinds of interpersonal relationships to be found in the companionship family is found in the selection by Burgess, Locke, and Thomes (*21*). Similar expressions about the intense, personal, or affectionate relationships to be found within the family have also been made by Parsons (see *22*).

As Straus (1962) and Kirkpatrick (1963, p. 84) have pointed out, a wide variety of terms are used to characterize the changing nature of the American family. One such term is the "colleague family," which has been proposed by Miller and Swanson (1958) as an alternative to the "companionship family." They see the colleague family, rather than the companionship family, as "the growing wave of the family's future." They acknowledge that "the tendencies which Burgess and Locke describe have, in part, been consolidated for large parts of the population. Women and men are increasingly equal." But, in addition, Miller and Swanson point out that women and men are different, and play specialized roles, and this is the essence of their disagreement with Burgess and Locke:

> The specialization on the job has entered the home, and the equal partners have been able to see that differences in talent, interest, and function, as long as they are complementary, do not threaten equality. Instead, they may enrich and promote the common life. For this reason we call this type of family the "colleague" family. As specialists at work may find in each other skills they lack, but skills they equally need, and as they may defer to one another's judgment on the grounds of differing competence without feeling that they have personally lost in prestige, so husband and wife may now relate in this way (pp. 199–200).

A more recent and more provocative model of the contemporary American family has been presented by Farber (1964). He refers to it as a "permanent-availability model," and contrasts it with the functional differentiation model of Parsons and the companionship model of Burgess. In essence, Farber's model assumes the permanent availability of all adults, regardless of marital status, as potential spouses for all other cross-sex adults who are not ruled out by the incest taboo. This means, among other things, that even a person already married is a potential spouse. Marriages are not arranged by kinsmen but are based upon personal choice. Personal welfare is the primary consideration, and as a result marriages take place early, the divorce rate is high, and remarriages are frequent. Having children is an indication, by the parents, that they intend to maintain their marital relationship, but children do not rule out divorce. This is merely a truncated account of Farber's model, but its elegance is attested to by its ability to account for such matters as a decreasing age of first marriages, increasing divorce and re-marriage rates, rising rates of illegitimacy, and rising rates of employment among women. It should be noted, of course, that Farber is talking about a *conceptual* model (which tries to describe trends in the American family) and not about an *ethical* model (which tries to promote virtue).

Disorganization or Reorganization?

Where there is change there is also a certain amount of chaos. As a consequence, the most widely debated question about the American family has been, and probably still is: Is it disorganized and deteriorating, or is it in a state of transition and reorganization?

Sorokin and Zimmerman are most closely associated with the view that the American family is disorganized and deteriorating. The basic facts that led them to their conclusion were the rising divorce rate, the declining birth rate, and the changing sex, marriage, and family mores. These facts were interpreted as a sign of the family's decay—individuals were overly selfish and were not prepared to play responsible roles as members of their families. As a consequence marriage was becoming more of a private contract between two individuals, and divorces were becoming easier to get; moreover, parents wanted fewer children, and many wanted no children at all (Sorokin, 1941, 1956, 1957; Zimmerman, 1947).

It is difficult to evaluate the issue on the basis of the statistics that are available. It is true that the divorce rate did not continue to rise, and that the birth rate did not continue to decline, as was generally predicted in the 1930's. This has been taken by some people to mean that Sorokin and Zimmerman were wrong. But we must also remember that the divorce rate which has leveled off is high (about one marriage in four presently ends in divorce); and that the birth rate is again on the decline (see Appendix). More-over, the question of what is happening to the American family does not merely rest on divorce and birth rates. As a result the debate about whether the American family is in a state of decay or a state of progress continues (Rutledge, 1956; Brinton, 1959; Sorokin, 1960; Winch, 1963; *15*).

But there is one view of the changing American family that appears to be predominant. In this view, a certain amount of disorganization is acknowledged, but it is the "disorganization of transition." The transition is toward a new type of family—a "companionship family" for some (*21*); an "isolated nuclear family" (*22*) or a "colleague family" (see p. 250) for others. In this view a declining birth rate was seen as an indication of the lesser utility of children—they were no longer needed for the family farm or the family firm. As a result, parents were beginning to have as many children as they "wanted" rather than as many as they "needed." Similarly, the rising (or high) divorce rate was seen as an indication of the greater mutuality in the relationship between husband and wife. No longer did they stay together because of social pressures, regardless of the quality of their relationship; they now were staying together because of their mutual affection, because they "wanted" to and not because they "had" to. The fact that the birth rate did not continue its decline through the 1930's and 1940's and that the divorce rate did not continue its rise (see Appendix) suggests that a reasonably good adjustment has been made by the American family to its changed conditions. The more ominous predictions that the society would die out as a result of the lack of incentive to raise children, or that lawful marriage would become indistinguishable from non-marital sexual relationships, have proven to be exaggerated.

On behalf of Sorokin and Zimmerman, however, it must be said that they have written about the family in much broader historical terms than their critics, and the changes they have spoken about have been changes involving centuries rather than decades. From this longer point of view, therefore, their predictions may yet be borne out. Moreover, Sorokin and Zimmerman have often been viewed over-simply as advocating "a return" to some older type of family organization. While this is true in part, it must be noted that both of them look forward to a *new* form of family organization. For them, the American family is in a state of crisis and decay; but it is also in transition. Sorokin, for example, sees some progress toward a more *integral* form of family life and society (from the currently *sensate* society in which we live) in which rational, spiritual, and sensory factors will all play their part. The "return" that is advocated by Sorokin and Zimmerman is to a type of family organization that has existed in the past, but it is not merely a wish to return to the past. As Sorokin points out:

> Any system changes incessantly during its existence: among all its properties something new is incessantly introduced and something old is incessantly lost from moment to moment of its existence. In this sense any sociocultural process is ever new and unrepeated (1957, p. 670).

Another difference that marks Sorokin and Zimmerman off from most sociologists is their acknowledged *moralistic* tone, and specifically their disenchantment with some of the new values that are developing. This, above all, has led to their unpopularity among many American social scientists.* As Sorokin himself remarks, "articles and books (including this one) that are critical in regard to the new mores are ridiculed and stigmatized as being hopelessly old-fashioned, unscientific and stupid" (1956, p. 44).

There are differences within American society, however, and in some circles the writings of Sorokin and Zimmerman are popular. Since they are critical of the ease of divorce and the over-use of birth control methods, it is understandable that they are rather popular among Catholic social scientists. But even among Catholics there is a good deal of controversy at present about matters of interest to family sociologists—and Catholic scientists and church officials are engaged in these controversies (cf. Bromley, 1965). Other churches are also engaged in these debates, and the issues of abortion, divorce, family planning (and the oral contraceptives), and interfaith marriages have all been discussed by various church officials in the press, in numerous books and articles, and at church councils. Although decisions on matters of morality must be reached by each religious group, and ultimately by each individual, it augurs well for the social sciences in the Western world that there are active debates and controversies about matters of morality in all segments

---

* I share Tiryakian's (1963, Preface) concern that Sorokin has not become as well-known as he should be to American sociology students. For additional commentary on Sorokin the reader should read the papers in the book edited by Allen (1963)—especially the papers by David R. Mace and by R. K. Merton and B. Barber.

of society. In this way the social sciences are perhaps left freer
to pursue matters of scientific interest without recourse to dogma,
while the churches remain free to make use of scientific findings in
a way that is consistent with their (possibly changing) morality.

The Present and the Future

It is possible to project present trends into the future, and a
number of writers, in an admittedly speculative manner, have done
so. The resulting picture is sometimes conservative and sometimes
radical, from the point of view of contemporary attitudes and morality. One of the strengths of American society has been its willingness and its ability to change, and it therefore seems worthwhile to
look dispassionately, but also critically, toward what the future may
hold for American family life. We shall very briefly discuss only two
possible areas of change—the status of the aged, and the status of
women.

One of the characteristics that Parsons has noted about the
American family is its rationality. Housework, child rearing, and
changing residential patterns are all seen in the context of rationality
(22). The "problem of the aged" is also seen in this context by
Parsons, who refers to a possible future solution of this problem in
American society. This involves a recognition of the special functions that the aged can play in our society—fiduciary functions—
and the assignment of these special functions to the aged. This is
perhaps the least convincing of the points that Parsons makes about
the American family.* Particularly in view of the pressure by American business and unions toward earlier retirement, it seems unlikely that more than a very small proportion of the aged can play
the kind of role that Parsons sees for them in the future.

Another type of solution to the "problem of the aged" has been
suggested by Theobald (1963) and others (see Burns, 1965).
Theobald sees little need to pay men for the work that they do,
in view of the tremendous productivity of the American economic
system. Because of cybernation "we will not be able to provide

---

* Parsons suggests that the aged would be especially prone to "take the
long view," but research evidence suggests that they are more likely to take
a short-range view. However, this is not true of the highly educated group
of which Parsons writes (see Gergen and Back, 1965).

everybody with jobs . . . but . . . we will be able to provide everybody with all the goods they need." He advocates that we "should provide for every citizen of the United States, as a birth-right, a guaranteed income sufficient to allow them to live in dignity." The future that Theobald projects involves much flexibility about the close tie between work and pay, and would therefore free many people in the society, young as well as old, to engage in activities of their own choice. If it actually comes to pass, then the distinction between work and non-work would be eliminated or blurred for many people, in the way that this is already so often the case for many people in professional and artistic occupations. As a result there would not be the sharp break between work and retirement—such a break would be mediated not merely by gradually reduced work loads or by "sabbatical" leaves for older workers, but by the very nature of the meaning of work, leisure, and retirement in society as a whole.

There are also several different predictions and suggestions about the future status of women in the United States. Miller and Swanson (1958, p. 200) state that "women and men are increasingly equal; they are also separate and different." Being separate and different, there is role specialization between them. Miller and Swanson imply that this role specialization may be based upon ability and interest or upon sex differences. If specialization is based upon sex differences then equality of status can be maintained, but the woman's role as a homemaker may become more important. Miller and Swanson indeed point out that this is one direction in which change is taking place, involving "the professionalization of the wife's functions":

> The women's magazines provide a kind of in-service training, supplemented with the post-graduate work of the mother's study clubs, the meetings with the specialists at the nursery school, the cooking classes, and the growing number of handbooks for preparing unfamiliar or exotic foods. . . .
> We believe there has been a general strengthening of some of the traditional family patterns along revised lines. We should guess that the requirements for personal stability made by large specialized organizations, together with the economic security they provide, will begin to slow and then lower the rate of divorce and separation in the population and will raise again the criteria of competence and the gifts of homemaking to renewed importance in the choice of a marriage partner. We find evidences . . . that the formal social controls of the large scale organizations are being

extended to shape the family and to provide a new sense of obligation (p. 201).

There are some distinct parallels in the above speculations by Miller and Swanson, and in those by Sorokin and Zimmerman, about the future of the American family.

In contrast to the prediction that the woman's role as home-maker will become more important is the prediction that this role will decline in importance. Miller and Swanson themselves see this as an alternative direction, and Foote (1961) much more sharply views this as a new role for women—such that "women can aspire to any kind of work there is without surrendering femininity." This involves a projection into the future where the tasks performed by middle-class husbands and wives are not determined on the traditional basis of what is a "man's job" or a "woman's job" but on the basis of the skills and inclinations of the spouses. This is also made explicit by A. S. Rossi (1965):

> We must educate boys and girls for all their major adult roles— as parents, spouses, workers, and creatures of leisure. This means giving more stress in education, at home and at school, to the future family roles of boys and the future occupational roles of girls. Women will not stop viewing work as a stopgap until meaningful work is taken for granted in the lives of women as it is in the lives of men. (p. 1201).

Rossi (1964a) deplores the current lack of feminist activity in the United States and the "conservative image of the woman's role" painted by experts in which the woman is supposed to find "complete self-fulfillment in her exclusive devotion to mar-riage and parenthood." Rossi ridicules Dr. Spock's advice to mothers of pre-school children that they should consult a social worker before making a decision to work; she emphasizes that "children of working mothers are no more likely than children of non-working mothers to become delinquent, to show neurotic symptoms, to feel deprived of maternal affection . . ."*; and she feels that too many American women follow the work pattern of withdrawal and re-entry many years later. She advocates complete equality between the sexes in the occupational and domestic worlds, with women pursuing a full-time career. "The major difficulty, and

---

* Contrary to what is commonly believed, research evidence indicates that children of working mothers do not suffer adversely in their personality development and adjustment (See Hoffman, 1963; Rossi, 1964b).

the one most in need of social innovation, is the problem of providing adequate care for the children of working mothers." For this, Rossi suggests two possible solutions: (1) upgrading the status of child-care jobs, perhaps with formal training that results in a certificate in practical mothering; and (2) "the establishment of a network of child-care centers."

Rossi's equality is one in which "intellectually aggressive women or tender expressive men" are not seen as deviants. It is, in short, a radical kind of equality that she looks forward to,* in which there is a complete departure from the traditional sex roles.

REFERENCES

ALBERT, ETHEL M. 1965. "The Role of Women: Question of Values," in Seymour M. Farber, and Roger H. L. Wilson, eds., *The Potential of Woman,* New York: McGraw-Hill, pp. 105–115.

ALLEN, PHILIP J., ed. 1963. *Pitirim A. Sorokin in Review,* Durham, N.C.: Duke University Press.

BERNARD, JESSIE. 1964. *Academic Women,* University Park: Pennsylvania State University Press.

BRINTON, CRANE. 1959. *A History of Western Morals,* New York: Harcourt, Brace, pp. 381–391.

BROMLEY, DOROTHY D. 1965. *Catholics and Birth Control: Contemporary Views on Doctrine,* New York: Devin-Adair.

BURGESS, ERNEST W., HARVEY J. LOCKE, and MARY MARGARET THOMES. 1963. *The Family: From Institution to Companionship,* 3d ed., New York: American Book Co.

BURNS, EVELINE M. 1965. "Social Security in Evolution: Toward What?" *Social Service Review,* XXXIX, 129–140.

FARBER, BERNARD. 1964. *Family: Organization and Interaction,* San Francisco: Chandler Publishing Co.

FOOTE, NELSON N. 1961. "New Roles for Men and Women," *Marriage and Family Living,* XXIII, 325–329.

FRIEDAN, BETTY. 1963. *The Feminine Mystique,* New York: Dell.

GERGEN, KENNETH J., and KURT W. BACK. 1965. "Aging, Time Perspective, and Preferred Solutions to International Conflicts," *Journal of Conflict Resolution,* IX, 177–186.

* For related but differing statements on this topic that are of special interest, see Maccoby (1963), Friedan (1963), Bernard (1964), Albert (1965), and Kirkendall (1965).

HOFFMAN, LOIS W. 1963. "Effects on Children: Summary and Discussion," in F. Ivan Nye, and Lois W. Hoffman, eds., *The Employed Mother in America,* Chicago: Rand McNally.

KIRKENDALL, LESTER A. 1965. "Captives to the Double Standard," *Pastoral Psychology,* XVI, 23–32.

KIRKPATRICK, CLIFFORD. 1963. "Housewife and Woman? The Best of Both Worlds?" pp. 136–152 in Seymour M. Farber, Piero Mustacchi, and Roger H. L. Wilson, eds., *Man and Civilization: The Family's Search for Survival,* New York: McGraw-Hill.

MACCOBY, ELEANOR E. 1963. "Woman's Intellect," pp. 24–39 in Seymour M. Farber, and Roger H. L. Wilson, eds., *The Potential of Woman,* New York: McGraw-Hill.

MILLER, DANIEL R., and GUY E. SWANSON. 1958. *The Changing American Parent,* New York: Wiley.

OGBURN, WILLIAM F. 1938. "The Changing Family," *The Family,* XIX, 139–143.

ROSSI, ALICE S. 1964a. "Equality Between the Sexes: An Immodest Proposal," *Daedalus,* XCIII, 607–652.

———. 1964b. "A Good Woman Is Hard to Find," *Transaction,* II, 20–23.

———. 1965. "Women in Science: Why So Few?" *Science,* CXLVIII, 1196–1202.

RUTLEDGE, AARON L. 1956. "Evidences of Strength in the Modern Family," *Journal of Home Economics,* XLVIII, 323–326.

SOROKIN, PITIRIM A. 1941. *The Crisis of Our Age,* New York: Dutton.

———. 1956. *The American Sex Revolution,* Boston: Porter Sargent.

———. 1957. *Social and Cultural Dynamics,* 1-vol. ed., rev. and abridged, Boston: Porter Sargent.

———. 1960. "The Depth of the Crisis: American Sex Morality Today," *Christianity Today,* July 4, 811–813.

STRAUS, MURRAY A. 1962. "Conjugal Power Structure and Adolescent Personality," *Marriage and Family Living,* XXIV, 17–25.

THEOBALD, ROBERT. 1963. "Needed: A New Definition of Work," *New University Thought,* III, 9–14.

TIRYAKIAN, EDWARD A., ed. 1963. *Sociological Theory, Values, and Sociocultural Change,* New York: Free Press of Glencoe.

WINCH, ROBERT F. 1963. *The Modern Family,* rev. ed., New York: Holt, Rinehart & Winston, pp. 740–752.

ZIMMERMAN, CARLE C. 1947. *Family and Civilization,* New York: Harper.

ஃ 21 ஜ~ The Companionship Family

by ERNEST W. BURGESS, HARVEY J.

LOCKE, *and* MARY MARGARET THOMES

The Revival of the Traditional Family Pattern. At a time of social crisis, one disposition on the part of the public is to advocate the preservation of the traditional form of organization or a return to it. One of the severest critics of present trends in the American family is Sorokin.[1] He holds that the new form of the family must be based on a "reconstruction of absolute moral values and norms, obligatory for all, universally binding, not to be brushed aside in the interest of relative, expedient, pseudo-values."[2] Essentially this is a proposal to return to the institutional family.

The black picture of the family and of present-day society painted by Sorokin arises from his failure to perceive that present trends represent not only disorganization but reorganization. He ignores the fact that the same forces which find expression in family instability are at the same time slowly creating a family unity based on neither compulsion nor on contract but on the binding affections and loyalties growing out of intimate associations in the companionship family.

The Companionship Family. The form of the family that appears to be emerging in modern society may be called the companionship family because of its emphasis on intimate interpersonal association as its primary function. Other characteristics of the companionship family are the giving and receiving of affection; the assumption of equality of husband and wife; democracy in family decisions, with

Reprinted from Burgess, Locke, and Thomes, *The Family: From Institution to Companionship,* 3d ed., New York: American Book Co., 1963, pp. 525–527. With permission.

a voice and a vote by the children; the personality development of its members as a family objective; freedom of self-expression which is consistent with family unity; and the expectation that the greatest happiness is to be found in the family.

This conception of the companionship family is becoming so much a part of our culture that it is difficult to consider it objectively and critically. In fact, many of the leaders in family welfare who are concerned with problems of marriage and child development are propagandists for the companionship family. Students of the family, however, find it necessary to view this new type of family in the same detached and impartial way that they examine the Apache or the ancient Chinese family.

The basic elements in the companionship family were derived from crude beginnings in the pioneer and frontier situations. It would be possible, of course, to go back to even earlier origins, especially in the ideological formulation of these elements.

The features of the pioneer situation making for the decline of the small-patriarchal family and the rise of modifications tending toward the companionship form may be briefly summarized. First of all, the pioneer situation resulted in a breakdown of status as determined by conventional and arbitrary standards, and the evaluation of individual members within the family on the basis of the initiative, originality, independence, and particularly the contribution each could make to the family. With free land available, not only were early marriages the rule, but the young couples established independent households, thus further departing from many aspects of the earlier patriarchal family.

In the second place, pioneer isolation operated to bring about a relaxation of the rigid patterns of control of the traditional family. An outstanding example is the decline in the influence of parents over the marriages of their children and the selection of mates by the young people themselves.

A third influence of the pioneer situation and, in the long run, perhaps the most important, was the emergence of political democracy. The patterns of political democracy, of course, were already present in the colonies. They had been derived from English sources. But pioneer society stimulated the spread of democracy downward until it reached nearly all the people.

The beginnings of democracy were evident in the family in the growing freedom of children and in tendencies toward equality in the relations of the sexes. Political democracy, although at first confined to adult males, later permeated all society with its ideology, and thereby was a powerful but indirect factor in raising the status of women.

The entrance of women into industry gave them actual or potential economic independence and thereby also raised their status. It made it unnecessary for a woman to marry just to secure economic support, and made it possible, if her marriage was unsatisfactory, for her to earn her own living.

This analysis of the emergence of the companionship form of the family as a result of a social process gives perspective for differentiating between familial disorganization that disrupts the family and that which mediates its reorganization. The concept of the family process suggests also that the family itself is a dynamic agent and not a passive, inert object. The term "process" also implies that the family structure is being modified by forces within it reacting to those impinging upon it. These considerations should give pause to the "well-intentioned friends" of the family who seek to intervene and reform it according to some preconceived program.

The companionship family is, in many respects, less stable than the previous forms of the family. This is true not merely because its unity is based on affection and comradeship instead of duty and social pressure, as in the institutional family, but because in the transition from a rural to an industrial society it has lost its security. Therefore, provision for the economic well-being of the family becomes a central problem.

NOTES

1. PITIRIM A. SOROKIN, *The Crisis of Our Age,* New York: E. P. Dutton & Co., Inc., 1941.
2. *Ibid.,* p. 203.

◄§ 22 ≥► Talcott Parsons' View of the Changing American Family

by H Y M A N   R O D M A N

Talcott Parsons is undoubtedly the most widely known contemporary sociologist. His writings deal with economic, political, psychological, and anthropological issues, as well as with sociological issues, and they are known internationally. His "general theory of action" represents an ambitious attempt to approach many disparate subjects with a single conceptual framework, and primarily as a result of the writings in which he has elaborated the "general theory of action" he has become an extremely controversial figure. His critics are correct that his writings are not always easy to follow; but some of his critics have been so vehement in their objections that they appear to be reacting to something other than Parsons' writings. Parsons has suggested that some of the criticism may be manifestations of "resistances to certain types of intellectual innovation" (12, p. 320). Another possible explanation for some of the criticism is a kind of anti-Parsons tradition that has developed, such that any two social scientists meeting for the first time can more quickly establish rapport by sharing their stereotypes about Talcott Parsons.

Written especially for this reader. Talcott Parsons has collaborated with Edward Shils, Robert F. Bales, Winston White, Neil J. Smelser, Kaspar D. Naegele, Jesse R. Pitts, Renée Fox, and others, as co-author or co-editor, and part of this account of Parsons' writings is therefore inevitably based upon the contributions of some of these associates. It is also based in part upon the contributions of other scholars, because some of the facts that Parsons has interpreted are also commonly referred to and interpreted by other social scientists. For the most part this paper is not a critical examination of Parsons' writings, but a straightforward exposition of his view of the American middle-class family. For critical examinations of Parsons' writings see Max Black, ed., *The Social Theories of Talcott Parsons,* Englewood Cliffs, N.J.: Prentice-Hall, 1961.

Even Parsons' severest critics, however, acknowledge that he has made important contributions to knowledge when he has turned his attention to empirical questions—the professions, prejudice, social stratification, McCarthyism, the mass media, the American family. Since Parsons makes use of his conceptual scheme in his approach to these more empirical areas, we must conclude that this scheme is not totally without merit. Parsons himself has agreed, in replying to his critics, that "any more ultimate judgment" of his work will have to be left to further scientific developments and criticism (12, p. 321).

This paper, however, is not a critical evaluation of Parsons' writings. It is, rather, an exposition of his view of the American middle-class family. Occasional critical comment is introduced with the intention of highlighting some essential point in Parsons' writings. The reader should also be aware that it is not possible to do full justice to Parsons' view in a short paper. For example, some of Parsons' theoretical writings about the family that are not specifically related to the American family—on the father symbol, or on the incest taboo—are not considered in this paper.

Some of the areas this paper covers are the isolated nuclear family, the youth culture, and aging. In order to follow Parsons' view of these and other areas it is extremely important to understand what Parsons means by the concept of "differentiation." This is the most central concept in Parsons' writings generally, as well as in his writings on the family.* By differentiation Parsons has in mind the increasing specialization that takes place so that certain functions formerly carried out by one unit are taken over by other specialized units, while the original unit concentrates upon fewer functions:

> Differentiation refers to the process by which simple structures are divided into functionally differing components, these components becoming relatively independent of one another, and then recombined into more complex structures in which the functions of the differentiated units are complementary. A key example in the development of industrial society everywhere is the differentiation . . . of the unit of economic production from the kinship household (18, p. 103).

* Cf. Farber (38, p. 122 *et passim*). Other writers, of course, have interpreted changes in society in terms of the concept of functional differentiation. See Durkheim (40); see MacIver and Page (39, chap. 11) on the American family. For a recent statement by Parsons, see (21).

Parsons emphasizes that American society is highly differentiated. This refers to the many different units performing highly specialized functions, unlike simpler societies in which the kinship group may also be a work group, a political group, and a religious group. In such simpler societies, in other words, a kinsman would be the work leader, the political leader, and the religious leader, and the kinship group would carry out many different functions rather than specializing in very few functions as in American society. Some critics of the process of differentiation in American society have seen the resultant as "an 'atomized,' mass society where the relations of one individual to another have become increasingly amorphous" (9, p. 77). Parsons, however, sees this as a fallacy, and he points out that "American society is one of the preeminent examples of a *pluralist* society in which—through the course of structural differentiation—an increasingly ramified network of criss-crossing solidarities has been developing" (9, p. 77).

Many of the critics of American society have, in other words, been disturbed by the increasing specialization and complexity that are involved in the differentiating process. They have seen this as a dehumanizing and fragmentizing process. Parsons, however, has emphasized that there are gains as well as losses in the changes that have taken place. He indicates that when functions are "lost" by one unit, that unit may thereby be freer to concentrate upon other functions. It is not merely a matter of "loss," therefore, but also a matter of what one is "freed for." Certain groups have come to specialize more than in the past upon certain of the functions that mass-society critics fear have been lost. The family and the peer group, for example, have become more specialized as groups in which emotional support is provided. As Parsons has put it: "When two functions, previously embedded in the same structure, are subsequently performed by two newly differentiated structures, they can *both* be fulfilled more intensively and with a greater degree of freedom" (11, p. 129).

The Isolated Nuclear Family

According to Parsons, the isolation of the nuclear family "is the most distinctive feature of the American kinship system and underlies most of its peculiar functional and dynamic problems" (2, p. 28). The isolation that Parsons has in mind is, above all, residential and economic. In other words, the nuclear family of husband, wife, and children neither lives with nor pools its money with the family of orientation of either the husband or wife—"the members of the nuclear family, consisting of parents and their still dependent children, ordinarily occupy a separate dwelling not shared with members of the family of orientation of either spouse, and . . . this household is in the typical case economically independent, subsisting in the first instance from the occupational earnings of the husband-father" (7, p. 10). Moreover, as a result of geographic mobility of the population, many nuclear families are separated from their relatives by large distances; as a result of social mobility, many nuclear families may have a higher social status (and a good deal more money) than related nuclear families.

The isolation of the nuclear family is seen as part of the general trend toward differentiation in American society. Parsons views this as related above all to the process of industrialization that has taken place. Industrialization requires large plants, large outlays for equipment, and mass production. The family, as a group, cannot be the primary source of labor in an industrialized economy. The individual worker, however, apart from his family, is ideally suited to the needs of an industrial plant. He can be hired and set to work on the basis of his skills and competence for a particular job, without any nepotistic considerations. While nepotism has by no means completely disappeared, it is now far less important than formerly. Kinship ties therefore interfere less with the efficient organization of an industrial society.

Not only has economic production been taken over by organizations other than the family, but also certain types of financial and educational responsibilities are being carried out by other organizations. The schools, the mass media, peer groups, hospitals, and voluntary associations have assumed functions formerly performed by the family. The family has therefore become a much more specialized group, and it now concentrates its functions on the socialization of the child and the emotional support and affection that is exchanged among its members.

A number of critics have taken issue with the emphasis that Parsons has placed upon the *isolated* nuclear family. Sussman has

emphasized that the nuclear family does maintain contact with its
kinsmen, and that help and assistance of various kinds is exchanged
by kinsmen (22). Zimmerman and Cervantes have stressed the importance of family "friends" and they have suggested that "isolated
families are largely a figment of the imagination" (32, p. 37).
Litwak has argued that extended family relations are not antithetical
to an industrial society, and he points out that such relations may
take place between kinsmen without interfering with occupational
or geographic mobility. He therefore prefers to speak of a "modified extended family" rather than an "isolated nuclear family" (23,
24, 25). To be accurate, however, we must point out that Parsons
has usually spoken of the *relative* isolation of the American nuclear
family, and he has contrasted the contemporary American case to
the American past and to more "primitive" societies. Therefore,
there does not appear to be any underlying basis to this "controversy"*—for Parsons emphasizes the relative isolation of the nuclear family, while others stress that the family is not altogether
isolated and have explicated in greater detail the nature of extended
family relations and the part they may play in aiding the mobility of
the family [see above pp. 204 ff. and see (47)].

I shall cite just one example to show that Parsons' emphasis upon
the isolated nuclear family is supplemented by his recognition that
there is still a continuation of relationships with extended family
members:

* At the level of describing the American family it is easy to reconcile
Parsons' views and those of his critics. For example, residential and economic independence are compatible with affectional ties and visits. However,
there is an underlying *theoretical* question: What is the relationship between
the economic and the family organization of a society? Several writers have
pointed out that some of the characteristics of American society—bilateral
kinship, neolocal residence, and "isolated" nuclear families—are also to be
found in non-industrialized and non-urbanized societies. Neither industrialization nor urbanization is therefore necessary to explain the "isolated"
nuclear family. Nevertheless, there may be a greater likelihood of finding an
"isolated" nuclear family in association with an industrialized economy (or a
hunting or gathering economy, which likewise requires mobility) because of
some of the functional reasons that Parsons and others have cited (see 35, 36,
and 37). What appears to be crucial is the differentiation of kinship and
occupational roles (44). Therefore, as Mogey (45) has indicated, industrialization and urbanization may be related to the non-corporate nuclear family
—as opposed to the corporate, working-as-a-group nuclear family often
found in hunting and gathering societies. Smelser (41) gives a particularly
good account of the differentiation of the British corporate nuclear family
engaged in handicrafts into the non-corporate nuclear family in an industrialized society.

Of course with the independence, particularly the marriage, of children, relations to the family of orientation are by no means broken. But separate residence, very often in a different geographical community, and separate economic support, attenuate these relations (7, p. 11).

Characteristics of the American Family

In dealing with the characteristics of the American family Parsons has pulled together information to support at least three different theses: (1) that the nuclear family is relatively isolated; (2) that the family is differentiated and not disorganized; and (3) that certain patterns of behavior within the family reflect the basic American value of "instrumental activism." These three will be dealt with below.

First of all, what are some of the characteristics of the American family that Parsons cites to back up his contention that it is relatively isolated? One type of evidence is terminological. Parsons points out that there is no kinship term that refers to a unit that cuts across nuclear families, including some members and excluding others. As he says: "It is significant that we have only the words 'family,' which generally refers to the conjugal [nuclear] unit, and 'relatives,' which does not refer to *any* solidary unit at all, but only to anyone who is a kinsman" (2, p. 24). (The traditional upper class is an exception to this, as Parsons notes.)

Additional evidence is the sense in which "the marriage bond is, in our society, the main structural keystone of the kinship system" (2, p. 30). In the first place, a person's major loyalty is to his spouse and children, rather than to his parents as in some societies. In the second place, an individual is largely free to choose his own mate— an important reason for this being that "the new marriage is not typically 'incorporated' into an already existing kinship unit" (2, p. 30). Since the newly married spouses ordinarily live neolocally, apart from either set of parents, and since they are ordinarily economically independent, their kinsmen have less of a vested interest in controlling their choice of a mate.

Another important characteristic is the impartiality that is maintained in the descent lines of the American kinship system. There is no established rule, for example, that a child should be closer to either his maternal or paternal grandparents. Nor is there any established rule that requires one or both parents to leave their property to one or another child, for example, an eldest son or a youngest son. The expectation is that all children will receive equal shares, but with testamentary disposition by parents there is also much leeway for taking into account affectional and financial circumstances. For these reasons there are, in the usual case, no special ties between certain kinsmen that are based upon a rule of descent or inheritance, and a married couple therefore is structurally required to "strike out on its own" (2, pp. 24–30).

Parsons also points out that it is not merely a matter of what the rules or expectations are, but also a matter of the practices conforming to the expectations. For example, "the actual practice of wills overwhelmingly conforms" to the pattern of "equal shares" (2, p. 28). In addition, the actual practice of neolocal residence conforms to the expectation, and a separate residence is also usually maintained by aged parents. Parsons cites evidence on the prominent place of the single family home in residential building (7, p. 7) and on the high percentage (16 per cent) of households that consist of individuals living alone (14, p. 128).

Another important point Parsons makes is that the stresses and strains to be found in the American family are indicative of a process of differentiation that is taking place, and not of the disorganization and decay of the American family. Critics have, in the past, cited a rising divorce rate, a falling birth rate, and the family's loss of functions as indices of the family's decline. Parsons, however, along with many others, has been able to point to a drop in the divorce rate since its post-war peak in 1946, to a rise in the birth rate from about 1940 to 1955, and to the fewer but still vital functions that the family performs. "The family is more specialized than before, but not in any general sense less important, because the society is dependent *more* exclusively on it for the performance of *certain* of its vital functions" (7, pp. 10–11).

To further support his view of the viability of the American family Parsons points out "there is today a larger proportion of the total population of marriageable age married and living with their spouses than at any time in the history of reliable census data; this is true in spite of divorces (since most divorced persons remarry) and separations. One of the reasons for this, of course, is increased longevity, which means that spouses have longer married periods before the death of one; another reason is that people are now getting married at an earlier age" (13, p. 275).

Finally, Parsons notes that within the family one can observe the workings of the basic American value of "instrumental activism." "Among other things, this means that members of the society ought to master their environment and develop its resources instead of resigning themselves passively to the way things are" (20). It is above all in the socialization of the child, which is discussed below, that we note some of the ways in which the family prepares the child for an adult role in a society in which achievement, mastery, efficiency, and rationality are important elements.

The use of electrical and other appliances in the house is indicative of the trend toward rationality and efficiency. So is the strong emphasis upon scientific child rearing. The kind of residential pattern that is becoming characteristic of an increasing number of Americans is also part of the stress upon efficiency and rationality. This pattern is "for the individual to grow up in a suburban home that his parents own . . . to go to college, to settle in the central city . . . and to remain there until married with a family started and the means acquired to make a down payment on a suburban home." Later on, when the children have left home, the parents "may choose to move back into the central city to enjoy its conveniences when they no longer need the facilities of the suburban community for family life and child-rearing" (20).

The Youth Culture

There are special strains placed upon American youth, notably the need to move from a state of dependence upon the parents to a state of independence in a job and family of one's own. These strains are intensified because of the extreme dependence initially fostered within the small nuclear family, and also because of the long period of formal education youth must go through before attaining complete independence. According to Parsons' view, the youth culture aids the American adolescent in overcoming these strains. It helps the adolescent to obtain and maintain a degree of independence from his parents, and it provides him with the emotional support he needs to make the transition from dependence to independence. While it is true that a different kind of dependence and conformity is demanded within the peer group, this is never-theless a group in which the adolescent is preparing to take on adult responsibilities.

Once again, Parsons sees youth groups "as part of the general process of differentiation" in which these groups "are coming to occupy an increasingly differentiated position" especially by virtue of the sharply segregating effect of the formal educational system (18, p. 120). Being thus age-segregated and also subjected to the need to attain independence, youth groups have developed a sub-culture that helps them to meet the strains they face. Above all, as differentiated units, they provide adolescents with the emotional support they need in order to take a stance that is independent of their parents.

Parsons believes that "important shifts of emphasis in American youth culture have occurred in the last generation" (18, p. 115), and his writings on youth culture reflect that belief. His early writings, which have been widely reprinted, stressed the elements of irresponsibility, pleasure-seeking, and (for males) athletics as major features of the youth culture (1, 2, 4, 5). Currently, how-ever, Parsons' view of American youth culture is quite different (18). He no longer believes that irresponsibility and pleasure-seek-ing are important characteristics of youth culture. Moreover, he points out that the emphasis upon athletics and physical prowess has declined. In their place, Parsons sees "the enormous develop-ment of serious cultural interests among students in the more elite colleges" (18, p. 117). He also sees a "resurgence of political interest and activity" that focuses "on specific issues in which moral problems are sharply defined, notably in race relations and the problems of nuclear war" (18, p. 117). Finally, he notes that "perhaps the most significant fact about current youth culture is its concern with meaningfulness" and with problems of identity (18, p. 119). From 1942 to 1962, therefore, Parsons has rather dras-tically shifted his view of American youth culture—in essence, he believes that the youth culture has moved from an emphasis upon irresponsibility and pleasure-seeking to an emphasis upon responsi-bility and seriousness.*

* In a critical vein, one might ask whether Parsons is noting an actual change in the youth culture, or whether he is merely changing his mind about a relatively unchanging youth culture. Grinder (34) provides a variety of references that suggest that the former is true.

It is important to note, however, that although Parsons sees a rather sharp change in the *content* of the youth culture, he does not see a change in its *function*. The present youth culture is much less antagonistic to adult values, and "youth has become better integrated in the general culture" (18, p. 116). Regardless of these values, however, the problem of achieving independence from one's parents remains, and the youth culture provides the emotional support needed to achieve that independence.

Another important change in Parsons' writings is his recent view of American youth culture as more differentiated than formerly. It is not merely a situation in which responsibility and seriousness are paramount; rather, there are different groups with different subcultures. In contrast to the past, Parsons sees a much greater responsibility on the part of youth. The average period of schooling is longer; the courses of study have generally been upgraded; there is less learning by rote and more learning for which the individual is himself responsible. In brief: "The educational process puts increased demands on the younger group" (18, p. 110), and these increased demands have been "largely met with a positive response rather than with rebellion or passive withdrawal" (18, p. 115). In addition, however, Parsons notes the fact that some peer groups lay much greater stress upon popularity than others. He cites a study which reports that in some peer groups popularity and friendliness are dominant, while in others popularity and friendliness are combined with an emphasis upon scholastic achievement (11, p. 125; 26). There are, in short, different types of peer groups, and although they may all provide their members with emotional support to maintain independence from the family, they also serve the function of sifting and sorting students out according to how far they are likely to go in the educational and occupational systems—"the youth culture helps to differentiate between types of personalities which will, by and large, play different kinds of roles as adults" (8, p. 315).

Parsons' view of the youth culture is at variance with Riesman's on the one hand, and with Elkin and Westley's on the other.*

* For critical statements (by Robert Hess, Bernice Neugarten, and eighteen other social scientists) on whether or not there is an adolescent subculture, see 42, pp. 60–75. For additional critical commentary, which indicates that one can point to "discontinuities of socialisation to prove the existence of a youth culture, or continuities to bear out the opposite contention," see 46.

According to Riesman the peer group is much more important than other socializing groups, and it has no stable normative structure. The members are other-directed and respond to each other on the basis of shifting norms and values (27, pp. 47–48; see *14*). Parsons, however, does see a fairly stable system of norms in the peer group, and he puts much less emphasis upon the importance of the peer group as a socializing unit.

According to Elkin and Westley's research in a suburb of Montreal, the concept of "youth culture" is very much open to question (28). In many areas, for example, they say that "no sharp distinction is made in the family between parental and adolescent activity" (29, p. 245). Moreover, they state that "the adolescent does not manifestly experience much storm and stress, and the peer group serves to reinforce rather than oppose parental values" (29, p. 249). In contrast, Parsons originally emphasized the storm and stress experienced by adolescents and the role the youth culture played in helping to alleviate that stress. His more recent view, however, in which he points to different types of youth groups, and in which he lays greater stress upon the responsible aspects of youth culture, suggests that he is now in essential agreement with Elkin and Westley. It is well to note, of course, that "whether or not there is a separate adolescent subculture is partly a matter of definition as to what constitutes a separate subculture" (33, p. 5).

A summary statement of Parsons' position, in his own words, runs as follows:

> Our main thesis is that the emergence of youth culture and peer groups is part of the general process of structural differentiation that has been going on in American society . . . and that within this framework the peer group has assumed a place that is *complementary* to that of the school on the one hand, the family on the other (11, p. 122).

> [The peer group] is the primary repository of the needs for emotional security and acceptance which have been so powerfully fostered in early childhood and then so sharply cut back . . . because of the imperative of achieving independence (13, p. 281).

Feminine and Masculine Roles

One body of research which provides empirical data substantiating Parsons' theoretical ideas is to be found in the small-group field. Bales and Slater have shown that a process of differentiation tends to take place in small, experimental groups such that two different kinds of roles emerge. One person in these small groups tends to become an "instrumental" leader, and another a "social-emotional" leader (7, pp. 259–306). The instrumental leader concentrates upon getting the group's task done, and the social-emotional leader concentrates upon handling the social and emotional needs of the members of the group. This parallels the important distinction that Parsons has drawn, in his treatment of the functional problems faced by a social system, between the problems that are posed by the external environment and those posed by the internal environment. According to Parsons, each social system must take care of these problems—it must carry out certain jobs in relation to the external environment, and it must also maintain a sufficient degree of harmony among its members so that they can continue to work together. The fact that Bales has shown a tendency toward differentiation along the lines conceptualized by Parsons—in spite of the absence of age and sex differences in the experimental groups—is important support of Parsons' view. Moreover, further support has been provided by Zelditch, who has shown that there is a cross-cultural tendency for role differentiation to appear within the nuclear family, with the husband usually playing an instrumental role and the wife an expressive or social-emotional role (7, pp. 307–351). As Seeley *et al.* (43, pp. 176–178) phrase it in their suburban study, the husband is, above all, "the earner of the income," while the wife is "the emotional hub of the family."

There may be a good deal of variation, however, in the degree to which a man's role is instrumental, not to say anything about the variation in the actual content of that instrumental role. In American society, for example, the wife is coming to take charge of or to share in an increasing proportion of household tasks. Does this mean, as many have suggested, that there has been a loss of masculine authority? Parsons believes that this is only part of the story. From his viewpoint, it is a misinterpretation of the changes taking place in the American family. The "loss of function" of the family has above all been in the productive area, and since the man is primarily involved in the production process his role has increasingly been carried on outside of the family. In the meantime the family has specialized in the functions of socialization and emotional support, and it is in these areas that the woman has taken major responsibility. It is thus true that the woman has come to play an increasingly important role in the family. This is to be interpreted, according to Parsons, not so much as a loss of masculine authority but rather as a resultant of the changes wrought by the process of differentiation. The kind of authority a man formerly had in the family can no longer be appropriately exercised because the family no longer engages in the kinds of activities (for example, a family business enterprise) over which a man exercised authority.

An article by Jourard and Richman lends support to Parsons' emphasis upon the emotionally supportive, "human relations" role played by women. They point out that women tell more about themselves and hear more about others than do males, so that they may be viewed as being more expressive, nurturant, empathic, and intuitive than men (30, p. 146).

It is Parsons' belief that the strains formerly associated with the feminine role are now much diminished. In his early articles he referred to "a good deal of . . . tension in the feminine role" and to the feminine role as "a conspicuous focus of the strains inherent in our social structure" (2, pp. 36–37). These strains were due to the strong emphasis "placed upon individual achievement" in the occupational world, a type of achievement that was largely denied to women. Women were thus relegated to the carrying out of "a set of utilitarian functions in the management of the household . . . a kind of 'pseudo'-occupation." This *domestic pattern* of the housewife was not highly valued, and women therefore increasingly sought other roles. One possibility was the *career pattern* in which the woman would "follow the masculine pattern and seek a career in fields of occupational achievement in direct competition with men of her own class." Another possibility was the *glamor pattern,* in which a "feminine form of attractiveness which on occasion involves directly sexual patterns of appeal" could offset "masculine occupational status and . . . its attendant symbols of prestige." Finally, there was the *good companion pattern,* with a humanistic emphasis on matters of "good taste" and art and a humanitarian emphasis upon community welfare obligations (1, pp. 609–613).

More recently, however, Parsons has placed much less emphasis upon the strains of the feminine role. Women, including married women, have increasingly entered the labor force, but on the whole this is a very special kind of phenomenon—these are largely "women who either do not yet have children . . . or whose children are grown up and independent." In addition they tend to be distributed in the less technical occupational roles (7, pp. 13–15). The inference that Parsons leaves us with is that the female is less likely to be forced into choosing *either* a domestic pattern *or* a career pattern *or* a glamor pattern *or* a good companion pattern. It has now become much more acceptable and possible for her to combine a variety of different role patterns during the course of her life. She can, for example, carry out her domestic duties with greater dispatch, and she can combine these with a good companion role or a career that may be flexible enough to give her more time with her children when they are young. This is a matter of changing attitudes, of the increasing help that a woman has as a result of time-saving household appliances, and of the woman's earlier completion of child care and her greater longevity and better health. Parsons notes that "overwhelmingly the central specifically feminine function is the rearing of children" (10, p. 169). But he also notes another interesting fact:

> This is the concentration of childbearing within a substantially shorter time period than before. As of the most recent information, women are on the average likely to bear their *last* child at the age of 26 or 27.* . . . It thus appears that special devotion to child-rearing, notably of course of younger children, is becoming a more differentiated role in the life-cycle of the mother. . . . Thus, she is freed for other functions partly by living longer in a better state of health and partly by concentrating her primary attention to motherhood within a shorter time-span (10, p. 169).

Aging in American Society

Parsons also takes note of a change in the position of the aged in American society from the 1940's to the 1960's. In his earlier writings he emphasized the structural isolation of the aged and their loss of functions. Retirement was abrupt and it "leaves the older man in a peculiarly functionless situation, cut off from participation in the most important interests and activities of society." In addi-

* [Although the figures of "26 or 27" were widely published, recent analysis by Glick and Parke indicate that the correct figures should be "30 or 31"; see Appendix, Table 3.—Ed.]

tion, the older person was isolated from his family—and this isolation was the obverse of the isolated nuclear family. Under such circumstances the aged may find that "there is no one left to respect them, for them to take responsibility for or have authority over." In short, their social isolation and their loss of functions was what constituted the major problems of the aged (1, p. 616; 2, p. 37).

In his recent writings Parsons has made a somewhat different interpretation of the position of the aged. They still are faced by problems resulting from retirement (loss of functions) and isolation, but there are now strong pressures in the direction of solving these problems. In an admittedly tentative way, Parsons suggests that some trends are now emerging which are indicative of the future direction the society will take.

First of all, Parsons' view about the isolation of the aged is now much more optimistic. As he says: "It is difficult to evaluate the implications of this isolation. There is an initial tendency to deplore it and to sympathize with the loneliness of the old folks." But he also notes that "given easy transportation and the telephone, there need not be too severe a lack of contact with . . . relatives and friends." In addition, he notes that "older people do in fact enjoy independence," so that it is usually not a matter of forced isolation but rather a matter of chosen independence (17, p. 23). In other words, it is now no longer merely a question of the young couple's right to independence from their older parents, but also of the older people's desire to maintain their own independence.

Parsons also takes a much different view of the loss of functions experienced by the aged. He suggests that recent trends perhaps indicate that older people have not merely lost functions, but that in sloughing off certain functions they have been freer to concentrate more exclusively on others. A "process of differentiation has been going on with respect to the life cycle" such that special functions are coming to be associated with certain stages of the life cycle (17, p. 27). In a very tentative way, Parsons suggests that "the technically specialized functions can most readily be performed . . . at the earlier age levels," that "functions of an executive or decision-making character . . . tend to be carried out above all by people in the middle years," and that "fiduciary and cultural responsibility" tend to be placed in the hands of older people (17, pp. 30–31). This is, of course, not an iron law of differentiation of functions by age, but it is a suggestion that certain age groups may specialize somewhat more than others in certain kinds of functions.

The technical functions of the earlier age levels involve a disproportionate amount of mechanical skill; the executive functions of the middle years require a greater degree of experience and judgment in order to make decisions; and the fiduciary functions of the older years involve responsibility not only for the interests of a particular organization but also "for fitting such interests into a wider and higher-order context." Parsons points to the trustee as an example of a role involving fiduciary functions—"the trustee is expected to have the interests of the organization very much at heart, but generally bridges these interests with others in the same community." He suggests that "there is evidence that the talents of many of the higher-status older people are being utilized more extensively than before, partly through postponement of retirement, but even more through employment in advisory and fiduciary capacities after retirement." He also notes that "there are important cases of fiduciary and cultural responsibility which have been lodged particularly in older people. Conspicuous examples include judges and religious functionaries" (17, pp. 30–31).

What is it that fits an older person for a fiduciary role? Parsons puts it as follows:

> Older people have two particular virtues, that is, if they preserve their integrity of character and their alertness of mind. They can take the long view partly because of personal experience and awareness of how things have changed. They can afford to act more disinterestedly than young people because their basic career commitments have been made, their levels of success are already determined, their decisions are not going to affect their personal fates in the same sense as is true for younger people (19, p. 15).

He takes note of the increasing life span and of the increasing proportion of the population that is over 65—from approximately 4 per cent in 1900 to more than 9 per cent in 1962. Potentially, this could lead to an increasingly severe problem of the aged in the United States. But Parsons suggests that "a society which has been increasing its 'production' of older people has at the same time been creating an increasing demand for their contributions" (17, pp. 31–32). It is this direction, involving important fiduciary functions for the aged, that Parsons sees as the long-run trend in American society.*

Socialization of the Child

A major function of the contemporary American family is the socialization of the child. Various commentators on the American family have been distressed by the way in which this function is presumably carried out, and a special focus of concern has been the "undisciplined" child. This has been seen by various writers, including David Riesman, as an indication that parents have not taken due responsibility for the socialization of their children. According to Parsons, however, there is another interpretation:

> The requirement of preparing the child for high levels of independence, competence, and responsibility means that as socializing agent the family cannot do its job unless it emancipates its children from dependence on the parents, an emancipation that precludes parents from being too definite role-models for the child's own life course. What Reisman interprets as the abdication of the parents from their socializing responsibility can therefore be interpreted in exactly the opposite way. If parents attempted to impose their role-patterns in a detailed way on their children, they would be failing in their responsibilities (11, p. 119).

Parsons' contention is that we have a type of socialization in American society that prepares the child for the autonomous role he will play in our achievement-oriented society. The problems of the child are taken into account and there is more concern with the child as a person. This involves a greater degree of permissiveness in child-rearing, but it is not permissiveness that permits the child to do anything he wants—rather, it is "a new way of 'leading' the child, rather than 'forcing' him, to higher levels of growth" (11, pp. 117–118).

Parsons points out that, to the child, the family is a "closed emotional corporation." The dependency upon the parents that this

* It is also worth noting that there are many welfare activities that the older person is beginning to engage in. This is coming to be thought of less and less as a strictly feminine activity, as exemplified by the increasing percentage of men now entering the social work field.

fosters is then converted into motivation for high-level achievement. This is brought about by the increased leverage that the parents have as a result of the child's extreme dependence upon them. As a result of the conditional love of his parents—conditional upon his achievement in school and peer situations—the child develops a strong motivational commitment to achievement (3; 11).

Parsons has looked upon the process of socialization as involving the internalization of social objects, by which he means the internalization of roles—"ego learns a patterned system of complementary actions toward alter" (7, pp. 56–57). Men learn roles, but this does not make them "merely obedient puppets," as Merton notes. Nevertheless they do "tend to develop the values and to channel their motivations in directions the institution defines for them" (31, p. 640). Merton's position, like Parsons', emphasizes the way in which men are guided by the norms and values of their society. This is the essence of the process of socialization. In Parsons' words it involves "the internalization of social objects and cultural norms and values in the personality of the individual," and "its discovery was an epochal turning point in social thinking" (16, p. 73). The reason for its importance is that it makes clear that social behavior is not merely a product of genetic or environmental or economic factors, but that it is also importantly influenced by the norms and values that an individual learns in his society. Since the basic value of American society is "instrumental activism," Parsons underlines the socialization techniques whereby the child is taught to play his role in such an achievement-oriented society.

Illness and the Family

Parsons has long been interested in the medical profession and in problems of health and illness, and some of his major insights have been in this area. He has shown "the similarity between illness and the status of the child in the family. . . . Both child and sick person [are unable] to perform the usual functions of an adult." In addition, "they are both dependent" and need "to be taken care of by stronger . . . persons" (6, pp. 31–32). Both statuses are also temporary, and involve the problem of motivating change to the status of a capable adult.

Parsons also points out that there are various problems that a person faces in contemporary life—especially within the family—and illness may be an escape from these problems. This is particularly so because "the state of illness is partially and conditionally legitimized. That is, if a person is defined as sick, his failure to perform his normal functions is 'not his fault,' and he is accorded the right to exemption and care" (6, pp. 32–33). On the one hand, this has a positive function, because it is a type of deviance that is less harmful to society than, say, crime and delinquency. On the other hand, it is still necessary to control this type of deviant behavior, because it does interfere with the performance of a person's normal roles.

How is illness controlled? In most cases the sick person is separated from his family and is treated by doctors and nurses in a professional setting. Parsons acknowledges that technological developments are involved in the shift of the setting for the care of the sick person from the family to a hospital. But he also suggests that something else is involved—that ordinarily the family is not the best agency to handle the sick person. For example, there are fewer motivational reasons for becoming sick or prolonging a recovery if the sick person is removed from the family—because with such removal he is not able to get the attention he may want from his loved ones. In addition, the small, isolated nuclear family would be severely strained by sacrifices called for in order to give most attention to the sick person. It may also be that because of latent dependency needs other members of the family will overreact or underreact in the amount of support given to the sick person. For these reasons—the motivational component of illness as well as the technical one—the sick person is usually best handled in a professional setting (6, pp. 33–38).

There is the danger, however, that a patient may receive too little support in a professional setting, and Parsons takes note of the trend to invite increased participation of family members in the care of a sick person in the hospital. In this way, through the judicious mixture of support (from the family) and discipline (from the professional team) within the therapeutic process, a patient may receive more effective care and he may be led toward a quicker recovery (6, pp. 42–43).

Summary

It is generally acknowledged that Talcott Parsons has made important contributions to knowledge in a variety of empirical areas, even though as a theorist he still remains highly controversial. For this reason, the present paper has focused upon Parsons' interpretations of trends in the American family, and has not attempted an elaborate exposition of his theoretical ideas. Moreover, Parsons has said that any theoretical statement, in our generation, is "destined to be superseded, and relatively quickly" (15, p. 79). This was further reason for concentrating upon Parsons' view of the American family rather than upon his more general theoretical position.

The concept of major importance in Parsons' writings, if we are to follow the insights he has brought to many different areas, is the concept of differentiation. This concept refers to the process whereby a system becomes increasingly complex. Functions formerly carried out by one unit in the system are taken over by a newly developed unit which comes to specialize in these functions, while the original unit specializes in the functions remaining to it. The American family, for example, was formerly the locus of many more functions, but as various functions came to be taken over by newly developed and specialized units such as manufacturing plants, protective agencies, and recreational and educational organizations, the family came to focus more exclusively upon the functions of socialization and emotional support.

Parsons places emphasis upon the isolation of the nuclear family as the most distinctive feature of the American kinship system. This is related to the process of industrialization which requires a work force that is relatively mobile and efficient. As the American nuclear family has become less tied residentially and economically to other nuclear families it has become a better source of supply of the kinds of workers required in an industrial society. An individual no longer works as a member of a kinship group that is also a productive unit; he works as an individual and can be hired on the basis of his skills and competence, aside from any nepotistic considerations.

Parsons has also emphasized that the youth culture is a distinctive feature of American society. Young people are being kept in school for an increasingly long time before making the transition to complete economic independence. In addition, young people must go through a transition from extreme dependence upon the few people in their family to the extreme independence required in an achievement-oriented society. It is within his peer group and its associated youth culture that a young person finds the emotional support and encouragement to make this kind of transition.

The man's role in American society, being primarily in the occupational world, has led to a big change in his role in the world of the family. He is no longer the boss of a family enterprise, and he has come to participate in the family's tasks of socialization and emotional support. At the same time, the wife-mother in the family has come to specialize in these tasks. However, since these tasks do not necessarily require a total commitment of her time, she has become increasingly freer to work or to participate in various kinds of cultural and welfare activities.

Increased longevity and earlier child-rearing have led to a long period of years during which the American woman is only minimally tied to domestic chores, and this has increased the trend toward combining some kind of career with her domestic duties. But increased longevity, and the policy of forced retirement, has also led to another distinctive feature of American society—the problem of the aged. Here, Parsons notes what may be the beginning of a trend. There is now more emphasis upon a flexible retirement age for higher-status workers and there is also more opportunity for using older persons in roles for which they are specially fitted. These roles are "fiduciary" roles, in which the older person, by virtue of his years of experience and greater objectivity, is able to take the long view and to see the place of a particular organization in context within the developing community.

Illness is viewed by Parsons as a possible expression of deviance, through which an older person, or any other member of the family, is legitimately able to find an excuse for not performing his role. Since the illness of one member may have a severe impact upon the family, Parsons notes that one way in which this form of deviance is controlled is through the existence of a professional setting in which the illness is taken care of. This cuts down on the possibility that a serious illness or a long period of recovery will have, as its motivational source, the desire for special care and attention from loved ones within the family setting. The professional person in a professional setting can more effectively exercise the discipline that may be required to push a sick person toward recovery.

In its briefest compass, then, Parsons relates the changes that have taken place in the American family to the changes that have taken place in American society. The process of differentiation that has been part of the industrialization of the country has had its impact upon the family. One result has been the isolated nuclear family specializing in the functions of socialization and emotional support. Another has been the changing nature of masculine and feminine roles, both within and outside of the family. A youth culture has emerged so that adolescents are aided in their transition toward independence by their peers. "The same basic processes of structural change that have differentiated out a youth subculture have begun to differentiate out an age subculture" that will help older people to maintain their independence (19, p. 10). And finally, the American child is being socialized so that he can come to play the independent and autonomous role required of him in an achievement-oriented society.

REFERENCES TO
TALCOTT PARSONS' WRITINGS

1. "Age and Sex in the Social Structure of the United States," *American Sociological Review*, VII, 1942, 604–616.
2. "The Kinship System of the Contemporary United States," *American Anthropologist*, XLV, 1943, 22–38.
3. "Certain Primary Sources and Patterns of Aggression in the Social Structure of the Western World," *Psychiatry*, Vol. X, 1947.
4. "The Social Structure of the Family," in Ruth N. Anshen, ed., *The Family: Its Function and Destiny*, New York: Harper, 1949. Based on (1), (2), and (3) above and reprinted in revised edition, 1959.
5. "Psychoanalysis and the Social Structure," *Psychoanalytic Quarterly*, XIX, 1950, 371–384.
6. "Illness, Therapy and the Modern Urban American Family" (with Renée Fox), *Journal of Social Issues*, VII, 1952, 31–44.

7. *Family, Socialization and Interaction Process* (with Robert F. Bales), Glencoe, Ill.: Free Press, 1955.

8. "The School Class as a Social System: Some of Its Functions in American Society," *Harvard Educational Review*, XXIX, 1959, 297–318.

9. "The Mass Media and the Structure of American Society" (with Winston White), *Journal of Social Issues*, XVI, 1960, 67–77.

10. "Toward a Healthy Maturity," *Journal of Health and Human Behavior*, I, 1960, 163–173.

11. "The Link Between Character and Society" (with Winston White), in Seymour M. Lipset and Leo Lowenthal, eds., *Culture and Social Character*, New York: Free Press of Glencoe, 1961.

12. "The Point of View of the Author," pp. 311–363 in Max Black, ed., *The Social Theories of Talcott Parsons*, Englewood Cliffs, N.J.: Prentice-Hall, 1961.

13. "A Sociologist's View," in Eli Ginzberg, ed., *Values and Ideals of American Youth*, New York: Columbia University Press, 1961.

14. "Comment on Trends Shown by Population Census," part of a Discussion of Trends Revealed by the 1960 Census of Population, in *Proceedings of the Social Statistics Sections*, Washington, D.C.: American Statistical Association, 1961, pp. 127–129.

15. "An Outline of the Social System," in Talcott Parsons, *et al.*, eds., *Theories of Society*, Vol. I, New York: Free Press of Glencoe, 1961.

16. "Individual Autonomy and Social Pressure: An Answer to Dennis H. Wrong," *Psychoanalysis and the Psychoanalytic Review*, XLIX, 1962, 70–79.

17. "The Aging in American Society," *Law and Contemporary Problems*, XXVII, 1962, 22–35.

18. "Youth in the Context of American Society," *Daedalus*, XCI, 1962, 97–123.

19. "The Cultural Background of Today's Aged," in Wilma Donahue and Clark Tibbits, eds., *Politics of Age*, Proceedings of the University of Michigan 14th Annual Conference on Aging, Ann Arbor: University of Michigan, Division of Gerontology, 1962.

20. *American Society*, 1963, mimeographed.

21. "The Normal American Family," in Seymour M. Farber, Piero Mustacchi, and Roger H. L. Wilson, eds. *Man and Civilization: The Family's Search for Survival*, New York: McGraw-Hill, 1965.

ADDITIONAL REFERENCES

22. MARVIN B. SUSSMAN, "The Isolated Nuclear Family: Fact or Fiction," *Social Problems*, VI, 1959, 333–340.

23. EUGENE LITWAK, "Geographic Mobility and Extended Family Cohesion," *American Sociological Review*, XXV, 1960, 385–394.

24. EUGENE LITWAK, "Occupational Mobility and Extended Family Cohesion," *American Sociological Review*, XXV, 1960, 9–21.

25. EUGENE LITWAK, "The Use of Extended Family Groups in the Achievement of Social Goals: Some Policy Implications," *Social Problems*, VII, 1959–1960, 177–187.

26. MATILDA W. RILEY, JOHN W. RILEY, JR., and MARY E. MOORE, "Adolescent Values and the Riesman Typology: An Empirical Analysis," in S. M. Lipset and Leo Lowenthal, eds., *Culture and Social Character*, New York: Free Press of Glencoe, 1961.

27. DAVID RIESMAN, with NATHAN GLAZER and REUEL DENNEY, *The Lonely Crowd*, abridged ed., New Haven: Yale University Press, 1961.

28. FREDERICK ELKIN and WILLIAM A. WESTLEY, "The Myth of Adolescent Culture," *American Sociological Review*, XX, 1955, 680–684.

29. WILLIAM A. WESTLEY and FREDERICK ELKIN, "The Protective Environment and Adolescent Socialization," *Social Forces*, XXXV, 1957, 243–249.

30. SIDNEY M. JOURARD and PATRICIA RICHMAN, "Factors in the Self-Disclosure Inputs of College Students," *Merrill-Palmer Quarterly*, IX, 1963, 141–148.

31. ROBERT K. MERTON, "Priorities in Scientific Discovery: A Chapter in the Sociology of Science," *American Sociological Review*, XXII, 1957, 635–659.

32. CARLE C. ZIMMERMAN and LUCIUS F. CERVANTES, *Successful American Families*, New York: Pageant Press, 1960.

33. JAMES S. COLEMAN, with JOHN W. C. JOHNSTONE and KURT JONASSOHN, *The Adolescent Society*, New York: Free Press of Glencoe, 1961.

34. ROBERT E. GRINDER, "Fidelity or Alienation in the Youth Culture?" *Merrill-Palmer Quarterly*, X, 1964, 195–204.

35. JULIAN H. STEWARD, *Theory of Culture Change*, Urbana: University of Illinois Press, 1955.

36. M. F. NIMKOFF and RUSSELL MIDDLETON, "Types of Family and Types of Economy," *American Journal of Sociology*, LXVI, 1960, 215–225.

37. SIDNEY M. GREENFIELD, "Industrialization and the Family in Sociological Theory," *American Journal of Sociology*, LXVII, 1961, 312–322.

38. BERNARD FARBER, *Family: Organization and Interaction*, San Francisco: Chandler, 1964.

39. R. M. MACIVER and CHARLES H. PAGE, *Society: An Introductory Analysis*, New York: Holt, Rinehart & Winston, 1949.

40. EMILE DURKHEIM, *The Division of Labor in Society*, trans. George Simpson, New York: Free Press of Glencoe, 1933.

41. NEIL J. SMELSER, *Social Change in the Industrial Revolution*, Chicago: University of Chicago Press, 1959.

42. DAVID GOTTLIEB and JON REEVES, *Adolescent Behavior in Urban Areas:*

A Bibliographic Review and Discussion of the Literature, New York: Free Press of Glencoe, 1963.

43. JOHN R. SEELEY, R. ALEXANDER SIM, and ELIZABETH W. LOOSLEY, Crestwood Heights: A Study of the Culture of Suburban Life, New York: Basic Books, 1956.

44. MORRIS ZELDITCH, JR., "Family, Marriage, and Kinship," in Robert E. L. Faris, ed., Handbook of Modern Sociology, Chicago: Rand McNally, 1964.

45. JOHN MOGEY, "Family and Community in Urban-Industrial Societies," in Harold T. Christensen, ed., Handbook in Marriage and the Family, Chicago: Rand McNally, 1964.

46. MARIE JAHODA and NEIL WARREN, "The Myths of Youth," Sociology of Education, XXXVIII, 1965, 138–149.

47. ALLAN D. COULT and ROBERT W. HABENSTEIN, "The Prediction of Inter-Family Ties in the American Kinship System," in Habenstein and Coult, The Function of Extended Kinship in Urban Society, Kansas City, Mo.: Community Studies, 1965.

✥ APPENDIX ✥

Some Figures on the Changing American Family

A good deal has been said in this book about the changing American family. At least some of the controversy about the future of the American family rests upon whether one takes a short-range or a long-range view of trends; it also rests upon the way in which one interprets the trends. Since there has already been much discussion about contrasting views of the American family— Is it becoming disorganized or reorganized?—it is well to be explicit about some of the figures upon which these different views are based. It would not be practical to attempt a comprehensive survey of the many figures we have on the American family; but it does make sense to single out a few of the most important figures that demographers use in order to note changing trends. In this way, students will be able to see the substance behind various interpretive remarks that have been made about the American family, and they will be in a better position to evaluate these interpretations.

In Table 1 we can see the changing birth and divorce rates in the United States from 1800 to 1964. The birth rate shows a steady decline from 1800 to the period of 1935–1940. From there it rises until the period of 1955–1960, and then it falls again. Seen in broad perspective, then, the birth rate in the United States has been falling since at least 1800. It remains to be seen whether the rise in the birth rate occasioned by World War II (and the expected rise in the late 1960's when the war babies themselves begin to have children) will prove to be exceptional. If this turns out to be the case then the presently declining birth rate will only be reversed

Written especially for this reader.

temporarily, and the historic decline in the American birth rate will again assert itself in the late 1970's and the 1980's. According to projections of the U.S. Bureau of the Census (*Current Population Reports,* 1964, p. 22) the birth rate will rise between 1970 and 1980, and then decline.

The divorce rate in the United States shows, in Table 1, a tendency to rise through the years. From 1860 to the period 1945–1950 there was a steady rise in the divorce rate, and the peak year of 1946, with a rate of 4.3 (per 1,000 population), was associated largely with marriages that took place during the World War II years. From that peak the divorce rate has declined to a level slightly above the rate found prior to the war, and it has remained quite stable from 1955 to the present time.

In Table 2 we can see the changes that have taken place from 1890 to 1963 in the percentage of people who are married. It is clear that there has been a steadily rising proportion of people in the United States who are married. In 1890, for example, 59.4 per cent of the females over 14 were married; in 1963 this figure was 68.3 per cent. The same trend is evident if one considers the percentage of people who had been married at least once (whether or not they were married at the time of the survey). In 1900, for example, 66.7 per cent of the females over 14 had been married at least once; in 1960 this figure was 81 per cent.

In Table 3 we can see that from 1890 to 1964 men and women have been marrying earlier and having their last child at an earlier age. This, along with increased longevity, has given both men and women a longer period of time at the end of their lives without the responsibility of raising children, and has been related to the rising percentage of women in the labor force and to the problems of old age and retirement. It is evident in Table 3 that the median age of a person's first marriage, for both men and women, has declined from 1890 to about 1950; since then the median ages have remained fairly stable.* The median age of men and women at the

* There is evidence of a slight upturn in 1964. The figures reported are based upon Current Population Survey data. The 1960 census data, however, show a slight decline from 1950, to a median age of 22.3 for males and 20.0 for females (see Rele, 1965). Much concern is expressed in many contemporary societies about early marriages. For excellent reviews, the first two on U.S. data and the third on cross-national data, see Burchinal (1960, 1965) and Moss (1964). Moss's article contains summaries of papers by Olivera Buric, Kenneth L. Cannon, Erik Grønseth, and Paavo Piepponen.

birth of their last child has also declined, although Glick and Parke (1965) have recently shown that the decline has not been as pronounced as prior publications have indicated. They also point to a temporary reversal for women born between 1910 and 1919, attributable to the coincidence of their marriages with the depression of the 1930's. It is also of interest to note that in 1880 the male was about four years older than the female, on the average, at the time of first marriage; by 1964, this figure had declined to about two and one-half years.

The rising percentage of married women who work is shown in Table 4. Here again there has been a steady increase through the years. In 1890 only 4.5 per cent of married women with a husband at home were working; by 1963 this figure was 33.7 per cent. When married women have young children in the home they are less likely to work, but even here there has been a steady increase in the percentage of working mothers. In 1940, approximately 4 per cent of married women with a child of their own at home under age 6 were working; by 1963 this figure had risen to 22.5 per cent.

Although the rise in the proportion of married women who are working has been very rapid, it should be noted that a good deal of this work is of a part-time nature. For example, 43.4 per cent of married women with husband present had had some work experience in 1960—this compares with 30.7 per cent of married women with husband present who were actually in the labor force in the week prior to their enumeration (Table 4). Of those married women with husband present who had had some work experience in 1960, 34.3 per cent worked at part-time jobs, and an additional 16.9 per cent, who were working at full-time jobs, were in the labor force for 26 weeks or less. As a result, we can see that the work commitment of a majority of the married women with husband present is partial, even though they have been entering the labor force in unprecedented numbers (Bureau of Labor Statistics, 1961).

TABLE 1

Birth and Divorce Rates in the United States, 1800–1964*

Year	Birth Rate	Divorce Rate	Year	Birth Rate	Divorce Rate
1800	57.8		1935	18.7	1.7
1820	55.2		1940	19.4	2.0
1840	51.8		1945	20.4	3.5
1860	44.3	0.3	1946	24.1	4.3
1880	39.8	0.4	1950	24.1	2.6
1900	32.3	0.7	1955	25.0	2.3
1910	30.1	0.9	1960	23.7	2.2
1920	27.7	1.6	1962	22.4	2.2
1930	21.3	1.6	1964	21.2	

* Both the birth rate and divorce rate are per 1,000 population. The birth rate for 1800 was estimated from the white birth rate on the basis of information available for the white population and the total population in 1820 and 1840.

Sources: U.S. Bureau of the Census, *Historical Statistics of the United States, Colonial Times to 1957*, Washington, D.C., 1960, pp. 23, 30; U.S. Bureau of the Census, *Statistical Abstract of the United States: 1964*, Washington, D.C., 1964, p. 48; U.S. Public Health Service, *Monthly Vital Statistics Report*, Vol. XIII, No. 12, Feb. 25, 1965, p. 1 (source of provisional 1964 birth rate); Paul H. Jacobson, with Pauline F. Jacobson, *American Marriage and Divorce*, New York: Rinehart, 1959, p. 90.

TABLE 2

Per Cent Married, by Sex, United States Population, 1890–1963*

Year	Males	Females
1890	61.2	59.4
1900	59.9	58.7
1910	60.4	60.1
1920	61.3	60.4
1930	62.1	61.2
1940	62.8	61.0
1950	68.0	66.1
1955	69.3	67.4
1960	70.0	67.8
1963	71.0	68.3

* The table presents per cent married of the U.S. population aged 14 and over. The 1950 age distribution is used as a standard for all years in order to eliminate the effects of changes in age distribution.

Source: U.S. Bureau of the Census, *Statistical Abstract of the United States: 1964*, Washington, D.C., 1964, p. 31.

TABLE 3

Age of Husband and Wife at Selected Stages of the Life Cycle, United States, 1880–1964

Year	Median Age at First Marriage		Median Age of Woman at Birth of Last Child	
	Male	Female	Year of Birth of Woman	Median Age
1890	26.1	22.0	1880–1889	32.9
1910	25.1	21.6	1890–1899	31.1
1930	24.3	21.3	1900–1909	30.4
1940	24.3	21.5	1910–1919	31.5
1950	22.8	20.3	1920–1929	30.5*
1955	22.6	20.2		
1960	22.8	20.3		
1962	22.7	20.3		
1964	23.1	20.5		

* This figure is tentative, and is based upon the incompleted childbearing histories of women born from 1920 to 1929.

Sources: Paul C. Glick, "The Life Cycle of the Family," *Marriage and Family Living*, Vol. XVII, Feb., 1955; Paul C. Glick and Robert Parke, Jr., "New Approaches in Studying the Life Cycle of the Family," *Demography*, II, 1965, 187–202; U.S. Bureau of the Census, *Historical Statistics of the United States, Colonial Times to 1957*, Washington, D.C., 1960, p. 15; U.S. Bureau of the Census, *Statistical Abstract of the United States: 1964*, Washington, D.C., 1964, p. 65. *Current Population Reports*, Series P-20, No. 135, 1965, p. 3.

TABLE 4

Married Women in the United States Labor Force, 1890–1963

Married, Husband Present		Married, Husband Present, with Own Children under 6 Years Old	
Year	Per Cent	Year	Per Cent
1890	4.5	1940	4*
1910	10*	1946	9.4
1930	11*	1948	10.7
1940	15.4	1950	11.9
1950	21.6	1952	13.9
1953	25.8	1955	16.2
1955	27.7	1957	18.2
1960	30.7	1960	19.2
1963	33.7	1963	22.5

* Estimated. The percentages for 1910 and 1930 are based upon the figures for all married women (husband present or absent), and the percentage for 1940 is based upon the figure for women ever married with children under

REFERENCES

BURCHINAL, LEE G. 1960. "Research on Young Marriage: Implications for Family Life Education," *Family Life Coordinator*, IX, 6–24.

———. 1965. "Trends and Prospects for Young Marriages in the United States," *Journal of Marriage and the Family*, XXVII, 243–254.

Bureau of Labor Statistics. 1961. *Special Labor Force Report No. 19*. U.S. Department of Labor, p. A–12.

Current Population Reports. 1964. U.S. Bureau of the Census, Series P–25, No. 286.

GLICK, PAUL C., and ROBERT PARKE, JR. 1965. "New Approaches in Studying the Life Cycle of the Family," *Demography*, II, 187–202.

MOSS, J. JOEL. 1964. "Teenage Marriage: Cross-national Trends and Sociological Factors in the Decision of When to Marry," *Acta Sociologica*, VIII, 98–117.

RELE, J. R. 1965. "Trends and Differentials in the American Age at Marriage," *Milbank Memorial Fund Quarterly*, XLIII, 219–234.

---

eighteen. The available rates have been used to estimate the desired but unavailable rates by making use of information from those years where both rates are available.

Sources: Janet M. Hooks (1947) *Women's Occupations Through Seven Decades*, Washington, D.C.: Women's Bureau Bulletin No. 218, p. 39; *Women as Workers* (1953) Washington, D.C.: Women's Bureau (prepared by Jean S. Campbell), Table 32; *Current Population Reports*, Series P–20, No. 53, 1954, and Series P–50, No. 87, 1959; U.S. Bureau of the Census, *Historical Statistics of the United States, Colonial Times to 1957*, Washington, D.C., 1960, p. 72; Jacob Schiffman (1961) "Marital and Family Characteristics of Workers, March 1960," *Monthly Labor Review*, 84: 355–364; U.S. Bureau of the Census, *U.S. Census of Population: 1960*, Vol. I, *Characteristics of the Population*, Part 1, United States Summary, Washington, D.C., 1964, Table 196; Vera C. Perrella, "Marital and Family Characteristics of Workers," Bureau of Labor Statistics, *Special Labor Force Report No. 40*, 1964, Table H.

thumbsucking, 105, 113, 117–18, 120–1, 125
Thurber, Emily, 109–10
Tibbits, Clark, 284
time in family life, 88
Tiryakian, Edward A., 253n, 258
Tocqueville, Alexis de, 31
toilet training, 105, 107–8, 113, 117–119, 123–5, 171
Tolstoy, Leo N., 93
Tomanec, Miroda, 210
Trost, Jan, 51, 65
Turbeville, Gus, 51, 63
Turner, Ralph H., 5–6, 16, 60, 65
Tyler, Leona E., 162, 165, 169

Udry, J. Richard, 60, 65
Undset, Sigrid, 87
unemployment, 214
upper class, 32, 35, 43, 49, 65–8, 174, 176, 214n, 220, 232, 267, 282
upper middle class, 92, 94, 100–2
urban groups, 100, 141–2, 173, 183, 187, 206, 209, 237, 266n

value stretch, in lower class, 215
values: middle class, 220–1, 227, 238; of social classes, 231, 235–44, 279
Vernon, Glenn M., 44, 68–72
Vincent, Clark E., vii, 54, 65, 106, 111, 214, 218
vitality in marriage, 82, 97–100, 102
Vogel, Ezra F., 108, 126–36, 142, 146
Vogel, Suzanne H., 142, 146

Waller, Willard, 9–10, 16, 77, 85–92
Wallin, Paul, 3, 16, 51
"war on poverty," 181, 213
Warner, W. Lloyd, 51, 65, 228
Warren, Neil, 286
weaning, 105, 107–8, 112–14, 117–118, 121–3, 125, 233
Weeks, H. Ashley, 69, 72
Weil, Mildred W., 5, 16
Weinstein, Karol, K., 213n, 217
West, James, 228
Westermarck, Edward, 49, 65

Western societies, xiv, 43, 139–40, 156, 158, 180–1, 203, 205–6, 253–254, 264, 275, 278, 282–3
Westley, William A., vii, 271–2, 285
White, Martha Sturm, 106, 111, 245
White, Winston, 262n, 284
Whiting, Beatrice B., 106, 111, 116
Whiting, John W. M., 116
Whyte, William F., 136, 144, 148, 197, 219, 221, 228–9
Whyte, William H., 78, 84
widowhood, 79, 94
Williams, M. J., 7
Williams, Robin M., Jr., 244
Willits, Fern K., 53, 65
Willmott, Peter, 210
Wilson, Bryan R., 144, 148
Wilson, Roger H. L., 15, 258, 284
Winch, Robert F., 8, 16, 48, 59, 61, 63, 65, 252, 258
Wolfe, Donald M., 76–7, 81–2
Wolfenstein, Martha, 105–6, 116–26
women: orientation toward marriage, 4–6; employment, 3–7, 23, 25–6, 29, 31–3, 39, 256–7, 274, 282, 288–9, 291; as sociometrists, 5–6, 37, 170, 172–3; sexual behavior, 7–11, 17–22, 36; sexual norms, 17–22; roles played by, 23–30, 250, 255–7, 274; status of, 31, 39, 75, 202, 250, 254–7, 259, 261; employment's effect on children, 109, 256, 289
Wootton, Barbara, 228, 230
working class, 31, 106–7, 128, 144, 176, 192, 215, 232–43; see also lower class
World Health Organization, 109, 111
Wrong, Dennis H., 284
Wylie, Philip, 80, 84

Yamamura, Douglas S., 52, 62
Yarrow, Leon J., 109, 111
Yinger, J. Milton, 52, 56, 64, 220, 229
Young, Michael, 180, 185, 210
youth culture, 263, 269–72, 282–3

Zavin, Theodora, 180, 185
Zelditch, Morris, Jr., 273, 286
Zimmerman, Carle C., 182, 185, 251–3, 256, 258, 266, 285

Date Due

NO 28 70				